*Psychotherapy of
Sexually Abused Children
and
Their Families*

Psychotherapy of Sexually Abused Children and Their Families

WILLIAM N. FRIEDRICH, *Ph.D.*

Consultant, Section of Psychology,
Mayo Clinic and Mayo Foundation;
Associate Professor of Psychology,
Mayo Medical School,
Rochester, Minnesota

W.W. NORTON & COMPANY • NEW YORK • LONDON

Library of Congress Cataloging-in-Publication Data

Friedrich, William N.
    Psychotherapy of sexually abused children and their families /
William N. Friedrich.
       p.   cm.
    Includes bibliographical references.
    1. Sexually abused children — Mental health. 2. Family
psychotherapy. I. Title.
RJ507.S49F75   1990   616.85'83 — dc20   90-32204

ISBN 0-393-70079-8

W. W. Norton & Company, Inc., 500 Fifth Avenue, New York, N.Y. 10110
W. W. Norton & Company, Ltd., 37 Great Russell Street, London WC1B 3NU

  2 3 4 5 6 7 8 9 0

To my wife

Contents

Introduction

A central and unifying theme in this book is the theory and process of coping with either acute and specific or sometimes chronic and pervasive adversity. Sexually abused children in our society are forced to cope with this phenomenon whose effects are frequently manifested throughout their life span. The same is true for their families. Only the minority of these children and families receive therapy. It is doubtful that there is any reason behind who does and who does not get referred and treated. Thus, the majority are left to adapt to this crisis, often a recurring one, and to use whatever resources they have to cope. Some do; many more do not.

Those of us whose work is primarily with these children and families also must cope with the recurrent evidence of inhumanity and depravity. Our styles, motivations, and relative success are extremely variable. Whether or not we cope successfully, as evidenced by continued empathic and reasoned therapy that brings hope and resolution, is dependent on how successfully we can cope with this persistent "gnawing down" feeling that comes with the territory.

Writing this book is one of my coping processes. From the beginning, my research and clinical interests have focused on the coping and resilience of chronically disadvantaged children and their families, including the physically abused, the chronically ill, the mentally retarded, and the sexually abused. Why do some people make it, even part way, and others do not?

What I have found helpful to me is to balance the emotional part of my work with an intellectual dimension. This book has been an excellent vehicle to do just that. An experience in therapy with a child, a mother, a sibling pair, or a family, rather than simply felt, is also wrestled with on an intellectual level. How does it fit with what I know of the family, of developmental theory, of child psychopathology? What does that now tell me would be a useful intervention? And by writing this book, I feel that I can also give at least a small voice to the lives of these people who are so often completely voiceless, but who have caused me to reach and grow.

There is a tension within the book between theory and technique. Both are present because I believe both are absolutely necessary. Yet we each have different needs, and when we are feeling pressed we usually want to know "What might I try next?" rather than the underpinnings of the technique. Read this book in the way that is best for you, whether in an orderly progression through the chapters or in a here-and-there reading of some technique and theory. You know best what you need and when.

Another type of tension in the book revolves around the utility of discriminating between intrafamilial and extrafamilial sexual abuse. My experiences have told me that the two are far more alike than different and that usually the same rules apply. Families compromise children and so does sexual abuse. Whether both of these compromising forces operate incestuously or not, the child must still cope, most of the time, with insensitive, marginal parenting along with sexual trauma. I hope that my combining the varieties of sexual abuse rather than discriminating among them does not lead to confusion.

This book is intended for a diverse audience—child therapists at all levels of skill and experience, therapist-researchers, family and group therapists, and researchers. Thus, some parts of the book will be more immediately relevant to you than to others, and portions that are basic to some will be advanced to others. I wrote this book with all of you in mind, and you can tell me the degree to which I succeeded for you.

Another coping resource which I could not live without in this work is the support of friends and colleagues. Not only was writing the book an intellectually and emotionally therapeutic process but the writing also reflects years of input from some people very dear to me. Beginning with the first sexually abusive family I saw in 1976, people too numerous to mention have helped to shape my thinking and practice. The mixture of support, stimulation, and challenge from friends and colleagues at the Harborview Sexual Assault Center in Seattle, North Seattle Youth Services, Seattle Day Nursery, Midwest Children's Resource Center in St. Paul, Department of Psychiatry and Psychology at Mayo

Clinic and Mayo Foundation, and Olmsted County Department of Social Services in Rochester, Minnesota, has been invaluable and sustaining.

This list of colleagues includes, among many others, Lucy Berliner, Sandra Hewitt, Carolyn Levitt, Paul Gerber, and Robert Colligan. All or part of the book has been read and helpful comments provided by Bill Luecke, Alison Einbender, Pat Fallon, Robert Beilke, Jon Conte, Lucy Berliner, Sandra Hewitt, Cheryl Lanktree, and Redmond Reams. Other colleagues and friends whose thinking and support have been instrumental include David Finkelhor, John Briere, Michael Nash, David Corwin, Gail Wyatt, Barbara Boat, and Sue White. Some of the conceptualizations in Chapters 1 and 2 are the product of a study group at the University of Washington that included Alison Einbender, Carol Cole, and Anthony Urquiza. I have also been taught immeasurably by the children and families I have seen, who have facilitated my personal growth in so many ways. Care was taken to hide the identity of all families and children in this book, but they exist in my heart.

Susan Barrows, my editor at W.W. Norton, has provided her typical mixture of support and remarkable incisiveness. Carol Kornblith provided sensitive editing at Mayo, and Gloria Mensink transformed my rough notes and dictation into a legible first draft with speed and professionalism. Thanks also to Margery Lovejoy, my editorial assistant, and Patricia Calvert, my proofreader.

Finally, my biggest thanks go to my family, my best support, who have proven again that love is sustaining. Thank you to my wife, Wanda, and my children, Hannah and Karl. You provided support and distraction, in equal measures, and always when needed.

*Psychotherapy of
Sexually Abused Children
and
Their Families*

1

Understanding the Impact

Not with a Club, the Heart is broken
Nor with a Stone—
A Whip so small you could not see it
Emily Dickinson

A book about psychotherapy is inherently a book about resilience and hope. As therapists, we must search for and nurture evidence of resilience in our clients and instill in them the hope for change and a cessation of the abuse cycle. Examples of resilience, or the ability to rebound in the face of adversity, are numerous in our practices. For instance, consider the mother of a sexually abused boy, herself sexually abused by her stepfather for many years, who seized on the opportunity for therapy along with her son in order to resolve long-standing guilt and animosity regarding her relationship with her mother. Her statement to me was, "My mom's not going to be around much longer. If I don't work on this now, I'll be blown away when she dies." A further example is the shy, anxious 6-year-old who steeled herself in order to confront her offender from the witness stand. When praised for her bravery, which resulted in conviction, she stated, "I decided not to be scared."

Further evidence for resilience comes from research which describes the marked variability of impact from one victim to the next, even given similar abuse experiences (Russell, 1986; Wyatt & Newcomb, in press). Or a child may initially appear to be coping adequately with the trauma, but given the onset of adolescence, or an event in adulthood, the seeming earlier resolution is not as certain. Resilience at one point in time may be viewed as premature resolution from another vantage point. Whatever the outcome, victims do vary widely in their behavioral responses and intrapsychic reactions to the potentially profound trauma of sexual abuse.

1

In a recent volume, it was reported that numerous diverse symptoms have been linked, at one time or another, to sexual abuse (Bolton, Morris, & MacEachron, 1989). A review of these symptoms will be presented later, but for now a conceptual framework that can be used to guide the therapy of a wide range of children and families will be described.

The tension in a book about therapy comes from our need as therapists for some "how to's" and techniques on the one hand and an equal need for a set of ideas and theories to guide the techniques on the other. When we reach an impasse with a child or family, as is often the case, the need for techniques seems paramount.

Yet, an integrated theory could help us understand the diversity and also appreciate the commonalities among these children. A framework allows us to learn more about these commonalities with each succeeding child, and we are not left with numerous, but nonintegrated, findings that may not help us with the next child who walks through our agency's door.

In the same way that a sexually abused child struggles to understand what has happened, or to "make meaning" (Kegan, 1982) of the abuse and to understand its effect, these first two chapters were written to help the reader make meaning out of the experience of traumatized children and their families. Your sensitivity as a therapist, the precision you bring to your work, and your increased empathy can be direct outcomes of a careful reading and integrating of theory.

The theories chosen reflect my own experiences and are distilled through my need for pragmatism. When I am wearing my clinician's hat, which I presume you are now wearing, I generally want to have some help on procedures and techniques. In addition, I need a framework or a model to help organize my observations of disparate children so that I can begin the "meaning-making" process and make sense out of their behavioral presentations.

Finkelhor (1988), who as a research sociologist has contributed more to our understanding of child sexual abuse than any practicing clinician, has written about how theories are built in this area. He believes that there is a need for a "modeling" phase in theory building, wherein models are proposed to explain why the particular short-term and long-term effects of sexual abuse occur. The model is to "connect what is known about the phenomenon of sexual abuse with what is observed in the attitudes, feelings, and behavior of victims of sexual abuse, using more general theories about the process of traumatization." Without a model, our understanding of sexual abuse remains superficial and intervention suffers.

A currently popular formulation, the Post-Traumatic Stress Disorder (PTSD) (American Psychiatric Association, 1987), has been reviewed by Finkelhor (1988), who dismissed the PTSD formulation as too narrow and atheoretical. It does not explain why only a small subset of sexually abused children actually exhibit PTSD symptoms. For example, the concept of PTSD does not help us understand the boy with aggressive acting-out problems and the girl with somatic symptoms, two diverse but frequently seen outcomes. Yet the PTSD diagnosis is enormously seductive. We deal always with society's and our "shared negative hallucination" (Summit, 1988), which obscures every aspect of child sexual abuse, particularly minimizing the extent and potential severity of impact. A diagnosis, such as PTSD, may fit only a small range of sexual assault victims (Finkelhor, 1988), but the implication of trauma forces people to sit up and notice.

Finkelhor's own model is a traumagenic factor formulation, which elegantly explains why it is that the diverse features of the act of sexual abuse — e.g., genital penetration, perpetrator's relationship to the child, frequency and duration of abuse, use of force, and lesser or greater erotization — have an impact (Finkelhor & Browne, 1985). The four traumagenic factors — betrayal, stigmatization, traumatic sexualization, and powerlessness — are made more or less traumatic by these sexual-abuse characteristics. However, as much as I admire this contribution, this model also remains too narrow. It relies primarily on the child's initial cognitive appraisal of the act(s) of abuse.

Yet, there is more to the impact of a traumatic event, or as is more often the case in sexual abuse, a series of events, than simply the child's cognitive appraisal of the event. For example, very young children may not even think about the abuse in a more adult fashion, and other children, particularly the more seriously traumatized, may have found the means to avoid any amount of recall. The context of the child, prior to the abuse and after, also contributes to impact.

A model needs to help us to understand:

1. the pre-abuse context of the child (e.g., was everything normal prior to the onset?)
2. what it is about the abuse that is traumatic
3. the post-abuse discovery reaction of the child, family, school, social services, and court
4. where development fits in
5. the nature of the sleeper effect, or the delayed onset of symptoms that is commonly reported by therapists working with adult incest victims.

A model that accounts for these various components is necessarily diverse, and a variety of findings from child psychopathology will be drawn on to build the model. But two central organizing principles are (a) coping, or the active adaptation to a stressful event or series of events, and (b) human ecology, or the fact that none of the events exist in isolation, but are embedded in various social relationships. The rudiments of this model were published earlier (Friedrich, 1988a) and I welcome the opportunity to expand on it here.

COPING THEORY

Coping theory goes counter to traditional perspectives on child psychopathology. The medical model, for example, stipulates that a disease agent (stressor) activates an illness state (behavioral response). The larger the stressor, the worse the illness state. The stressor of sexual abuse would traditionally be expected to result in a negative behavioral response that persists into adulthood (Meiselman, 1978).

We need to adjust our perspective on stress and coping from a simple, individualistic view, to a more complex, systemic view. Researchers (Garmezy, 1983; Hetherington, 1984) suggested that we must adopt a view of stress and coping that includes the individual and family characteristics and resources, the patterns of family structure and interaction, the social and physical context of the child, the coping modes, how the child and family appraise the event, and the existence of potentiating and protective environmental factors.

In fact, recent research suggested that children vary widely in their immediate and long-term responses to sexual abuse, from neutral to very negative (Friedrich, Urquiza, Beilke, 1986; Gomes-Schwartz, Horowitz, Sauzier, 1985; Mannarino & Cohen, 1987). This variability is probably related to differences in the nature of the abuse, individual differences in the children, and differences in the families (ecology) of which they are a part (Finkelhor, 1984).

Three recent studies document the importance of family differences. In a study of 248 adult women victimized as children, Wyatt and Mickey (1988) found that "level of family support" nullified some of the harmful effects of abuse. In addition, the attributions the individual made regarding the victimization were strong protective factors against later symptomatology. These two variables, support and attribution, may be why overall lasting effects of abuse and severity of abuse were not correlated in their study.

In a study of adult women who had experienced contact sexual abuse, Peters (1988) found that maternal warmth was a stronger predictor of psychological difficulty than three aspects of abuse: number of incidents, age at last incident, and duration of the abuse.

Finally, in a sample of young children sexually abused in the previous 18 months, Friedrich (1988a) found that both family conflict and family cohesion were primary predictors of both internalizing and externalizing behavioral problems (as measured by the Achenbach Child Behavior Checklist in Achenbach and Edelbrock, 1983) and more important than abuse characteristics.

A coping model does not diminish the very real and negative sequelae of sexual abuse. In fact, it says something about the triumph of the human spirit and the healing potential of families—something that we as therapists must believe in. Coping theory also emphasizes again the active nature of the child's and family's adaptation to this trauma. This adaptation process will vary from individual to individual, and as clinicians we are interested in those variables that contribute to both positive and negative adaptation.

The model discussed in this chapter is presented in Figure 1-1. It is broadly applicable to both intrafamilial and extrafamilial sexual abuse. Briefly, all components are interrelated, but for purposes of simplicity and ease of understanding, they are divided into four sections.

The first section includes variables pertaining to *functioning prior to abuse*. These include risk factors, which explain why sexual abuse is rarely a random event; preconditions of abuse, another contribution from Finkelhor (1984) that explains why abuse occurs in some families and not in others and at certain times and not others; and also family variables, wherein variables of incestuous and nonincestuous families will be discussed with respect to how they predispose a child to one of several possible outcomes of sexual abuse.

The second section represents the *nature of trauma*, dominated largely by the traumagenic factors of Finkelhor and Browne (1985) and those variables that exacerbate the four factors they have identified.

The third section illustrates the *initial response* by the child and the family. Some perspectives from cognitive coping theory and ego psychology will be presented in this chapter. Although development is discussed in greater detail in Chapter 2, we will address it here somewhat as we try to understand symptoms that might emerge later, particularly as the child moves through the developmental transitions into adulthood.

Finally, the fourth section shows that the degree to which these *long-*

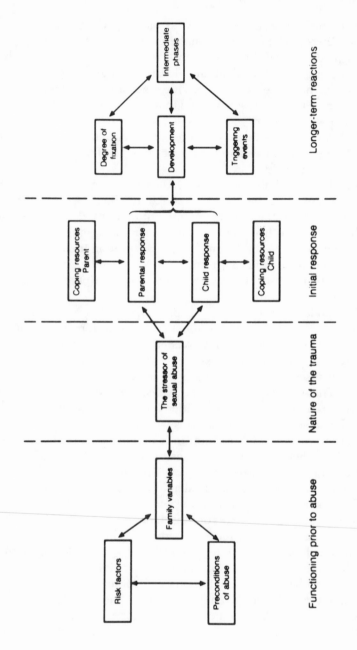

1-1. Schema for coping model.

er-term reactions occur is presumably dependent on all preceding events and the opportunity for appropriate therapy.

Functioning Prior to Abuse

A thorough discussion of this component of our model would not be complete without a statement to the effect that "human behavior is not random." The same is true for both intrafamilial sexual abuse and non-incestuous sexual abuse. Despite the fact that sexual abuse occurs in all demographic strata, it is not randomly distributed. Pelton (1978) made the same statement about physical child abuse. However, as clinicians, we know that for a large subset of families who see us, whether for intra- or extrafamilial sexual abuse, there is a prior history of sexual abuse in the parental generation, the caregiving is chaotic and offers little consistent protection for the children, or there are life events that precipitate a reactive type of sexual abuse. These characteristics represent risk factors that increase the likelihood of sexual abuse.

Risk Factors

Several studies of varying quality have been done that surprisingly produce quite similar findings regarding those variables related to increased risk for abuse. A study by Finkelhor (1979) retrospectively examined 795 undergraduates. They completed questionnaires about childhood sexual experiences. The eight strongest independent predictors of sexual victimization were:

1. presence of a stepfather
2. ever lived without mother
3. not close to mother
4. mother never finished high school
5. sex-punitive mother (sexually repressive)
6. no physical affection from father
7. income under $10,000
8. two friends or fewer in childhood.

These risk factors were cumulative, with each additional factor increasing a child's vulnerability between 10% and 20%.

Paveza (1987) identified four risk factors for intrafamilial child sexual abuse: two similar to the above, i.e., a lack of mother-daughter closeness and lower income, and two somewhat different, i.e., marital dissatisfaction and spousal violence.

Using a very small sample, Gruber and Jones (1983) reported three risk factors that were similar to those already mentioned: poor marital relations, living with stepfather or foster father, and poor relations with mother.

Gale, Thompson, Moran, and Sack (1988), with a sample that was largely nonincestuous, noted femaleness was a risk factor, along with absent biologic mothers and biologic fathers, larger original families, and more children in foster care when these children were compared with a demographically similar non-abused group.

Finally, Parker and Parker (1986) found three clear risk factors that followed from biosocial theory: abusive fathers performed fewer nurturant caregiving activities with their daughters, were more frequently absent for prolonged periods during the child's first three years of life, and had received greater abuse themselves, as children, from both of their parents. The first two factors point to impaired parent-child attachment between the abusing parent and the child victim, with the result that the child cannot be viewed as accurately or empathically.

There is overlap with several of Rutter and Quinton's (1977) six risk factors identified for psychiatric disorder in children. Rutter and his colleague found that foster-care placement, severe marital disruption, a large original family, low income, a biologic father with prior legal problems, and a biologic mother with a previous psychiatric history would predict psychological disturbance in children.

Neither psychiatric disturbance nor sexual abuse is a random event. Rather, there are variables that predict a greater likelihood of occurrence. Although this may not be stated as definitively for extrafamilial sexual abuse, there is also a nonrandom quality to its occurrence. If you conceptualize extrafamilial sexual abuse as a type of childhood accident, particularly when it is repeated, there is ample research that shows that childhood accident repeaters also come from distressed families (Matheny & Fisher, 1984). These statements in no way remove the responsibility for the act from the perpetrator. They simply are facts of which we must be aware.

Rutter (1983) also identified a triad of protective factors that, in concert, seem to be linked with positive adaptation of children to stress: (a) child's disposition, (b) family cohesion and warmth, and (c) external social support system. These findings are supported by studies of competent urban black ghetto children who are characterized by social skills with peers and adults, positive self-esteem, internal locus of control, impulse control, cognitive skills, good physical and psychological home environment, and one adequate adult identification figure (Garmezy, 1983).

These findings regarding risk factors are correlative and cannot be interpreted as causative. What they do explain is the fact that the therapist is likely to be confronted with various therapeutic challenges, including correcting failed parent-child relationships over several generations. Rather than removing blame from the perpetrator, this perspective illustrates the actual complexity of sexual abuse, effectively making it both individual and systemic. For instance, an impaired mother-victim relationship was found in several of the studies reviewed. Mothers get blamed for "everything," as do victims (Salter, 1988), and that is not my intention. An example may be helpful here.

A mother brought her 10-year-old daughter to see me after the girl disclosed molestation by her father, who had left the mother almost one year earlier. Two older brothers had not been involved, and the mother appeared to be doing a credible job with all three children. During the second interview, the mother stated the following to me.

> I was molested by my adoptive father when I was younger. I prayed with each of my pregnancies to have a boy. I didn't think I could raise a girl, protect her from abuse, or be as close to her. To me, girls were weak, unprotected, and just brought heartache to their mothers. It doesn't help that my mother and I don't get along either. And now here I've had my worst fears come true. I am such a failure.

It took considerable time before the woman saw the positive in (a) her prompt response to her daughter's disclosure, (b) her overall adequate parenting, and (c) the mother-daughter relationship maturing now that both were resolving similar abuse experiences. But her eloquent statement illustrated several points about the mother-daughter relationship in some of these families. For example, rather than deliberate unprotectiveness, many mothers have been taught to believe that abuse of daughters is practically inevitable, protection is not likely, and they protect their own shaky sense of self by withdrawing, making the hurt less intense. In addition, this woman's model for mother-daughter relationships had never been adequately developed because of her own relationship with her mother. Thus, she did not know what should happen between mother and daughter. She could handle sons; she had observed her mother do that.

The central importance of the mother-child relationship is a given. Winnicott (1975) stated that there is no such thing as an infant, only a "mothering couple." The child with a secure attachment to his or her mother has an arena in which to develop social skills, self-esteem, and a secure base to return to in time of need. The mother is not expected to be perfect, but to be "good-enough," another phrase from Winnicott. Good-enough mothering means that the child gradually, and as it is able, experiences opportunities to succeed on his or her own and to develop a sense of self-efficacy and of the availability of mother if the need arises.

The parenting role continues beyond this first epoch described above. The provision of a consistent and predictable environment is central to healthy development (Sameroff, Seifer, & Zax, 1982). It is useful to consider a quote from Erickson (1986) when making a determination of what helps a child adjust adequately to sexual victimization. In a prospective study of 267 children born to high-risk mothers, 11 children were identified as having been sexually abused during their 4- to 6-year follow-up appointments. Erickson devoted some of her paper to a description of the extremely bleak outcomes of the children.

> Of this group only one child appeared to be making steady gains in competence. . . . Several factors seemed . . . to facilitate her coping with . . . the abuse her natural father perpetrated: *the solid formulation of an early secure attachment with her mother*; superior intellectual ability; a stabilizing home environment following her mother's divorce of the abusing father and subsequent remarriage; ongoing family therapy; close cooperation between home and school.

These variables are protective factors (Rutter, 1983). Children can do well when these factors are present. Erickson identified factors provided by the girl, her home, and the school environment. But a central factor is the secure mother-daughter relationship.

Further support comes from Rutter and Quinton (1977), who studied a small group of families of psychiatric patients and found that the presence of one good parent-child relationship made little difference in families without discord. However, of the children from discordant homes in which there was one good parent-child relationship, only one-quarter of the children showed conduct disorders compared to three-quarters of the children who lacked such a relationship. It seems that in addition to the protective effect of a good parent-child relationship, good relations with peers and other significant adults (e.g., relatives, teachers, therapists, or caseworkers) may mitigate the effects of stress for children. The risk factors identified by Finkelhor (1984) — the absence of close parental relationships in sexually abused children — are directly related to these findings and articulate how these children are predisposed to psychological disorder, even before ever experiencing sexual abuse.

The other risk factors deserve some mention also. Lower socioeconomic status (SES) is probably the single variable that correlates routinely with psychiatric problems in epidemiologic research, and its presence here is only further evidence of its robustness as a variable (Graham, 1979).

Following closely in importance is educational level; the lower the maternal educational level, the more likely it is that the mother married early, that she married a similarly educationally disadvantaged male, and that she was too rapidly caught up in the important task of parenting. The risk factor of "few friends" is a product of an isolated family in which the child's natural social development with peers is circumvented because of family needs. Finally, the presence of a stepfather or non-biologic father speaks in part to what Parker and Parker (1986) found. Not only is the taboo against incest less strong in these men but also there is something about the early rearing experience that creates empathy for the child's position and habituates the father against acting on sexual urges.

Preconditions of Abuse

Referring back to Figure 1-1, you can see that a second dimension of the child's functioning prior to abuse is the preconditions to abuse. This is also a contribution from Finkelhor (1984) who, in an attempt to organize the multiplicity of ideas regarding why sexual abuse occurs, developed an integrated perspective. The four preconditions are:

1. the motivation to abuse
2. overcoming internal inhibitors
3. overcoming external inhibitors
4. overcoming resistance by the child.

Each one of these states something about the nature of the context around the child prior to the abuse and, as such, is important in our coping model.

Motivation to Abuse The first precondition, motivation to abuse, is the necessary condition without which abuse would not occur. For example, some offenders have deviant sexual arousal patterns that make them sexually attracted to children. The percentage of incestuous fathers, for example, who would also meet diagnostic criteria for pedophilia, is still a focus of research (Langevin, 1983). Other sexual abuse occurs as an acting-out response for nonsexual problems. It is here that the role of stress is thought to be an important precipitant, and thus the distinction between fixated and reactive offenders has been created (Groth, 1979). The fixated offender is thought to be primarily attracted to children, whereas the reactive offender is situationally compromised by some stressor, resulting in the abuse of a child. However, little empirical data exist to support this duality and, in real life, it appears that here again there is a broad continuum or spectrum of men who molest children, with various levels of fixation and reactivity.

The point I would like to make is that in some families, a "culture of sexuality" may have been developing prior to the act of molestation. For example, pornography may be present, and the child's behavior may be sexualized or eroticized, thus blurring further the distinction in the child's mind about the nature of what is happening. The sexualization of the relationship may invite sibling abuse to occur as well. The father's parenting role with the child is also likely to be minimal, leaving the mother overworked in this regard and paving the way for behavioral problems that emerge via inconsistent parenting, e.g., oppositionality and conduct problems.

Overcoming Internal Inhibitors   The second precondition, overcoming internal inhibitors, also pertains to the offender, and it illustrates more of the nature of the context prior to the abuse. Data from research on sex offenders illustrate the fact that these men have more stereotyped views of sex role behavior (Overholser & Beck, 1986). In addition, these individuals lack empathy for the child. They view the child unrealistically and put themselves in situations, e.g., drink too much, in which abuse becomes increasingly likely.

Again, roles are distorted and out of balance. It is here that some of the "grooming" behavior prior to abuse most likely fits, e.g., time alone with the child and making the child "special." The child cannot establish an accurate self-perception from this behavior, and the betrayal dimension of abuse is probably more profound. Sibling relationships may be deeply affected because of jealousy. The degree to which drinking is part of the family dynamic also influences the vulnerability of the family and of the victim to additional risk factors for emotional problems.

Overcoming External Inhibitors   The third precondition pertains to overcoming external inhibitors. This usually includes the mother as a primary external inhibitor, along with social and legal agencies. The degree to which the family is able to protect its children is the degree to which the child is safe from abuse. However, a physically or emotionally absent or overwhelmed mother, in addition to the other preconditions being met, may complete the combination resulting in sexual abuse. The child, even prior to the abuse, is becoming "parentified," or pseudo-mature, stepping into a parental void. This has the effect of limiting the child's natural development and ensuring that the child feels hyper-responsible for everyone's behavior. This is a difficult problem to correct. Other consequences are inconsistent parenting, with the resulting predisposition to behavioral problems.

Overcoming Resistance by the Child   The final precondition is overcoming the child's resistance. There are vulnerable children, made more so by risk factors and preconditions. Finkelhor (1979) noted several risk factors that pertain directly to this precondition, e.g., living on a farm and having few friends. Both of these are related to isolation and decreased socialization, made more likely by the absence of a secure attachment to a parent figure. Offenders have described their recruitment techniques and they include identifying those most vulnerable (Conte, Wolf, & Smith, 1989). Some physically abused children exhibit indiscriminate affection-seeking, seeking physical contact from any potential provider (Friedrich & Einbender, 1983). The relationships are transient and shallow, but they are what the child has learned to expect. The same has been noted for neglected children, and those sexually abused children who also were physically abused or neglected prior to the sexual abuse may be vulnerable because of this style of affection-seeking.

However, Finkelhor (1986) stated that if the first two preconditions are not present, i.e., motivation to abuse and overcoming internal inhibitors, and the father is neither inclined to abuse nor uninhibited, the remaining two contributing factors are not sufficient for sexual abuse to occur.

Family Variables

This is the last component of the model's first stage and comes prior to the onset of abuse. The model is drawn so that the risk factors and the preconditions channel through these variables. Family dynamics will be discussed in far greater depth in Chapter 6, but they need some mention here. Gelinas (1988) described incestuous families as being characterized by role imbalances. Fathers do not function as fathers, mothers do not function as mothers, and children do not function as children.

This type of blurring of generational boundaries is also called enmeshment and role reversal. The longer this occurs, the more one or several of the family members get "stuck" in these maladaptive roles. For example, an extremely role-stuck family began to see me after the four children returned home to their mother and the oldest, a 14-year-old girl, recounted a history of sexual abuse during the preceding six years while living with the natural father in a distant state.

From the beginning of the family therapy, I was confronted by two mothers, one quite talented at parenting, the 14 year old, and the other quite reluctant at parenting, the actual mother. School nonattendance by one of the sons was resolved after the sister assumed control over the behavioral program that had been put in place and was failing in the mother's hands.

The family then drifted out of therapy for several months. The daughter's depression and suicide attempt approximately one year after leaving the father brought the family back into therapy, and I could see that my efforts at elevating the mother and demoting the oldest daughter had probably helped to precipitate the depressive episode. Over several more months of family sessions, a joint parenting agreement was reached with the daughter involved in much of the mothering of her younger siblings, and the mother fulfilling more the role of breadwinner. As Mrazek and Mrazek (1987) pointed out, the daughter's overt competence became maladaptive over time, because she and the family could not give up this role at the cessation of abuse.

Other features of sexually abusive families commonly include (Alexander, 1985):

1. their frequent and unresolved losses that serve to organize their daily functioning (e.g., a previous history of victimization in one or both parents or strained multigenerational relationships resulting in further isolation among family members)
2. poor conflict resolution, with the accumulated resentments only adding to the isolation the parents experience between themselves
3. poor communication avenues, explaining in part why so many victims feel unable to report the abuse when it begins
4. isolation, both within the family and also between the family and the larger community, effectively removing the family from the benefits of "curative" or "corrective" impact (e.g., the importance of children being allowed to be children or the fact that fathers act differently in other families).

This is only a very brief, capsulized description of some critical family variables.

There is developing empirical support for impaired family functioning. Several recent studies found that adult women who were sexually abused rated their families as significantly more dysfunctional than did nonabused controls on several dimensions of family functioning (Harter, Alexander, & Neimeyer, 1988; Sexton, Hulsey, Harralson, & Nash, 1989).

I hope the result of reading this section on the initial component of the model, although it is not true for every family that has a sexually abused child, is that you are impressed with the likely context in which abuse occurs. The risk factors interact with and occasionally duplicate the preconditions, all of which occur within a family system that likely is either recently stressed, impaired in structure, or both.

Nature of the Trauma

Let us turn now to the second component of the model. It is useful to think of sexual abuse as a stressful event, defined as a change in the environment that induces a high degree of emotional tension and interferes with normal patterns of response. This does not necessarily reach the point of being diagnosed as traumatic in a PTSD perspective, although for a subset of children it may reach that point. Whatever the intensity, the stressful event activates individuals to either modify or adapt to their situation, a process we call coping. Coping can be adaptive or maladaptive.

Types of Heterogeneity

A fundamental difficulty in understanding how children cope with sexual abuse is that the range of phenomena covered by the term is enormously varied. Sexual abuse subsumes heterogeneous sexual acts. A similar heterogeneity is seen in physical abuse, in which three types of heterogeneity have been reported (Cicchetti & Rizley, 1981): (a) the resulting symptom patterns, (b) the type of maltreatment, and (c) the child's/family's response to treatment. I would like to add a fourth type of stressor: the sociolegal response to the child's assault. Legalism has entered into the treatment of sexual abuse and can be disruptive (Conte, 1989).

The first type of heterogeneity acknowledges the existence of a spectrum of different symptoms which are thought to be a function of the maltreatment and often will act as continuing stressors to the child. This is a useful concept because it illustrates the fact that stressful events can continue to be stressful to the child, even after they have ceased. For example, a child becomes isolated from peers because of his or her increased aggression and is removed from an important socialization experience (Strassberg & Dodge, 1989). The more this persists, the greater the likelihood that this socialization failure results in involvement in a deviant peer group (Patterson, DeBaryshe, & Ramsey, 1989). Thus, an additional set of problems emerges.

The second type of heterogeneity recognizes the existence of different causal networks, giving rise to different types of abuse. The expectation is that the symptom pattern will vary with the nature of the abuse act. For example, sexual abuse includes acts as diverse as talking sexually with the child to sexual intercourse. Frequently, the child may be the victim of several types of sexual abuse, and physical abuse and neglect may be occurring concurrently, particularly for males (Finkelhor, 1984).

The third type of heterogeneity acknowledges that families vary widely in their response to interventions aimed at decreasing maltreatment. The same is true for the larger community. The responses in each of these ecological contexts can range from openly antagonistic and unsupportive of the child to the opposite extreme, characterized by support and regard.

Finally, the sociolegal response to the sexual abuse has been identified by Conte (1984) as system-induced trauma. Some clinicians write that this trauma revictimizes each family member and may be more negative than the abuse itself (Giaretto, 1982). This trauma may stem not only from unskilled clinicians but also from the poor handling of cases, e.g., the child remains out of the home or the system fails to work toward reunification in those cases in which it is possible. In some jurisdictions, law enforcement discourages treatment due to a defense belief that children are contaminated by treatment, thus risking the loss of the case (Conte, 1989).

Sources of Trauma

In a recent paper (Finkelhor & Browne, 1985), a typology of the sources of trauma in child sexual abuse was posited. This model seems to complement the types of heterogeneity outlined in the previous paragraphs and adds to our understanding of how sexual abuse is traumatic.

Four general sources of trauma are identified, including traumatic sexualization, stigmatization, betrayal, and empowerlessness. Characteristics of the abuse experience contribute to these sources of trauma differentially.

For example, the perpetrator's relationship to the child can be the primary contributor to betrayal if the relationship is emotionally close. Duration of the abuse contributes to both powerlessness and sexualization. Both the type of act and the use of force are thought to contribute to powerlessness, with penetration engendering a greater sense of powerlessness. Sexualization may be enhanced by the duration and also particularly by the erotic nature of the abuse.

In fact, a recent study indicated that sexual behavior problems were directly related to both the number of perpetrators and the frequency of the abuse (Friedrich et al., 1986). Multiple perpetrators add to the child's self-perception of being a sexual object.

Stigmatization can be a function of parental reaction to the disclosure of sexual abuse, along with the child's interpretation of her or his own role in the abuse. This source of trauma is similar to Porter, Blick, and Sgroi's (1982) concept of "damaged goods," in which the child views herself or himself as broken, useless, and bad as the result of the abuse.

The sources of trauma are clearly attributional in nature, with the child actively processing what has happened and why. It is disconcerting to see the extent to which these are internalized and come to form the child's functional map of relationships. The child becomes aware of relationships and how to negotiate them and develops a certain set of expectancies about people. When trauma is experienced repeatedly, the child's internalized map of relationships provides little room other than to become involved in situations that result in further victimization.

Multiple Stressors

Rutter (1980) reported that a single stress typically carries no appreciable psychiatric risk for children. When children are exposed to multiple stressors, however, the adverse effects increase. Thus, stress is cumulative and, as this model indicates, looking solely at the act(s) of abuse does not help to fully appreciate the possible impact.

A further confounding factor is that there is no event which is uniformly stressful for all people under all circumstances (Maccoby, 1983). Although an event's intensity is an important factor in its stress potential, the familiarity and predictability of the stressful event are also of great importance. We know that sexual abuse varies in intensity, familiarity, and predictability. Researchers have written that an explicit taxonomy of stressful events is difficult to create because of the multidimensional nature of most stressful situations (Garmezy, 1983). An aspect of this is that stressors do not exist in a vacuum. Rather, there is a transactional effect or a person/environment interaction. Despite the fact that Browne and Finkelhor (1986), in their excellent review, were unable to find definite relationships between specific dimensions of sexual abuse and behavioral outcomes, some characteristics of the stressor of sexual abuse seem more critical than others.

Clinicians have long speculated on what types of abuse have the most serious impact on the child victim. Groth (1979) contended that the greatest trauma occurs when sexual abuse is of long duration, occurs with a close relative, involves penetration, and is accompanied by overt aggression. However, Browne and Finkelhor found that the limited empirical data available on the dimensions identified by Groth were contradictory for the variable relating to frequency or duration and age at onset. Available empirical data were more conclusive about a greater likelihood of negative impact when the offender was the father (or a primary father figure), the molestation involved contact with the genitals, and the use of force accompanied the molestation.

The reader needs to be aware that the data regarding the specific dimensions of the sexual abuse act(s) are derived from interviews with victims. Recent data indicated that a large minority minimize the nature and the extent of the abuse, thus providing error-ridden data for the types of studies reviewed by Browne and Finkelhor (Friedrich, 1988a; Koverola, 1989).

Given this information, these results raise a question as to whether any specific dimension of the abuse is the most powerful contributor to behavioral sequelae. For example, in a pilot study of victims of sexual abuse, abuse-specific variables correlated less strongly with behavioral problems in the abused child than did clinician ratings of family variables, i.e., family conflict and parental support of the child victim (Friedrich, 1988a). If some aspect of the sexual assault was the single most important variable, the reverse would be true, e.g., greater force accompanying the abuse would be associated with more behavioral problems. This study does not deny the importance of abuse variables. Again, part of the difficulty in relating abuse variables to behavioral outcome is the under-reporting of the extent of abuse. However, this study does underscore the complexity of the coping process and the need to study the "protective factors that can act to contain the expression of deviance or pathology" (Garmezy, Masten, & Tellegen, 1984).

Transactional Effect

Before we complete our discussion of the nature of the trauma, it would be useful to discuss what I mean by a transactional effect. The transactional approach (Sameroff & Chandler, 1975) views development as a series of transactions. The impact of the abuse is part of one transaction; the child's and the parents' reaction to the abuse is the other part. This reaction sets the stage for another transaction between child and parent, with the child being a bit different as a result of the prior transaction. Thus, the individual and parental responses to sexual abuse, particularly attributions made over a long-term series of transactions, will modify the child's response and subsequent recovery. The attributions made by the parents and the child regarding the abuse, the child, and the support of the parents are seen as central. To be fully appreciated, these transactions should be viewed prospectively. Sameroff and Chandler (1975) clearly indicated that retrospective analyses provide a distorted view of the relationship between a stressor and subsequent behavioral outcome.

An example of a nontransactional approach would be the study in which prostitutes reported a high incidence of child sexual abuse (Benward & Densen-Gerber, 1975). This finding has been interpreted as meaning that child sexual-abuse victims have a high probability of becoming prostitutes. This particular conclusion, arrived at retrospectively, is misleading and has never been documented. In addition, it does a disservice to the many successful survivors of sexual abuse. There are numerous opportunities for corrective transactions or their inverse, negative and destructive transactions.

The transactional perspective is useful to our understanding of the impact of sexual abuse. For example, the transactional nature of stressful events can lead to an increase in the probability that a series of other stressors will follow the occurrence of the first stressor. This is called generativity and is a commonly seen clinical phenomenon (Hetherington, 1984). Generativity can be identified frequently in situations of physical and sexual child abuse. For example, because of diminished self-esteem and a learned response that makes them familiar with violence, many abused children will become involved in abusive relationships and have a child who in turn is abused (Friedrich & Wheeler, 1982).

Initial Response

Relevant to our coping framework is the fact that beginning with the initial response, the coping process is under way (Figure 1-1). Coping is defined as the way in which people respond to stressful events or situations, including loss. Lazarus and his colleagues (Folkman, Schaefer, & Lazarus, 1979) wrote that coping serves the dual functions of problem solving and regulating emotional distress. Additionally, it must be considered as a process extending over time. Some coping processes increase the risk of maladaptation whereas others decrease it. Furthermore, there is not one but rather multiple routes to both adaptive and maladaptive outcomes in response to stress.

Child Response

How do children cope with stressful events? Coping styles are thought to be different from behavioral reactions, although there is some overlap. Still in its relative infancy, some literature exists on children's coping mechanisms or styles. Haan (1977) proposed three subtypes of coping mechanisms: (a) those that are healthy, reality oriented, and conscious; (b) defense mechanisms, which are rigid, distorting, and unconscious; and (c) fragmentary processes, which are repetitive, unresponsive to requirements, and determined by emotional needs.

Zeitlin (1980) also studied coping styles in children. These styles include productive-nonproductive, active-passive, and rigid-flexible. These styles were derived from normative and non-normative samples of children, and relate to how the child copes with both self and environment. An example of a self-productive coping behavior is the child appropriately using language to express needs or feelings, e.g., disclosing abuse. An environment-flexible example is the child drawing on various external resources to achieve a goal or to solve a problem.

Billings and Moos (1981) suggested several other styles of coping drawn from studies of adults. These include emotion-focused, information-seeking, and denial. The first and second coping styles describe a more affective and a more cognitive style, respectively, with denial being characterized by a more escapist style, e.g., sleeping too much. Although the relevance of coping styles to childhood response to sexual abuse is only now being documented empirically (Wolfe, Gentile, & Wolfe, in press), it would be useful to determine what styles and which environments promote those styles that are most effective in bringing about a return to a preabuse level of functioning. Research with adults who were victimized as children has begun to deal with mediators of the stress and is including coping mechanisms in the variables studied (Wyatt & Powell, 1988).

A contribution to coping theory from ego psychology comes from Karen Horney (1950). She described three resolutions to conflict: The child can learn to "move toward" the individual, "move away" from the individual, or "move against" the individual. The nontraumatized child, developing under normal circumstances, learns how to use all three of these resolutions without emphasizing any one of them. A child who is traumatized, and possibly arrested in development, may learn to rely on only one style to the relative exclusion of the other two. Using only one of these modalities is not beneficial to the individual. Therapists often see victims of sexual abuse becoming hyperaffiliative, overemphasizing moving toward adults, often failing to learn to balance this with good judgment for those times when moving away might be the most adaptive outcome, preventing further victimization.

I am particularly drawn to Horney's schema because it also parallels the three general categories of parent-child attachment that have been formulated by developmental psychologists (Feiring, 1983). Children attach securely (move toward) and insecurely to parents, with the latter group divided into ambivalent (move both against and toward) and avoidant (move away from) attachments to the parent.

I have been following, via irregular therapy sessions over the past two years, a young girl now 5 years old, who epitomizes Horney's moving against resolution. She refuses help from me to open the heavy playroom door or to get toys from around the room, did not take offered stickers until recently, will not eat a snack at the same table with me, and on visits to her biologic mother, is actively resistant to her. This spilled over into her foster-care setting, for at least a time, resulting in aggression and defiance, and some self-destructiveness. Yet, my clinical impression is that once some safety and predictability enter into her life, with termination of parental rights, her prognosis is more favorable than that of another child who was "indiscriminate" in affection-seeking.

More specific to sexual abuse, what might be an appropriate way to cope with the experience? There is a wide range of adaptations. Consider the case of an 8-year-old, fondled on one occasion by a preadolescent nonacquaintance, who informs a school nurse at the urging of a friend one day after it occurred. By the time the detective arrived, the child had told her friend, the school nurse, and her mother. She refused to talk to the detective, and still refuses to this day, some several months later, on the grounds that she had talked about it enough and wanted just to forget about it.

How would her response be classified? Haan (1977) might describe her initial reporting as healthy but somewhat fragmented because of her reluctance to talk to the detective. She was not denying the abuse and has, on one occasion, asked about the status of the perpetrator, who was interrogated, partially admitted, but not charged. The child has not been in therapy, and my advice to the parents, who have used me as a consultant, has been to use her behavior as a guide— if it deteriorates or shows signs of regression, some further discussion, including a police statement, would be warranted. But I am not proposing that she be further coerced into talking.

It also is possible to view the child's behavioral response to the sexual abuse as reflective of a coping style. The literature on classification of child psychopathology suggests two broad factors that subsume the majority of behavior disorders in children (Achenbach & Edelbrock, 1983): internalizing and externalizing. The child who internalizes is likely to be depressed, anxious, and withdrawn, whereas the externalizing child is aggressive, cruel, and delinquent. Sexually abused girls more frequently exhibit the former pattern and boys, the latter (Friedrich et al., 1986).

Some recent evidence suggests that sexually abused children's behavior may change over time, from depression to aggression or vice versa (Friedrich & Reams, 1987). The variation appears in part to be related to parental reaction and family context. One of the children described by Friedrich and Reams had been pulled into a caretaking role, i.e., parentified, and exhibited pseudomaturity, demonstrated in the absence of behavioral problems at initial referral. An example of the role reversal present is that when the abuse was discovered, the mother went into a psychiatric hospital. The girl began to regress significantly only after her mother was released from the hospital and was presumably able to take care of the child's distress.

In addition, many sexually abused children display persistent sexual behavior problems. In fact, sexual behavior problems, when present, are probably some of the few reasonably reliable indicators of sexual abuse. The behavior can take a number of forms, including:

1. sexually aggressive behavior
2. behavior that reflects a distorted sense of personal boundaries (boundary permeability)
3. gender confusion
4. self-stimulatory behavior (excessive masturbation) long after the abuse has stopped
5. inhibited behavior.

Sexual behavior problems are frequently identified in adult incest victims and the roots of the problems are derived from the early abuse. The persistence of these problems reflects not only a learned response but also efforts at coping with the abuse experience (Friedrich et al., 1986).

Another coping conceptualization consistent with what I have seen clinically is empirically derived from research on manifestations of competence in children, many of whom were under high stress (Earls, Beardslee, & Garrison, 1987). Four categories of children were noted, classified on the dimensions of control (overcontrolled and undercontrolled) and flexibility (resilient and brittle). For example, a resilient undercontroller was active, energetic, curious, expressive, liked by adults, and recouped after stress. It is in this group that you might see some of the repetitive trauma play described by Terr (1981), particularly in younger traumatized children. A brittle overcontrolled child might be inhibited, withdrawn, avoidant of any disruption of routine, and unable to master any energy for peer relations or school activities.

Another increasingly mentioned reaction to child sexual abuse falls under the PTSD rubric. For some sexually abused children this nosology is quite apropos, and we will discuss this further. I also believe that the PTSD diagnosis allows us, as practitioners, to give vent regarding the never-ending stream of victims we see. It enables us to shout, "There are bad things happening to our children; take notice," in the same manner that we were forced to notice PTSD in Vietnam veterans.

The percentage of sexually abused children that would actually qualify for this diagnosis is uncertain. The criteria are listed in Table 1-1. Three different studies reported research on sexually abused children with this possibility in mind (Kiser et al., 1988; McLeer, Deblinger, Atkins, Foa, & Ralphe, 1988; Wolfe et al., in press).

Kiser et al. evaluated 10 children, 6 years and younger, who were abused in a day-care setting. Nine of the 10 children met PTSD criteria, with the most commonly noted behaviors being avoidance of activities stimulating recollection and intensification of symptoms after exposure to events symbolizing the traumatic event.

In McLeer and colleagues' sample of 31 children, almost half met PTSD criteria. Children abused by adults, including natural fathers, were more likely to receive this diagnosis. Children with PTSD also had significantly more externalizing and internalizing behaviors than those without. Interestingly, the time elapsed since the last abuse episode was not related to the development of PTSD.

Finally, Wolfe et al. studied 54 children with an impressive array of

TABLE 1-1
DSM-III-R Criteria for Post-Traumatic Stress Disorder

---

1. The existence of a recognizable stressor that would evoke significant symptoms of distress in almost anyone.

2. The reexperiencing of the trauma, through one of the following:
   (a) recurrent intrusive recollections
   (b) dreams
   (c) sudden feelings.

3. A numbing of responsiveness or reduced involvement in the external world indicated by the following:
   (a) diminished interest in activities
   (b) feelings of estrangement from others
   (c) constricted affect.

4. In addition, at least two of the following set of symptoms must also be present:
   (a) hyperalertness
   (b) sleep problems
   (c) survival guilt
   (d) problems with memory or concentration
   (e) avoidance of activities
   (f) intensification of symptoms when exposed to stimuli related to the traumatic event.

---

standardized measures, including a child self-report instrument assessing the presence of intrusive thoughts and numbing, along with the child's attributions regarding the abuse. Their sample displayed a substantial number of PTSD-related symptoms, but the exact number meeting DSM-III-R criteria was not determined.

Although the PTSD diagnosis appears to be relevant for some sexually abused children, its greatest utility is probably that it identifies the existence of specific behaviors that should be addressed in therapy. It does not apply to all sexually abused children, but then no single nosology does. For those who remain uncomfortable with its use, Terr (1988) described two PTSD classification systems: Type I disorders follow from a single traumatic event and Type II disorders result from multiple or long-standing experiences with extreme distress, such as sexual abuse. Four symptoms are characteristic of both types: visualization, reenactment, fear, and futurelessness. Additional problems, e.g., denial or psychic numbing, rage, and unrelenting sadness, may be evident in those people who have experienced Type II PTSD.

Recently, some empirical research on behavioral consequences of child maltreatment has emerged, including comparison group research and studies in which results on standardized measures were contrasted with test norms. Sexually abused children, as a group, exhibit more serious behavioral problems, as reported by parents, than test norms would predict (Gomes-Schwartz et al., 1985; Friedrich et al., 1986; Mannarino & Cohen, 1987) or compared to normal samples (Friedrich, Beilke, & Urquiza, 1988a; White, Halpin, Strom, & Santilli, 1988; Einbender & Friedrich, 1989), but they exhibit fewer parent-reported behavioral symptoms than psychiatric samples (Friedrich, Beilke, & Urquiza, 1987; Friedrich et al., 1988a). The problem with parental report of behavioral problems in sexually abused children has been documented quite convincingly by Everson, Hunter, Runyon, Edelsohn, and Coulter (1989) who found that parents who were supportive of their child after the disclosure of sexual abuse were far more accurate about their child's behavior than unsupportive or neutral parents. They compared parent reports with independent ratings of the child by using an extensive diagnostic interview.

There is also evidence that sexual abuse is negatively related to overall child development (Erickson & Egeland, 1987; White et al., 1988), cognitive abilities, and subsequent school achievement (Erickson & Egeland, 1987; Einbender & Friedrich, 1989; Hewitt & McNaught, 1987). The degree to which sexually abused children differ from other maltreated children or children from chaotic and violent households may be small (Erickson & Egeland, 1987; Wolfe & Mosk, 1983; Wolfe, Wolfe, & LaRose, 1986). In the best study to date (Erickson & Egeland, 1987; Erickson, Egeland, & Pianta, 1989), 267 children were followed prospectively, and 60 to 86 were identified as maltreated at different ages through age 6 years, including 11 sexually abused children.

> There are more similarities than differences among the groups of maltreated children. . . . All have difficulty meeting task demands at school, all seem to have an abiding anger, all are unpopular with their peers, and all have difficulty functioning independently in school and laboratory situations.

The problems are not abuse-specific; the authors go on to state,

> The common problems . . . all can be tied to the lack of nurturance . . . all [parents] failed to provide sensitive, supportive care for their child.

The lack of consistently sensitive caregiving disrupts basic psychosocial development, beginning with attachment and the establishment of basic trust and autonomy (Erikson, 1963).

The importance of these findings reminds us not to lose sight of the need to intervene with sexually abusive families; in many ways, their needs are the same as those of other maltreating families. Referral of the children for treatment seems based not so much on need as on age, sex, race, and the parent with whom they are residing (Adams-Tucker, 1984). At those families' core is insensitivity by critical caregivers. The resulting symptoms are diverse and range from few to many. Focusing only on the abusive events is usually insufficient.

Coping Resources: Child

Just as there are risk factors predisposing children to sexual abuse, there are also protective factors or factors that *modulate* the impact of the abuse. One factor that arises in the family context (parent) and is derived from transactional theory (Sameroff & Chandler, 1975) is parental attribution. For example, it was long believed that premature birth was a major risk factor for learning difficulties because studies found that primary-school children with learning difficulties had a higher likelihood of having been born prematurely than children without learning difficulties.

However, prospective studies of prematurely born children did not find that to be the case. Why? Transactional researchers found that parental attributions about their child's potential were also critical. If the parents perceived and acted on the belief that their child's birth status would not impede normal development, that was often the case. Rather than believing that the infant's crying "sounded neurologically impaired," the parent believed it was a sign of their child's "fighting spirit," and they responded with greater attention and stimulation. Transactions like these during the child's first years had a positive impact. Because sexually abused children do not exist in a vacuum, parental attributions about the abuse and their child's believability and resilience are a coping resource.

Three types of factors that affect coping responses in children are currently being studied (Garmezy, 1983):

1. predisposing factors (e.g., vulnerability) such as low IQ, low SES, and single-parent families
2. potentiating factors (e.g., the stressor itself)
3. protective factors (e.g., stress resistance) that assist coping such

as family environment, school achievement, problem solving, and peer relations.

These protective factors are of great interest to us in this section.

> Research of this sort is more likely to yield significant data through longitudinal-development studies of various high-risk groups in the search for those processes that underlie resilience versus inflexibility, competence versus incompetence, active coping versus passive retreat in the face of stressful experiences. (Garmezy, 1983)

It would be useful to see what features make some children more resilient to the impact of sexual abuse. There is some evidence that intelligence and scholastic achievement may exert a protective effect in the presence of chronic psychosocial adversity (Rutter & Quinton, 1977). Little is known about how these factors operate and whether this is true for children's responses to acute stressors. More research along these lines is clearly warranted. Rutter (1983) hypothesized that the effect may operate through one or all of the following mechanisms:

1. the protective influence of high self-esteem and a sense of achievement
2. greater problem-solving skills
3. intelligent children are constitutionally more resilient.

Coping and the study of protective resources continue to be a difficult research area, and results are slow in coming.

> Intuitively, it seems that the coping process ought to play a role in determining the outcome following stress events. But, up to the present, both the concepts and the measures have proved elusive, and there is a lack of evidence that the particular coping mechanism adopted in fact matters at all in terms of risk . . . but it may matter and the possibility should be studied. (Rutter, 1983)

It is also probable that for the young child, external relationships may be far more critical. Research on invulnerable children, or children who seem to do well despite enormous adversity, routinely indicates that these children have a supportive and nurturing adult as part of their life (Werner & Smith, 1982).

Other protective factors that are contextual in nature are simply the degree of sameness, consistency, and predictability in the child's life. Chaos is a powerful disorganizer, as found by Sameroff et al. (1982) in a study of the developmental outcome of children, followed prospectively, who were born to mothers having varying psychiatric diagnoses, including psychoses. Rather than a specific diagnostic category being more predictive of a child's outcome, much better predictors were measures related to sameness and stability in the child's life. Although these were only young children, the degree to which sameness and stability can be preserved in the families of sexually abused children is probably also related to adequate coping. Young children in foster care ask to return home despite the need we perceive to protect them. They want a return to sameness and predictability, not to further abuse.

Only one study specifically looked at coping resources in the sexually abused child: attributions about the abuse (Wolfe et al., in press). Children with self-enhancing attributional styles were more likely to be rated as socially competent by parents, and greater fearfulness regarding the abuse was related to children who externalized rather than internalized the source of negative events. Clearly, this interesting line of research should be followed.

Parental Response

Mothers have been routinely blamed for colluding in the sexual abuse. Therapists and caseworkers roll their eyes at each other when reviewing cases in which the mother reportedly does not know about abuse that was occurring in the house while she was present in a separate room. The mother is described as passive-aggressive or dependent, or both, or worse. Her own unresolved abuse experiences are thought to create an unconscious or even conscious motivation for her to allow her children to be molested.

However, I believe that parental, particularly maternal, responses are much more complex and diverse, ranging from supportive to unsupportive, and varying from the nonabusing parent knowing to not knowing about the abuse. Clearly, parental support is critical, outstripping abuse characteristics in predicting at least short-term behavioral reaction to the abuse (Conte & Schuerman, 1987). We gain far more leverage as therapists if we also realize the dilemma of women in our culture. The socialization process of women is such that we "train" them to accommodate to adverse events and to put relationships above independence and autonomy.

An example of developmental research that clearly illustrates this early training comes from a study that attempted to determine the age at which male and female children expressed displeasure at gifts that are inferior or broken (Cole, 1986). Cole found that girls as young as 2 years old already inhibit their displeasure, whereas boys are much more outspoken. Evidently, this expectancy our society has of girls not responding with overt distress is inculcated at a very early age. We also ask mothers to choose between relationships, i.e., boyfriend or husband vs. child, when their experiences and our socialization of them have trained them to value both above personal choice or autonomy. Once I was able to see this more clearly, it was much more difficult for me to maintain a tacit assumption of blame.

One mother deliberately married a man who, from her perspective, was different from her incestuous father so that her own children would be safe. When confronted with the reality of her children having been molested by her husband, she reported tremendous confusion because this man neither beat her nor drank and was religious, three salient features discriminating him from her father. Blaming her was neither therapeutic for her nor accurate, given the efforts she had made to create safety from her perspective about husbands and fathers.

The data support the existence of far greater diversity of mothers than our original beliefs allowed. Data about mother offenders, for example, rarely show them operating alone; usually they are in a coercive relationship with a male perpetrator that Faller (1987) labeled a "polyincestuous family situation." In addition, a considerable amount of sexual abuse occurs after divorce when the mother is not even present.

For example, in a recent study, 67% of children reporting intrafamilial sexual abuse came from families in which the parents were separated or divorced, compared with only 27% of children reporting extrafamilial sexual abuse (Mian, Wehrspann, Klajner-Diamond, LeBaron, & Winder, 1986). Rather than opting for the belief of Lustig, Dresser, Spellman, and Murray (1966) that spouses are more responsible than the offender, it would be useful to adopt the belief of Salter (1988) that there is a spectrum of spousal involvement and reaction. Spousal reaction ranges from supports child (slightly above 40% according to both Peters, 1976, and Everson et al., 1989), to denies the possibility of occurrence, to sides with spouse, to did not stop abuse even though aware of its occurrence, to the other extreme — sets up or participates in the abuse.

Although denial of the abuse is not the response clinicians need in order to work toward resolution, and certainly it invalidates the child victim, it is relatively easy to understand that to believe the accusations shatters the mother's world view about relationships and what they mean.

If it is true, the spouse's internal map of the world changes. She must reassess her relationship with the trusted spouse, and must now doubt her judgement. She will feel considerable guilt that her daughter was abused and she was unable to protect her. She must wonder why her daughter did not tell her immediately. (Salter, 1988)

We also know all too well the more negative response in which knowledge existed along with lack of support. This usually reflects a maternal history of victimization and a subsequent, long-standing alienation from her child. It is not a given that an abuse history automatically results in parenting that "allows" abuse to occur. A recent prospective study found that 30% of a sample of economically disadvantaged mothers who were physically abused as children provided adequate care for their children (Egeland, Jacobvitz, & Sroufe, 1988). Another study found that 53% of parents abused as children did not abuse their own children (Herrenkohl, Herrenkohl, & Toedter, 1983).

Why is abuse transmitted from one generation to another? Obviously, the predisposing factors described by Finkelhor (1986) are more likely present in the children when they are present in the parents. Another perspective is derived from attachment theory. Working models of the self, others, and self-other relationships are derived from early relational histories and carried forward. An abused mother is less likely to have a representational model of herself as a potentially lovable and valuable person (Bowlby, 1980). The power of these early relationships was noted in the study by Egeland et al. (1988), in which they found that all but one of the economically disadvantaged mothers with a history of supportive and loving parental care provided adequate care for her child.

As clinicians, our response of rejection to these mothers is an anticipated, expected response that does not contribute to change. When we respond with acceptance of them and their dilemma, it sets up an internal contradiction that can create movement toward change.

Coping Resources: Parent

Research with adults has identified several resources that facilitate coping with a wide variety of acute and chronic stressful situations. No research has empirically examined parental coping with sexual abuse in a child, and the closest approximation is research on parents coping with a chronic illness or condition in a child (Friedrich, Wilturner, & Cohen, 1985).

Specific coping resources include (Folkman et al., 1979):

1. social support
2. specific belief systems that are positive and realistic
3. financial resources
4. ability to solve problems
5. physical health and energy
6. good morale
7. absence of depression.

Psychiatric epidemiologic studies support the greater likelihood of psychopathology when financial distress is present (Graham, 1979). It acts as a chronic stressor and further decreases the likelihood of available resources, e.g., health, education, and good morale. Data from a small sample indicate that job loss and need for public assistance are a possible outcome of sexual abuse investigations, effectively impacting overall coping resources (Tyler & Brassard, 1984).

The importance of several of these coping resources has also been documented with research germane to child maltreatment. In a study I recently completed (Friedrich, Luecke, Beilke, & Place, submitted), approximately 40 sexually abused boys and their families were treated in a program ranging from 6 weeks to 18 months, depending on need. The boys and families were assessed prior to the onset of treatment and at follow-up. The predictors of positive behavioral change included lower initial depression in the mother, greater social support reported by the mother, and fewer behavioral problems in the unabused siblings. Each of the variables represents essentially the increased availability of resources or decreased level of competing stress.

In the study by Egeland et al. (1988) of at-risk mothers with a history of physical abuse during their childhood but who did not repeat this with their own children, the abused mothers who were able to break the abusive cycle were significantly more likely to have participated in therapy at some time in their life and to have had a more stable, supportive, satisfying, and nonabusive relationship with a mate. Abused mothers who reenacted their maltreatment were more distressed, anxious, dependent, immature, and depressed. One would suspect that parents who had some of the resources identified would also be more able to enlist and follow through with support from social services.

Longer-Term Reactions

Once the acute phase of abuse discovery, investigation, and social service involvement is over, what can we expect? Is it a common occurrence for the adolescent who had an earlier history of sexual abuse to now present as a truant or a runaway? Is there such a phenomenon as a sleeper effect?

These chronic sequelae certainly exist and persist for various reasons, and they include various reactions. As Steele and Alexander (1981) stated, "the first thing to be said concerning the long-term effects of sexual abuse is that we do not know nearly enough about them," although some retrospective studies exist. One prospective follow-up study of sexually abused children has been reported (Tong, Oates, & McDowell, 1987). A total of 49 children were followed up an average of 2.6 years after an initial evaluation subsequent to the discovery of abuse. Interviews led to the finding that even after this lapse of time, 76% were rated as less confident, 30% had fewer friends, 20% were more aggressive, and 24% were more sexualized. Teachers also verified the persistence of these problems: 28% still had behavioral problems, 17% had repeated a year in school, and 17% had further deteriorated in their schoolwork.

What might explain these findings? First, there simply is the never-ending, inexorable process of development. Earlier in this chapter, the phenomenon of generativity was mentioned. The impact of the stressful event can increase the probability that a series of other stressors will follow the occurrence of the first stressor. For example, the social withdrawal and increase in fearfulness seen initially may, after the passage of time, be identified as school refusal and subsequent decrease in academic achievement.

Second, sexual abuse, whether intrafamilial or not, has an impact on the parental relationship leading possibly to marital dissolution and the increased likelihood of economic stressors. Many of us are familiar with the "feminization of poverty" that has occurred with the increase in single-parent families headed by a woman. Some of us have even seen economics used as subtle or not so subtle coercion in these families. In a family session with a mother and two children, the 14-year-old girl who had been molested by her adoptive father, in response to the mother's statement that she wanted "Kris to know that I support her telling me what was going on," retorted, "So why did you blame me for the lousy Christmas?" It emerged, after some denial, that the mother had frequently said to the younger brother's complaints about so few toys, that he "had his sister to thank for that."

What made intervention at this point so difficult with this family was that I knew if I confronted the mother about this strongly and directly, Kris' role in the family was to recant, support the mother, and attack me for being insensitive to her mother. The tack I took instead was to help the family identify those times the mother was supportive of Kris' disclosure, and there had been some instances, and those times when she had not been supportive. The contradictions were now out in the open, and some more congruent support of Kris could now be planned and discussed.

Rieker and Carmen (1986), in an excellent paper titled "The Victim-to-Patient Process," discussed the individual and familial processes that lead to the abuse victim becoming a psychotherapy patient. Both authors, in fact, believe that the "original defenses employed by both child and adult victims are viewed as adaptive survival strategies that later form the core of the survivors' psychopathology." The process involves:

1. accommodating to the judgments about the abuse provided by the members of the victim's environment, e.g., abuse denied
2. altering the affective response to the abuse, e.g., anger at perpetrator not allowed
3. changing the meaning of the abuse, e.g., abuse as "discipline."

This results in a sense of fragmentation and nonreality, but does accommodate to the demands of an unsupportive context.

Degree of Fixation

Although traditionally a word that has narrow theoretical origins, fixation will be used here to describe those children whose normal developmental path has been derailed or stuck subsequent to the abuse. It is expected that this will have an impact on longer-term reactions to the abuse.

To the degree that children have a chance to talk about the abuse and to find ways to think positively about themselves vis-à-vis the abuse, the extent of their feelings of fragmentation or lack of integration will be affected. Werner (1948) is a developmental psychologist who has described development in terms of two pathways, one resulting in greater differentiation of roles and functions within the child, and the other leading to a greater integration among the various parts of the child's functioning. When differentiation occurs without subsequent integration, one can actually see fragmentation of self. Specific to sexual abuse, differentiation taken to an extreme is the phenomenon that we see all too frequently, usually in female victims or oldest-child victims; the children develop a part of themselves, sometimes academic, sometimes parental, to the exclusion of their other parts, e.g., social, personal, and playful.

Because of my interest in child sexual abuse, I began to see adult victims with increasing frequency about 10 years ago. I was initially surprised to find that a large number of these people had an eating disorder and I developed a specialty in working on bulimia. Recent research (Root, Fallon, & Friedrich, 1986) has indicated the high percentage of victimization experiences among bulimics. These victimization experiences are most often sexual abuse or physical abuse, and frequently the bulimic woman has been revictimized when older, e.g., battering or rape, or both.

But what struck me with my adult, and even my adolescent, bulimic patients was the fact that the majority had a very compulsive side to them that had enabled them to succeed, usually academically or vocationally, at a level that was much greater than one would expect given their often profound histories of victimization. I was also impressed with the degree to which the competent components of the self were segregated from the more self-destructive parts of the self. This certainly paralleled the fact that when I would ask a bulimic patient about her view of herself, she would ignore the industrious and positive side, discounting it as if it were not even present. In tracing backward, however, I saw this as being a function of the fact that differentiation, probably better described as fragmentation, occurred after the sexual abuse. In some manner, development was still continuing but the child had become somewhat of a caricature of a normally developing child. These various fragments were not being integrated. Werner (1948) described this as a breakdown in the two complementary avenues of development.

Development

Several specific cases made me appreciate the developmental perspective offered by some schools of ego psychology. For example, working with children who denied the experience of abuse, despite pediatric evidence to the contrary, taught me again the reality of defense mechanisms and their intractability. When I began to see more and more dissociative symptoms or episodes in children, I found object-relations theory helpful. Following their victimization some young boys reflected a continuing inability to move into Erikson's (1963) stage of industry versus inferiority and were demonstrating decreased school performance and lower self-esteem; a rereading of Erikson's classic work was quite helpful for me.

One of the concepts from ego psychology that I have found particularly useful in understanding longer-term reactions pertains to the way a child deals with "overwhelming anxiety." For some children, sexual abuse creates difficulties in how these children "regulate" their emotions and behaviors. Sexual abuse will generate various reactions in children: for some it will be overwhelming; for others, puzzling and disorienting; and for others, the physiologic dimensions of the abuse may be most salient.

Theoretical formulations from both Sullivan (1953) and Winnicott (1975) indicate that a young child does not have the emotional or cognitive repertoire to adequately process extremely threatening events. These threatening events may be outside the child's "interpersonal map of relationships." For those children for whom sexual abuse constitutes an overwhelming experience, Sullivan has written about how the child may develop a "not me" persona so as to exclude these experiences from memory. As an interpersonal theorist, Sullivan believed that our personality reflected our interactions with other people. Positive interactions lead to a sense of a "good me," negative interactions to a sense of self (persona) as a "bad me," and overwhelming experiences to a "not me" persona. Because they are overwhelming to the child, they are not processed in the same manner as more easily processed input (e.g., "you are a good student") and are perceived by Sullivan to be largely out of the child's awareness, unless triggered by a precipitating event.

Winnicott, along with several of the English object-relations theorists, has developed a strongly interpersonal theory. The notion of splitting was developed and elaborated in part by these theorists. Children divide their experiences into good and bad, and with the proper nurturing they grow more complex (differentiated) and can see the "gray" in life and rely less on extremes. Overwhelming experiences are out of the child's frame of reference and create extraordinary anxiety. In introductory psychology class, most of us learned that a little anxiety potentiates the learning process, but we lose efficiency as we become more anxious. Multiply that manyfold for the young child who is being traumatized. This child is highly anxious and has no frame of reference. Thus, the event may be completely out of awareness or "split-off."

As the result of the child's inability to integrate these "overwhelming" experiences, the victim has less access to them, even in the therapist's office. This makes it more difficult for a therapist to help the child access these memories and experiences.

Triggering Events

Another unfortunate effect is that what is not integrated may come into the child's conscious awareness at moments of stress or when life experiences approximate the abuse experience, e.g., when a child moves into sexual activity or when a further loss is experienced. This reexperiencing of the traumatic event is a feature of PTSD. What is disheartening about the PTSD symptoms in traumatized children is that Wolfe et al. (in press) found little relation between passage of time and a decrease in these intrusive symptoms. It is as if sexual abuse contributes to a breakdown of the child's ability to regulate his or her reactivity and internal emotional states.

An example of not-me experiences comes from the book *Incest and Sexuality* (Malz & Holman, 1987), in which the authors report an exchange between two girls in a teen group.

Girl 1:   He used to stick his penis in my bottom. It would have this stuff on it so it would slide. . . . He'd make me stand over the counter and I'd tell him it hurted so bad and he'd say, "Bite on this washrag" or something. It was just terrible. When he'd sodomize me . . . he'd have his hands on the back of my head . . . so I couldn't really pull away to breathe.

Girl 2:   I'd bite him!

Girl 1:   When he's about 200 pounds heavier than you, you can't bite him or tell him no. He'd say it's all in your head that you don't like it . . . if you'd just change your attitude. . . . It's your attitude that's bad. You've got the wrong attitude! And I'm sitting there thinking, my attitude! He shouldn't even be doing this!

Gelinas (1983) borrowed heavily from Sullivan in her concept of "disguised presentation." In an excellent paper, she writes that the girl victim develops a disguised presentation or a veneer of propriety in social relationships that conceals the despair, powerlessness, and betrayal that accompany the abuse. I gave Gelinas' paper to one of my adult outpatients, a 45-year-old nurse with a history of sexual abuse as a child and adolescent, and she immediately knew what the phrase disguised presentation meant without having to read the actual definition. She stated to me, "That is my life. I have been a disguised presentation. No one knows what it is I am thinking or feeling. I just keep on a happy face." It is at developmental triggers in the child's or adult's life that more primitive and regressive behavior emerges. That was the case with the above patient. Her husband had recently died, her oldest child was leaving for college, and she finally was forced to realize her intrusive thoughts indicated she had been sexually abused.

The lack of integration can be profound. Gelinas (1983) described a patient who taught herself to not feel.

> She was 11 years old at the time and her stepfather was squeezing together the four fingers of one of her hands until she cried. She remembered looking straight into his eyes and holding her breath so that this time she wouldn't cry, telling herself not to feel her hand. As she began feeling the pressure of her lack of breath, it became easier not to feel her hand. Later that night, the stepfather came into the bathroom and asked to see that hand. She put it down on the edge of the sink and he abruptly brought his fist down onto it. The patient states that during the short interval of time between the beginning of his motion and the impact, she had been able to "not feel" her hand. Since that episode she has been able to induce and reinforce anesthesia when she felt she needed it.

The types of phenomena described in this section are not easily resolved, but frequently will cause a recurrence of distress at different periods in the life cycle. Naturally, any onset of intimate sexual activity could be problematic, as could parenting and the need to be supportive to and empathic with one's children.

Research in developmental psychology has provided support for the overwhelming and disorganizing effect of parental intrusiveness and inconsistency on young children (Jacobvitz & Sroufe, 1987). From a prospective study that included regular parent-child observation, greater maternal intrusiveness and inconsistency with these children was related to the onset, by age 6 years, of behavior very similar to attention-deficit disorder, characterized by inattention, overactivity, and distractibility. The authors concluded that the widely variable maternal style made it difficult for these children to develop and internalize self-control. Few adult behaviors are more intrusive than sexual abuse.

Another intermediate phase, which will be discussed in greater detail in Chapter 9, is the development of aberrant sexual behavior, including the child shifting from victim to victimizer. Becker (1988) reported that 59% of a large sample of adult sexual offenders had the onset of their paraphilic behavior during adolescence. Several researchers (Friedrich & Luecke, 1988; Johnson, 1988; Powell, 1987) have identified the onset of sexually aggressive behavior as early as preschool years. There is evidence that the younger the onset of the sexual behavior the more likely that sexual abuse is the primary precipitating factor.

Finally, literature exists on truly long-term sequelae: the psychological impact reported in adult victims (Wyatt & Powell, 1988). In fact, it is in this area that coping research has begun to develop, with social support (Peters, 1988; Wyatt & Mickey, 1988) and coping style (Cole, Stadler, & Mahnke, 1989; Wyatt & Newcomb, in press) demonstrating an ameliorative effect. Heterogeneity in outcome exists (Russell, 1984; 1986); women who request treatment as adults are more symptomatic than those who do not seek treatment (Tsai, Feldman-Summers, & Edgar, 1979). These differences appeared to be due, in part, to a longer duration and greater frequency of abuse. More importantly, eight non-clinical studies of adults, including three random community-based studies, found identifiable impairment when victims were compared to nonvictims (Browne & Finkelhor, 1986). Not all the impairments were severe, but they were present in the group.

DIRECTIONS FOR INTERVENTION

A clinical model is only as useful as its ability to facilitate new understanding of the clients we see and to guide interventions with the child and the dysfunctional system. Briefly, several points can be made with this model that are pertinent to the therapist.

1. Many of these children were compromised prior to the abuse and predisposed for some type of psychopathology. Ignoring these variables, most typically family in nature, in your therapy is not in the child's or family's best interest.
2. Intervention can occur at any phase and must be guided by each of the stages, knowing that there are premorbid variables that have operated long before many of these children were born, and knowing that intervention, although seemingly successful immediately after the abuse, may need to be reintroduced at later stages of development.
3. The response to sexual abuse can best be understood through a coping paradigm.

Summit (1988) wrote eloquently about "a shared negative hallucination" that blinds even sensitive clinicians to the potential impact of child sexual abuse. I firmly believe that, although this theory emphasizes active adaptation and coping, it does not obscure the profoundly negative effects that many sexually abused children experience. Rather, I hope that it articulates the multiple pathways, the multiple outcomes, and the opportunities for resiliency in children and families, not only as a function of our intervention but also as a function of the natural therapy that can be provided by positive social relationships, family support, and an individual constitution that copes positively.

It was with this in mind that the checklist in Table 1-2 was developed. Not only can this be a guide for therapists to understand the true scope of some of the factors that accompany the child to the treatment room, but it can also be a tool for researchers (a list of variables that appears to be related to coping outcome). I have developed this checklist into a more specific research/clinical tool that is available for research use.

Finally, sexual abuse is about relational problems and role imbalances. Strained and distorted attachments are commonplace. The therapist's greatest contribution to these disrupted attachments is to provide acceptance, consistency, and openness. The degree to which this can be provided is the extent to which change can occur and the cycle of abuse can be interrupted.

TABLE 1-2
Areas of Possible Change Identified in Coping Model

(Check all that apply)

Risk Factors
____Presence of stepfather
____Ever lived without mother
____Not close to mother
____Low maternal education
____Sexually repressive mother
____Low family income
____Few friends for child
____No physical affection from
      father

Preconditions
____Motivation to abuse
____External restrictions removed
____Internal restrictions removed
____Child's resistance

Family Response to Abuse
____Supportive
____"Neutral"
____Nonsupportive

Coping Resources
____Social support
____Locus of control
____Financial resources
____Interpersonal problem-solving
      skills
____Physical health
____Morale/absence of depres-
      sion

Developmental
Considerations

Any book on behavioral problems and intervention in children must consider developmental factors. Not only is a developmental perspective essential for children, but families also go through developmental stages of increasing organization and even disorganization. This fact also clearly argues for a developmental perspective to be present when discussing child sexual abuse. Beginning with the fact that abuse can occur at any age, it is important to examine the various perspectives regarding the role of age at onset of abuse or subsequent outcome. The child's cognitive and social developmental course can be derailed by abuse, and this in turn can foster a more negative or positive outcome, e.g., the risk factor of few peer relationships (Finkelhor, 1979).

There are several reasons why a developmental perspective is needed in the study of child behavioral problems (Gelfand & Peterson, 1985). Differences exist in the assessment of children and adults, the nature of the therapy process as related to cognitive development, prevention techniques, and also the ongoing developmental process, which continually brings changes with new developmental stages.

Rather than provide a generic primer on child development, however, I would like to discuss several developmental processes and make direct links between the theory and research data and any potential implications for the assessment or treatment of children who have been sexually abused. For example, in the area of cognitive development, the topics to be covered include the child's memory for events and the child's developing capacity for self-blame, perspective-taking, and understanding emotion; these three capacities all have implications for therapy.

Social development will be reviewed from an attachment perspective, particularly how the child's primary relationship provides a map for future interpersonal functioning, e.g., assertive and competent versus victimization-prone. Sexual development is also reviewed for obvious reasons and also the issue of age at onset of abuse, a variable frequently believed to be of importance in understanding long-term sequelae. Both cognitive and social developmental perspectives can bring insight to this issue. The issue of sex differences as it relates to differential symptoms is reviewed, and, finally, some direct clinical-developmental examples are provided so that the theory can truly come to life for the reader.

COGNITIVE DEVELOPMENT

Several developmental factors exert an influence on the child's response to stress. One such factor is the child's cognitive appraisal of the stressful event, i.e., the idiosyncratic, personal meaning of the event to the child. For example, Rutter (1983) wrote that bereavement should not automatically be considered an unpleasant event because it might signal the release from an intolerable relationship. Writing about children, he stated that "stress responses must be viewed in terms of a transaction between the individual and the environment with the meaning and appraisal of the event intrinsic to its definition."

Several options that younger children (i.e., preoperational, concrete operational) have regarding their cognitive reactions to out-of-control events, such as traumatic events, are to either blame themselves or to blame others. A study of 83 bereaved children and their families found that, when seeking a cognitive explanation for the parent's death, many of the children blamed themselves whereas others blamed the surviving parent (Arthur & Kemme, 1964).

It is interesting to speculate about whether we might see this same pattern in incest cases, with some victims blaming themselves and others blaming their mothers and absolving fathers. Is it somehow safer to feel anger toward the parent who is still there than toward the absent parent? Arthur and Kemme (1964) further noted that from the standpoint of coping with stress, the child's view of a predictable world has dissolved, at least temporarily, after the loss of a parent. The old view was replaced by an element of unpredictability and a pervasive fear that such events could recur. This was an out-of-control experience for the child, as is sexual abuse, which might possibly leave the child with a pervasive sense that the world is unpredictable and out of the child's control.

An area that is central to a child's cognitive appraisal of a stressor is the extent of the child's social knowledge (Maccoby, 1983). On one hand, younger children are protected from the stresses that require sensitivity to the meaning of others' actions, e.g., perceiving subtle slights. On the other hand, their defenses are poor against being manipulated by others, and they may not be able to take advantage of early signs of impending interpersonal crises in such a way as to forestall them. In conceptualizing child sexual abuse, we would do well to ask, "How does a child's lack of or incomplete knowledge about sexuality affect the child's vulnerability and reaction to sexual abuse?" For example, a preschool child insisted to me that her father "kicked my butt," although medical evidence indicated anal intercourse.

Researchers acknowledge that there is great individual variability with respect to the way in which children at any given age respond to trauma. This variability makes it unlikely that syndromes, reflecting a constellation of symptoms, can ever capture the behavior of any more than a minority of traumatized children (Garber, 1984).

Nonetheless, there is much controversy in the stress and coping literature regarding the age(s) at which children are most vulnerable to being negatively influenced by stressful events. Maccoby (1983) presented several compelling arguments. She pointed out that if the unfamiliarity of situations increases their stress value, then young children experience greater stress because so much is unfamiliar to them. Unlike adults, they have only a small repertoire of coping skills to help protect them from being disorganized. For example, after an extended abuse experience, they may generalize that all adults are abusive and be less able than an adolescent to sort people into more discrete categories.

There are counterbalancing factors. Young children cannot be upset by events if they do not understand their harmful implications, so they are buffered in that sense (Maccoby, 1983). However, the younger the child, the greater the importance of environmental structure in reducing the child's vulnerability to behavioral disruption under potentially stressful conditions. By structure we mean the presence of routines and a predictable, understandable physical and social environment.

Steinglass (1987), for example, found that family rituals buffered children in alcoholic families, resulting in a lower alcoholism rate when they became adults. Thus, the young child may not fully understand the sexual abuse and may be partially protected because it does not get integrated into the child's functional map of relationships; however, the subsequent family disorganization may be more wrenching than for an older child.

Another counterbalancing factor is that with an arousing event leading to strong negative affect, the younger the child, the greater the likelihood of extensive behavioral disorganization (Maccoby, 1983). Maccoby hypothesized that, in part, it is the maturation of the nervous system during early childhood that contributes to a child's increasing ability to inhibit crying and frustration reactions and to maintain behavioral organization.

The literature pertaining to children's response to divorce is relevant to these developmental concerns because parental divorce is experienced by the child as a stressful event over which the child has no control. Like sexual abuse, it is unwanted by the child and the child is helpless to change the situation. In addition, when sexual abuse occurs within the family, separation of the parents often follows discovery of the abuse. Kurdek (1981) wrote that infants are seen as being affected largely through the emotional state of their caregiver. Stress experienced by the caregiver may interfere with the child's forming a secure attachment and with the quality of care provided. Infants who are thus affected are therefore likely to respond by becoming anxious about feeding and exploring their environments and by developing separation anxiety.

Several authors (Kegan, 1982; Kurdek, 1981) reported that preschoolers experiencing the divorce of parents are at the greatest risk because of their level of cognitive functioning. Preschoolers are prone to form faulty perceptions of the reasons for their parents' separation, assuming responsibility for the breakup and, therefore, experiencing intense guilt. Kegan also added that the preschooler has a primary interpersonal need, more so than a school-age child, for inclusion and for the family "to remain in place." This then adds greatly to the disruption.

Wallerstein and Kelly (1980) also found that children's responses to parental divorce, both in terms of themes and coping styles, were clearly related to the age (developmental level) of the child. Predominant themes among preschoolers were fear, macabre fantasy, bewilderment, replaceability, guilt, and emotional need. These children attempted to cope with their feelings by regression (especially loss of the most recently acquired skills), fantasy denial, increased aggression or inhibition of aggression, and mastery. Whether or not this also occurs with sexually abused children has yet to be explored systematically.

Kurdek (1981) suggested that because school-age children have an affective investment in both parents, they too experience a profound personal loss when one parent leaves. Wallerstein and Kelly (1980) found common reactions of pervasive sadness, disorganized behavior, feelings of deprivation and yearning for the departed parent, inhibition of aggression toward the father and anger at the mother, and loyalty conflicts. Children in this age group were less likely to feel responsible for the separation, but wishes and fantasies of reconciliation were widespread and enduring.

In the older school-age group, Wallerstein and Kelly (1980) found a fully conscious and intense anger, a shaken sense of identity, somatic symptoms, and a tendency to align with one parent. These children attempted to cope with their underlying feelings of loss, rejection, helplessness, and fear of loneliness in many ways—denial, trying to understand, courage and bravado, keeping busy, and reaching out to others for help. They were more likely to use vigorous activity, sometimes addressed at undoing the divorce, than were the younger children, who were more likely to become depressed and to regress.

An explanation for these differences is that adolescents have the cognitive maturity to understand the reasons for the parents' separation (Kurdek, 1981). They may turn outside the home for comfort and advice and, therefore, be minimally affected by the separation. In other cases, the adolescent may be maximally affected because of exposure to longer periods of parental conflict.

Wallerstein and Kelly (1980) reported that the adolescents in their sample expressed grief, anger, and loyalty conflicts. Their perceptions of and relationships with their parents often changed significantly. Some attempted to cope by becoming detached from their families. Others evidenced greater maturity and moral growth. Those who failed to cope experienced temporary to prolonged interference with entry into adolescence, regression following the loss of external values and controls, and pseudoadolescent behavior such as sexual acting out.

Elkind (1979) discussed a cognitive development in adolescents that may explain why stigmatization as a traumagenic factor may be more salient in this developmental period. He saw adolescence as a period of renewed egocentricity; not only do adolescents perceive themselves as the universal objects of attention, with every flaw noted, but also every experience is unique to them and only they have suffered as much. Thus, despite a greater capacity for sophisticated thinking, the adolescent's psychosocial needs collide with this development and seemingly result in a world view that seems more primitive and clinically worrisome.

Whether response to sexual abuse follows a similar pattern across preschool, school-age, and adolescent age groups is yet to be determined. The review by Browne and Finkelhor (1986) found no clear relationship between age at onset of sexual abuse and the degree of behavioral disturbance. They stated that the age at onset may be less important than the stages of development through which the abuse persists. This latter variable would be related to the duration of the abuse.

It may be that changes in how children perceive adult authority figures affect their reactions to stress (Maccoby, 1983). Maccoby hypothesized that the obedient stance of most preadolescent children toward adult authority constitutes a buffer against stress:

> When children are following the instructions of others whom they trust, they experience little anxiety about the outcome, and are at least partially protected from guilt or a sense of failure over negative outcomes. However, throughout the preadolescent years, there is a gradual shift from reliance on external guidance to reliance on self-regulation.

But is this true of sexual abuse, in which the child may have great anxiety about participation in the act as well as a sense of the taboo nature of it? You could argue that sexual abuse is far more personal and intimate, and we may have no real useful comparison other than physical abuse to help us understand differential impact. It also seems clear that the obedient stance of preadolescents may actually be a potentiating factor in the case of sexual abuse.

Maccoby (1983) concluded that it is unlikely that there is any linear increase or decrease with age in vulnerability to stress. This concurs with the findings of Wallerstein and Kelly (1980) that although children of different ages tend to react to different aspects of the divorce and their patterns of coping differ, vulnerability is not different among age groups. Essentially, their findings support a transactional perspective in which cognitive development is but one contributing variable to a child's response to stress.

A directly applicable contribution of cognitive development to the psychotherapy of sexually abused children comes from Miller and Aloise (1989), who reviewed the literature on young children's understanding of the psychological causes of behavior. It is believed that children shift from external and situational causal attributions to internal and psychological attributions by the time they are school age. The question of

"Why did somebody do this to me and what does it mean?" is of great importance.

Actually the authors found that preschool children have greater awareness of psychological causes of behavior than is generally acknowledged. Their understanding of people's emotions, intentions, and motives is more sophisticated than originally believed. They assume, correctly or incorrectly, that people should have personal control over their behavior. They are not as capable as older children, who more easily infer psychological causes even when this information is not explicit, but the potential for preschoolers to have this awareness certainly exists.

Directly related to this is research by Harter (1980) on the child's understanding of emotions. The child's understanding progresses from being singular to sequential and finally to simultaneous. Children need to be 8 to 9 years of age before they can conceptualize several emotions simultaneously (Harter, 1981). These observations have obvious implications for whether a child can benefit from therapeutic interpretations. This has definite relevance to sexual-abuse victims, who may be ambivalent and confused about their feelings. Some direct application of this will be shown in Chapter 5.

Bierman (1983) also reviewed the literature on cognitive development and its applicability to clinical interviews with children. Oftentimes the child's own description of the problems is not considered a necessary or useful part of the assessment procedure, which is quite surprising given the weight the clinical interview is given with adults. Social cognition does develop over time. For example, how a child takes in, integrates, and organizes information about other people is something that develops gradually and shifts in nature and scope. Children also develop with regard to their ability to understand social roles and interpersonal relationships.

Bierman (1983) suggested some procedures to follow in interviews with children. For example, the typical use of open-ended questions as with adults should be discouraged because organizing a coherent answer to these questions requires a fairly high level of comprehension and expressive abilities. In addition to using shorter, more specific questions, Bierman recommended the use of pictures and dolls to present familiar situations to children and to provide a focus for interview questions. Children should also be given various options for responding, with one option being pointing to pictures that might have several affective labels on them. As the children grow older, particularly by grade school, they may have more advanced verbal and organizational skills but they also recognize that their thoughts and feelings are their own and can be consciously withheld, concealed, or denied.

Finally, an entire theory of child psychopathology has been developed that is based on the notion of children's need for control. This theory is derived from cognitive development and is related to children's beliefs about causality and intentionality (Rothbaum & Weisz, 1989). The authors of the theory believe that children's level of cognitive functioning may predispose them to develop certain psychological problems. Immature thinking can lead to illogical conclusions and resulting psychological problems.

For example, the authors believe that the emergence of what is typically viewed as depression may reflect the child's level of cognitive maturation. Not until adolescence are children truly able to contemplate a distant future and begin to eliminate possibilities for some effective change in that future. Thus, depression as we usually know it may really be possible only after the cognitive wherewithal is available to think in that manner. That does not mean that young children do not get depressed. They do. However, the adult type of depression is what is being discussed here.

In explaining the development of children's problems, Rothbaum and Weisz (1989) highlight the child's quest for control. "At each stage of intellectual development, children are predisposed to certain kinds of problems and protected from others because of their beliefs about, and desire for, control." An example directly related to sexual abuse would be the powerlessness that Finkelhor and Browne (1985) wrote about as a traumagenic factor. In the same manner, it would also reflect sexually abused children's search for control, e.g., victims becoming victimizers. Although a somewhat narrow perspective, this theory regarding the child's quest for control is derived from cognitive development and does reflect some problems germane to sexual victimization.

Children's Memory for Events

The accuracy of the child's report of abuse is a central issue in our field, one that has developmental, clinical, and legal implications. Cognitive development, in particular, comes into play in a discussion of how accurate children are when reporting traumatic events. Laboratory research that bears some relation to real life is rather difficult to perform, given the need to be sensitive and ethical. However, solid research is forthcoming and some things about children's recall can be stated with some certainty.

Of greatest concern to clinicians is the fact that children tend to minimize and underreport the extent of their abuse experience. Younger children lack the language sophistication needed, and older children have a more keenly developed sense of shame and embarrassment. However, in our role which takes us into court, we need to know about the accuracy of what children do tell us (see Goodman, 1984; Ceci, Toglis, & Ross, 1987 for more information). The most relevant research to sexual abuse focuses on both the accuracy of recall and the suggestibility of the child. Accuracy includes the child's ability to recall central and peripheral details. A central detail obviously would be "Who did it?" A peripheral detail might pertain to the room furnishings where the abuse occurred.

Recent research by Goodman, Aman, and Hirschman (1987) has been particularly relevant because they attempted to examine children's memory for events that approximate events about which they may testify in court.

One study found that 6-year-old and 22-year-old subjects were similar in their ability to answer questions and identify a photograph of an unfamiliar man with whom they had had interaction four days earlier (Goodman & Reed, 1986). However, 3 year olds were significantly poorer at each of these tasks. In the same study, both the 3 and 6 year olds were more suggestible than the adults when answering questions about the interaction, but their suggestibility was primarily on questions concerning peripheral information.

Another study examined 3 to 7 year olds about a frightening event (venipuncture) or a nonfrightening event (having a drawing rubbed on their arm) (Goodman et al., 1987). After 3 days, the groups were similar regarding overall recall; the frightened group was actually able to recall more peripheral details. Arousal did not seem to compromise memory function in these children; rather, it appeared enhanced.

A final study involved memory for events pertaining to an inoculation received by 3 to 6 year olds (Goodman et al., 1987). No significant age differences emerged, nor did recall deteriorate from the 3-day follow-up to the 7-day follow-up. Overall accuracy was quite high.

In summary, one of the more important conclusions to be drawn from research on memory and suggestibility is that whereas young children are generally more vulnerable to misleading suggestions than older children and adults, they do not appear to be more suggestible when it comes to a recall of the most salient and memorable aspects of the events—e.g., who, what, and where (Garbarino et al., 1989).

SOCIAL DEVELOPMENT

The broad area of social development refers to the child's expanding interpersonal world and, thus, is directly related to the child's attachment to its parents and subsequent caregiver and to peer relationships. Given the increased likelihood of the various risk factors being present in these families, the likelihood of a secure attachment to a parent figure is reduced.

For example, depression, one of the external inhibitors from Finkelhor's (1984) protective factors, discussed in Chapter 1, is common in a significant percentage of mothers in families in which intrafamilial sexual abuse occurs. The literature on the quality of attachment between children and mothers who are depressed definitely points to the increased likelihood of anxious attachment in 2 and 3 year olds (Radke-Yarrow, Cummings, Kuczynski, & Chapman, 1985). Cicchetti (1987) also found that children of depressed parents have difficulty with arousal modulation, self-control, and relationship formation.

Children who are reared in chaotic or stressful home environments may be less well equipped to negotiate successfully the critical developmental tasks that need to be accomplished. They may be more prone to becoming incompetent and thereby at greater risk for encountering problems in the resolution of subsequent issues throughout childhood. As a result, they may be more vulnerable to developing alternative modes of functioning that allow for a unique adaptation to environmental conditions. For example, physically abused infants may be more likely to develop an anxious-avoidant attachment relationship with a caregiver as a means of protecting themselves against future incidents of maltreatment (Cicchetti, 1987). This may not be the optimal outcome, but it may be adaptive.

It has been documented that maltreated children are significantly more likely to form insecure attachment relationships with their primary caregivers. Egeland and Sroufe (1981) found that the offspring of psychologically unavailable mothers shifted dramatically toward an increase in anxious-avoidant relationships between 12 months and 18 months of age. This was paralleled by a dramatic decline on the Bayley Mental Scale scores in those children with psychologically unavailable mothers. Thus, not only were social relationships impaired but cognitive development and related future learning prospects also suffered. Neglect actually had a more pernicious effect on these young children than physical abuse.

After the internalization of a sense of secure attachment with a caregiver, the next important task is the development of an autonomous self. The child gradually learns to differentiate between self and others and develops an emerging awareness of capabilities, goals, activities, and feelings. As this ability evolves, the child is able to understand environmental occurrences more fully and can comprehend himself or herself as a separate and independent entity.

Directly related to psychotherapy with sexually abused children is the fact that children who are insecurely attached, have an impaired sense of self, and are abused early on have an impaired ability to share information about intentions, cognitions, and feelings (Cicchetti, 1987). Maltreated toddlers use proportionately fewer internal-state words, attempt more strenuously to master feelings, and experience themselves in more negative ways. Troy and Sroufe (1987) noted a relationship between preschool children's attachment history and a relational pattern labeled "victimization." Children with an avoidant-attachment history were victimizers. Children with a resistant-attachment history were victims in play pairs. Children who were securely attached were in neither group. Depending on the role they assumed, insecurely attached children may organize their behavior around the expression of their anger and hostility in the role of victimizer or around their sense of unworthiness and poor self-image in the role of victim.

The revictimization that occurs in some of these children has been labeled counterphobic by some clinicians (de Young, 1984), but a more parsimonious explanation is that victim behavior is congruent with their map of relationships. Clearly, the internal working model that the child develops as a result of repeated interactions with the caregiver has long-term implications for successful social development.

The initial attachment paradigm and subsequent parent-child relations have long-term implications for future behavior. Patterson (1986) developed a model for antisocial behavior in children, particularly boys. The development of antisocial behavior in boys begins with something "as ordinary as the level of the parents' family-management skills." Accompanying this is parental rejection and a lack of parental warmth. These become the children whom we see after they have been sexually abused and in turn sexually abuse another child. But the roots are there from the beginning.

Emotional development is a gradual process of self-definition (Garbarino, 1982). Research focused on the sexually abused child must ask how sexual abuse impacts this emerging sense of self. Self-esteem is a variable related to this question, as is depression, both of which seem to have some of their origins in loss and learned helplessness. The peer group serves as an important socializing arena, and children who view themselves very negatively are going to be either cut off from this potentially positive socializing influence or involved in a peer group that confirms the negative self-image.

PSYCHOSEXUAL DEVELOPMENT

Increased sexualized behavior is one symptom that investigation suggests may be related to child sexual abuse (Browne & Finkelhor, 1986; Conte & Schuerman, 1987; Friedrich et al., 1986). In order to fully understand the implications of this finding, we need to review briefly the literature that is available on sexual development.

Sexual Development of Nonsexually Abused Children

Several studies have identified the presence of sexual behavior in children from the general population from infancy through 12 years of age. Although there are no major changes in physical sexual development between birth and puberty, it seems clear that psychosexual development begins in infancy.

In a review of normal sexual development, Rutter (1971) reported various sexualized behaviors seen in younger children, including the following: erections in male infants, "orgasmic-like responses" by males as young as 5 months of age, thigh rubbing by female preschoolers, exhibitionism and voyeurism with other children and adults by male and female nursery school children, undressing or sexual exploration games in males and females by the age of 4 years, and asking about sex by males and females by the age of 5 years. Genital interest for both sexes increases in the 2- to 5-year-old period and genital play is common. He also reported findings of sex play or genital handling by male and female preschoolers, with males exhibiting significantly more masturbatory activity than females. The observation that young males engage in more masturbatory activity than females may be because genitalia are more visible and thus more easily accessible (Gallo, 1979).

Exhibitionistic and voyeuristic activities with other children and adults are also common in the 4- to 6-year-old period (Gallo, 1979). According to Money and Ehrhardt (1972), 3 to 6 years of age is "the developmental stage when children can be outrageously flirtatious and seductive, impersonating mannerisms of parents, older siblings, television actors, or whoever." Confirmation for this comes also from factor-analytic studies of children's behavior problems (Achenbach & Edelbrock, 1983). Masturbation is much more common in younger children and is part of a separate factor, Sex Problems, on their Child Behavior Checklist for younger ages.

It seems likely that sexual interest and probably some form of sexual activity continue to be common and widespread but that as children learn the cultural standards these interests are concealed. Money and Ehrhardt (1972) described school-age children as going through "a developmental stage in which modesty and inhibitions are the watchwords." For example, they begin to demand bathroom privacy and are unlikely to discuss romantic fantasies with an adult. Because these children are now subject to nonfamilial socialization experiences, they are likely to assume cultural mores and restraints even if their families possess liberal sexual/nudity values.

Data from a normative sample of approximately 900 2- to 12-year-old children, rated by their mothers on a 42-item questionnaire of sexual behaviors thought to be exhibited by sexually abused children, indicated a mean total score of 0.5 at 2 years of age, decreasing steadily for both males and females until 12 years of age when the mean total score was 0.2 (Friedrich et al., 1989). This indicated that specifically sexual behaviors, e.g., attempting intercourse, inserting objects in vagina or rectum, touching breasts of adults, were unusual in normal, nonabused children.

However, sexual interest and exploration will flourish during the later school years. Rutter (1971) reported a gradual increase in masturbation and heterosexual play in the prepubescent years, from about 10% at 7 years of age to about 80% at 13 years of age for the former and from about 5% at 5 years of age to about 65% at 13 years of age for the latter. Homosexual play also increases during these years, being reported in up to 25% to 30% of 13-year-old boys.

During adolescence, there is a marked increase in sexual activity and interest in both sexes. Schofield (1965) found that by 13 years of age, 25% to 30% of boys and girls had had their first date, with the majority having experienced dating by 16 years of age. The figures for kissing were similar, and by 18 years of age about 30% of the boys and 15% of the girls had had sexual intercourse. He also found that sexual "appetite" was to some degree learned, in that adolescents for whom the first sexual experience was unpleasant were less likely to try again for some time, whereas those for whom is was pleasurable were likely to repeat the experience regularly and frequently.

Sexual Development of Sexually Abused Children

How does the sexual development of sexually abused children compare to that outlined above? In a recent paper, Finkelhor and Browne (1985) discussed the element of "traumatic sexualization." This refers to a "process in which a child's sexuality (including both sexual feelings and sexual attitudes) is shaped in a developmentally inappropriate and interpersonally dysfunctional fashion as a result of sexual abuse." The degree of sexualization will vary with the abuse experience and the child's level of development. The authors contended that a younger child, who understands less of the sexual implications of the abuse, may be less sexualized. This also may partially explain how childhood sexual trauma may result in the later development in the victims of a sexual interest in children (Russell, 1984).

It appears that for the age range of 3 to 12 years, sexual behavior, most notably sexual preoccupation and masturbation, is significantly more evident in sexually abused children than in either normal or psychiatric outpatients (Friedrich et al., 1986; Friedrich et al., 1988a,b; Friedrich et al., 1989; Yates, 1982). In addition, these behaviors may persist even after therapy (Friedrich & Reams, 1987). The earlier than average introduction to sexual activity appeared to "prime" these children to behave in a sexual way, and the decrease normally seen in latency was not seen in this sample.

The presence of a single sexual behavior is not an indication, however, that a child has been sexually abused. For example, the fact that a child touched a parent's genitals on one occasion was recently introduced in child custody cases as supportive evidence of molestation (Rosenfeld, Bailey, Siegel, & Bailey, 1986). The authors surveyed the parents of 576 children, 2 to 10 years of age, and found such activity "is not uncommon on an incidental basis."

Children who experience precocious physical puberty, or the onset of puberty before 9 years of age in girls and 11 years of age in boys, are another group who are "at risk" for being treated sexually. Consequently, they seem to provide a useful comparison group for sexually abused children, particularly with regard to their degree of sexual behavior. In fact, early sexual involvement has been suspected as a risk for children with precocious puberty (Solyom, Austed, Sherick, & Bacon, 1980).

The first, controlled, long-term follow-up study of psychopathology in female subjects with a history of idiopathic precocious puberty found increased risk for the patients in some areas of psychological distress. These included increased menstrual distress symptoms, somatic symptoms, and conduct problems (Ehrhardt et al., 1984). The authors concluded that the differences were not definitive with regard to psychopathology, but they did support the conclusion of increased risk in this sample. Regrettably, sexualized behavior was not assessed in this study.

Directly related to this finding of increased sexualization in sexually abused children is a recent paper on erotic orientation development (Storms, 1981). Storms wrote that "erotic orientation results from an interaction between sex drive development and social development during early adolescence." Although the paper was written to explain theories on the development of heterosexual/homosexual orientation, it is applicable to sexually abused children whose sex-drive development is accelerated and whose social environment may reinforce sexual behavior. Storms also stated that earlier sex-drive maturation appears to encourage homoerotic development, a finding that is supported in clinical research on latency-age, sexually aggressive boys (Friedrich & Luecke, 1988).

Two studies have examined sexualized behavior manifested by children referred for conduct disorder who reportedly have no history of sexual abuse. Pomeroy, Behar, and Stewart (1981) reported on behaviors seen in 16 children who received inpatient psychiatric treatment at the University of Iowa. A few of the children reportedly had been sexually abused, and for others no record of sexual abuse existed. Thus, the likelihood that some of the so-called non-abused children had actually been abused is quite high because there is no mention of specific inquiry ever being made and more recent literature suggests a much higher baseline of sexual abuse in child and adolescent inpatient units than in the general child population (Sansonnet-Hayden, Haley, Marriage, & Fine, 1987).

The varieties of behavior these children exhibited seemed quite significant. These included kissing of peers by a 12-year-old girl; excessive masturbation by girls 2, 3, 4, and 8 years of age; drawing nude figures; and attempted sexual manipulation with peers by two boys 5 years of age. Bates, Skilbeck, Smith, and Bentler (1974) also studied five 10- to 13-year-old boys referred for gender disturbance problems. No history of sexual abuse was reported but some boys were rated high on a scale related to effeminacy, e.g., cross-gender dressing and feminine voice and gestures.

The eroticization of the mother-infant relationship, although rarely described as sexual abuse, has also been shown to have markedly disorganizing effects on young children (Sroufe & Ward, 1980; Sroufe, Jacobvitz, Mangelsdorf, DeAngelo, & Ward, 1985). A small sample of primarily boys has been identified who, at a very early age were "used" in a sexual manner by their mothers. The disorganization and hypersexuality noted in these children, despite seemingly normal cognitive development, is remarkable, and it became more evident over time. This suggests that personal boundary dissolution of a sexual nature, while the child was still immature, can have a significant effect.

Some clinical support for this also comes from a family I saw in which the 11-year-old boy had a highly erotic relationship with his mother. As an infant, his father abandoned his mother, and the two were enmeshed. At 5 years of age, he interrupted an attempted rape of his mother by her ex-brother-in-law. This prompted severe somatic concerns and later school refusal in this young boy, who was clearly the most conflicted and immature child during his stay in the child psychiatry inpatient unit. During family therapy sessions, his mother frequently touched him, he could not keep his eyes off her, and their hugs at parting were quite sensual in nature. An initial goal of therapy was to interrupt that type of relationship and the dilemma was presented to the mother as "How can you get your son to quit making you his girlfriend?" Some initial success in clarifying boundaries was obtained, although the son resisted vigorously.

Of central importance to the ecological position developed in Chapter 1 is the fact that sexual behavior does not emerge in isolation. From the earliest period of life, the child's family will reciprocally influence the sexual characteristics of the child (Mrazek & Mrazek, 1981). The family establishes a "psychosexual equilibrium" that is a function of (a) the parents' sexual adjustment, (b) the child's developing sexuality, (c) the impact of the child's sexual development on parental sexual adjustment, and (d) the interaction that is developed as the child's sexual development activates parents to reexperience their memories and feelings related to sexual development.

For example, as families develop, the adaptive capacities of each individual change over the course of sexual development. Mrazek and Mrazek (1981) provided several insights into how a family, in which parenthood begins in adolescence, has different psychosexual issues over time than a family in which parenthood begins in young adulthood or middle life. For a family in which the parents feel trapped, their sexual experiences are curtailed, and marital instability exists, the emergence of a child's sexual interest can set off a series of transactions leading eventually to sexual misuse.

AGE AT ONSET OF ABUSE

A developmental consideration with important implications for treatment planning is the age at onset of abuse, and the subsequent developmental epochs that the child moves through while the abuse is ongoing. Psychoanalytic theory has as a basic tenet that the earlier the onset of the conflict or trauma, the more likely the child is to be arrested at an earlier psychosexual stage of development (Freud, 1966). Subsequent fixation is thus more primitive in nature. The earlier the fixation, the less available the child is for psychotherapy and a greater impairment of ego functioning is anticipated.

The impact of an event is influenced by the appropriateness of its occurrence in the life cycle of the individual. Research suggests that events in adult life are experienced as more disruptive and result in a more negative behavioral response if they occur at a non-normative age (Bourque & Back, 1977). For example, the sudden death of a parent due to an accident or heart attack is likely to be far more disruptive than death due to old age. One could draw a parallel for children, particularly in relation to sexual abuse, in which a child is prematurely exposed to adult sexuality.

The question of whether there are critical developmental periods that make the impact of a stressor more severe has been investigated in relation to childhood bereavement (Garmezy, 1983). The data are equivocal, probably because of the many factors other than age which mediate the experience of bereavement, e.g., family closeness preceding the loss, prior relationship of child to deceased parent, and suddenness of event.

Research on whether early stress sensitizes an individual to later stress is also equivocal. Freud and Dann (1951), in their account of children who had experienced a concentration camp, wrote of the sensitizing effect of this experience which was evident even in those who adapted well after liberation. Almost all of them were described as emotionally "scarred" in certain ways. This was reflected mainly in their increased vulnerability, e.g., minor changes in their life situations tended to produce breakdowns. Their description fits the brittle overcontroller from the work of Earls et al. (1987).

Bowlby (1969) suggested that early loss sensitizes an individual, making him or her more vulnerable to later loss or threats of loss. Brown and Harris (1978) reported a similar finding in the role of early loss in the etiology of depression in women. Bowlby emphasized that the impact of loss is mediated by the process of mourning at the time of the death and by the pattern of family relationships before and after the loss.

The lesson from Bowlby's research that is directly applicable to our topic of adjustment to sexual abuse seems clear. The child must have an opportunity to mourn the abuse and the subsequent loss of personal integrity. In addition, major changes in the child's immediate family will interfere with the necessary mourning process and add further predisposing factors that may exacerbate the stress. Yet there does not appear to be any one developmental period that is clearly more facilitative of the child "working through" a loss.

A confounding issue in understanding the impact of various stressors is our difficulty identifying what reactions specifically constitute a response to a given stressor; children exhibit reactions to any given stimulus in a number of ways. For example, in the sexually abused child who is having post-assault learning problems, how do we know whether these problems resulted from the sexual abuse per se? Children will manifest conflicts differently at different developmental levels, and we need to educate ourselves to know how to recognize emotional trauma in its many forms.

Research on depression suggests that immediate grief reactions are milder or of shorter duration, or both, in younger children than in older children. This may reflect the cognitive level of children, i.e., their limited ability to conceptualize the past and future and the full implications of the loss. Rutter (1983) wrote that although immediate grief reactions seem to be shorter in young children, the delayed consequences in terms of psychiatric disorder may be greater. These long-term effects may reflect other factors that occur after the death, e.g., breakup of home, frequent changes of caregivers, and effects of bereavement on surviving parent as well as the actual loss of the parent.

These secondary changes are similar to those seen frequently in sexually abusive families. Rutter (1983) reported that early events may influence later outcome in at least three ways:

1. They may cause altered patterns of behavior which persist.
2. They may lead to changed family conditions which, in turn, predispose to later disorder.
3. They may sensitize or steel the person to the effects of later stressors (e.g., become more vulnerable to later victimization).

He felt that the way in which children deal with stress is perhaps a more salient factor in their adjustment than is the number of stressors they encounter.

So what specifically do we know about age at onset of sexual abuse and differing outcomes? Despite statements to the contrary by Browne and Finkelhor (1986), some individuals believe there is a relationship. For example, Gomes-Schwartz et al. (1985) reported that preschoolers are not aware of the nature of the abuse so they are less affected. Yet the fact that they identified few behavioral problems in preschoolers may have more to do with the test construction difficulties encountered when we attempt to measure behavioral problems in very young children than with the preschoolers' awareness.

Uherek (1986) reported that in her sample of children who had been victimized in a ritualistic manner at a day-care center, behavioral responses differed depending on the age of the child at onset of abuse.

Older children in her therapy sample appeared to be more overtly embarrassed and conflicted about their participation in the abuse. Although she did not explicitly state this, the embarrassment seemed related to the onset of the children's ability to take a perspective separate from themselves: to see themselves through another person's eyes and anticipate the adult's response to their disclosure regarding participation in the abuse. The older children were also more reluctant to discuss the abuse. It appeared that they had an awareness that the acts were clearly wrong and could appreciate what an adult might be thinking about the same acts.

Younger children in her sample seemed to be more disorganized in general, but they assumed less blame in the therapy and did not demonstrate the inhibitions or embarrassment seen in the older group.

A recent paper (Zivney, Nash, & Hulsey, 1988) examined the Rorschach results of females, 9 to 16 years of age, and divided them into an early-abuse group (3 to 8 years of age), a late-abuse group (9 to 16 years of age), and a clinic patient comparison group. The authors hypothesized greater preoedipal psychopathology in the early-abuse group. They found that the late-abuse group did look more like the typical child clinic patient, with at least half of the early-abuse group having Rorschach results characterized by disturbed cognition, greater damage to the self, and preoccupation with issues of nurturance and relatedness. These age differences were unrelated to the child's age at testing or to the abuse variables of duration, frequency, and force.

One could argue, however, that the earlier abuse may be symbolic of greater pathology in the offender and the non-offending caregiver, and that may be one reason why earlier onset of abuse may lead to more severe behavioral problems. The younger the child the more embedded that child is in the context and the more likely it is that the child is going to be contaminated or influenced by everything that is going on in the family, e.g., chaotic disorganization.

Koverola (1989) clearly found that there was a link in her subjects between early onset, more unsupportive mother, *and* more frequent abuse. Age at onset of abuse, although it may be important purely from a cognitive viewpoint, is a highly confounded variable in the types of families we see.

In a different light, the complexity of this question regarding age at onset of abuse and its relationship to subsequent symptomatology is shown in my work with Luecke (1988) with sexually aggressive young children. It is our contention that the type of sexual aggression seen in very young sexually abused children who then are sexually aggressive is much more amorphous and reactive than the type of sexual aggressiveness seen in a child who was molested at 6 years of age and who then was caught molesting his sister and her friend when he was 9 years of age. His abuse of these two girls seemed to be much more planned and organized and reflected his own increasing awareness of the sexual and power aspects of the abuse.

It is true from an egopsychological perspective that the young child has fewer and more primitive defense mechanisms to use in the face of overwhelming assault. However, much of the sexual assault of young children begins with sexual pleasuring and with the types of grooming behavior that offenders use as they develop increasing compliance from their child victims. Consequently, younger children are not abused in as "forceful and severe" a manner, and less penetration is likely.

Thus, the question of developmental differences is a difficult one to answer because not only the age but also the types of abuse tend to be different. The simple statement of age at onset is very important and must be examined critically to determine whether or not the therapist is dealing with similar situations across two different age groups.

Finally, psychological speculations regarding the impact of sexual abuse are based on the behavioral manifestations of the abuse. A very young child, whose behavioral repertoire by nature is disorganized and not well developed, could look much more chaotic and disturbed than a child who is older, who has acquired the type of emotional modulation that one sees in elementary school children, and whose behavioral manifestations may be much more of the constricted or internalizing type. The therapist should not be fooled by this type of seemingly in-control stance on the part of the child.

SEX DIFFERENCES

The stress and coping literature generally concludes that males are more vulnerable than females to the negative effects of stress (Hetherington, 1984). Wallerstein and Kelly (1980) found that with divorce, disturbance tended to be more severe and prolonged in boys. Rutter (1983) found that boys showed more behavioral changes in response to daycare and more aggressive behavior in relation to parental discord and disharmony.

The reason why boys appear to be more affected by stressful events is unclear. It is also unclear if this sex difference holds for all stressors. Possibly echoing these findings is a statement by Kempe and Kempe (1978) that the impact of sexual abuse was usually more severe for males than for females. However, they provided no empirical support for that statement.

Bolton et al. (1989) reported several reasons why the impact may be more severe for males. These include a greater sexual orientation conflict in male victims due to the usually homosexual nature of the victimization, and a possibly greater impact of the powerlessness dimension of the trauma.

Kiser et al. (1988) found sex differences in the PTSD presentations of 10 2- to 6-year-old children who were sexually abused in a day-care setting. The boys in the study initially presented more clinically significant symptoms than did the girls. A partial follow-up one year later suggested that the girls were more symptomatic at that time. These initial findings parallel a study of fifth graders after a blizzard and flood (Burke, Moccia, Borus, & Burns, 1986). Boys in this study of behavioral reaction to a traumatic event reacted more intensely and their symptoms resolved slowly, whereas in girls a recurrence of symptoms developed at a later time.

A recent paper exploring sex differences in children's behavioral response to having lived in a home in which their mother was battered reported that boys exhibited more externalizing behavior and girls exhibited more internalizing behavior, with both exhibiting lower social competence (Jaffe, Wolfe, Wilson, & Zak, 1986).

The existence of sex differences is clearly in need of investigation in the sphere of sexual abuse in which 80% of the reported victims are female. Data from one recent study (Friedrich et al., 1986) found sex differences in 3- to 12-year-old sexually abused children, e.g., greater internalization in females and greater externalization of behavioral problems in males. These differences parallel other findings of sex differences in the psychopathological behaviors of children (Eme, 1979).

It has been reported to me by a colleague, Sandy Hewitt (1988) from the Midwest Children's Resource Center, that the developmental impact of sexual abuse on boy victims can be understood from Erikson's (1963) stages of ego development. The boys she sees frequently have a reduction in activity, and they present as much more quiet and shy and overly inhibited. In particular, the stage of industry versus inferiority, or a sense of mastery, appeared to have been derailed at an earlier age in them. Schoolwork suffered, along with their greater timidity and reduced autonomy.

Before we conclude that males are more adversely affected by sexual abuse experiences as a result of some function either of the abuse or the male child's inherent vulnerability, there is some attributional research which suggests that females may actually be far more self-critical in their attributions about their abuse experience.

Although he did not study a sexual abuse sample, Higgins (1987), in a study based on his self-discrepancy theory, found that the contrast between a child's actual self and ideal self is related to depression. Essentially, individuals, including children, repeatedly evaluate themselves with regard to an "ideal," or wished-for self, and with an "ought self," or a self that conforms to basic social standards. Although the actual-ideal contrast is related to depression, the actual-ought contrast is related to social anxiety. Higgins believes that the socialization of females results in more strongly defined standards. Thus, the actual-ought and actual-ideal contrasts tend to be greater, resulting in greater anxiety and depression. Sexual maltreatment, which has as an outcome a sense of being stigmatized or damaged, would directly affect the actual-ought and actual-ideal discrepancies. Conceivably this would result in greater anxiety and depression. Given that girls' standards are more strongly socialized than boys', Higgins' theory suggests the impact would be greater for females.

CLINICAL EXAMPLES

Some clinical issues that must be examined from a developmental perspective are related to sexualization. For example, a 3 year old who was compulsively masturbating (at baseline, at least one episode during every 15-minute period of observation while he was awake) was also bothering his somewhat erotophobic foster mother. Her perception of his behavior was that it was exclusively adult sexual in nature. After meeting with him, I saw him as extremely dependent. This observation, coupled with my knowledge of his concomitant history of physical neglect in addition to the sexual abuse, led me to the alternative conceptualization of this boy's masturbation as reflecting in part his emotional deprivation and neediness. The intervention attempted to address this issue. We began to increase his physical closeness with the foster mother and emphasized to her his need for affection. A teddy bear was introduced into the situation, and he was shaped to substitute holding the teddy bear for the compulsive masturbation. The success of the intervention added to my belief that this behavior was not simply sexual for him. There was a sexual dimension to it, but in his case it also had a comforting, familiar, and soothing nature.

The same type of new awareness came when I was involved in a consultation involving a boy who had daytime enuresis. (Daytime wetting has become a red flag for me for sexual abuse in older children.) The 7-year-old boy was from a chaotic and disrupted family and was both enuretic and oppositional. He also had a history of encopresis. After some questioning about the enuresis, he told me that when he would wet himself, he did not mind because "it felt warm." I had to change my perspective. The warmth met some dependency needs, in addition to its oppositional component. Once I could appreciate his basic neediness, we could talk about things in his life that were comforting and warm and the absence of them.

I think the treatment approach also will be dependent on age considerations. A mother recently came to me about her 4 year old and 2½ year old. My contact with her led me to believe she was a very adequate and confident caregiver who talked a great deal to her children. Each was touched 1 to 2 times by the 11-year-old son of the day-care provider. The decision was, after an initial observation of each child, that she could do a good job of natural therapy. Part of helping these very young children may simply be to empower their mother more and have her transmit that new confidence to them.

Symptom presentation can vary with the child's age. This case again involves sisters, one 7 years of age and the other 3½ years of age, each fondled one time, on the same night, in apparently the same manner, by a teen-age baby-sitter. They reported what had happened to their mother when she came home, after the baby-sitter had left. They repeated it to the pediatrician the next day, and had no overt symptoms or physical evidence at that time. Several weeks later, the pediatrician called me because she had just seen the girls again; each presented with a different symptom picture, presumably abuse related. The younger girl was now complaining of leg pain and had an exaggerated limp on occasion. The other girl was fearful of going to school. It could be argued that the younger girl's somatic complaint reflected her more naive view of her body, i.e., "something down there was hurt," whereas the older girl's symptom, albeit separation related, was occurring in an age-appropriate (school) context. The symptoms resolved after a single session held with the mother and her daughters which focused on a discussion of the abuse, some anger at the baby-sitter, and some problem-solving about future baby-sitters.

Clearly, developmental theory can inform us regarding the meaning of symptoms and appropriate interventions.

3

Evaluating the Child and Planning for Treatment

He's always in my head. Everywhere I go. I can't get
rid of him.

An 11-year-old victim

This chapter focuses on assessment that assists in the planning of therapy, and it largely ignores the initial "forensic" interviews done to determine whether sexual abuse occurred. Although the two are frequently
related, therapy-related assessment is discussed here. Separating the
roles of investigative interviewing and assessment for therapy often occurs, and sometimes it is legally mandated.

I strongly believe that a careful, theoretically sound assessment that is
geared to developing appropriate interventions marks the beginning of
therapy. Too often, assessment is dismissed by therapists who are convinced that all that is needed for therapy to proceed is their personal
presence. Other therapists have never learned how to assess a child or
family, either behaviorally or psychometrically. However, the assessment of sexually abused children is an important topic and probably
deserves its own book. The recently published chapter by Wolfe and
Wolfe (1988) would be an excellent paper to review as a companion to
this chapter.

There are reasons why assessment is often dismissed. Traditional psychological assessment is frequently presented in a not very useful fashion
to nonpsychologist therapists. Arcane numbers and jargon may be used
too freely in the report. I have certainly read several relatively useless
evaluations that report IQ scores and make some vague comments about
what a child's drawings might suggest about self-esteem and superego
functioning or lack thereof. However, assessment that is directly *linked
to intervention* and is *ecological* in focus can be extremely useful to
therapists.

64

When I speak of assessment being *linked to intervention*, I intend that the assessment should identify target behaviors and issues that are amenable to treatment. For example, it should examine the child's available resources (e.g., IQ, school achievement, and peer relations) so that efforts can be made, if areas of need are identified, to bring support to the child. Assessment should also give the therapist some idea about the child's cognitions, internal processes, and predominant coping style.

Consider, for example, a 6 year old referred to you because she was fondled by her baby-sitter's 13-year-old brother. The parents are extremely upset and guilt-ridden, even more so because the child had indirectly resisted going to the baby-sitter on one occasion before she told her parents, and the parents had urged her to go with the sitter, resulting in one more instance of fondling. Your task is to determine the need for intervention with this system.

You may operate at any position along a continuum, anchored on one end by the belief that all sexually abused children need therapy, and lots of it, and on the other end by the belief that "if the system returns to normal, the child will do fine." My position is somewhere in between these two extremes, most typically in favor of some intervention. I do feel that an assessment can and should be done in each case, and, when done skillfully, it provides useful information that may suggest only minimal therapy needs. Actually, the assessment process can be made therapeutic and the brief contacts revolving around the evaluation may be all that is needed at that particular developmental stage.

Ecological assessment, simply put, requires an understanding of each of the parents and caregivers involved with the child. What is the psychological status of the parents in cases of incest? A nonabusing mother, who initially responds adequately, but who suddenly shows a lack of advocacy for the child, might have been anticipated by her MMPI profile that indicated passive-aggressiveness and chronic depression. The offending father's psychological status may never be adequately evaluated, and when he applies pressure to resume visits, your job as therapist for the child victim may include advocating a more thorough assessment that targets his treatment needs. If we eschew assessment in general and fail to realize that the father's brief treatment left many issues untouched, our hard-earned progress in therapy is for naught.

Other ecological areas of assessment include school and daycare. Although parent-teacher correlations on behavioral ratings can vary widely, if good baseline data are obtained in the child's day-care and home setting, improvement can be documented or behavioral regression can be noted when the offender begins contact with the child again.

This latter function of ecological assessment has served several of my child clients quite well in the past. With one child, for example, her behavioral improvement could be seen clearly at home and in the day-care, via two separately administered behavior checklists. The first set was completed at the time abuse was discovered, and the second set was completed six months later. Thus, her continued regression after visits resumed with her untreated father could also be charted and the contrast was clear and significant. This evidence was introduced into court, visitation was stopped, and the child began again to improve.

We have all heard nonabusing parents report behavioral deterioration after visits with the abusing parent. However, because it is unsystematic reporting by parents who are presumed to be biased, and the behavioral observations are not done in a more reliable manner, these are dismissed by the welfare workers or the judges who are approached. But when the observations are systematized and are congruent in several settings, it is easier to persuade the appropriate people to act in a manner supportive of the child.

A final introductory comment about assessment is needed here. Do not take the view that assessment is static. Rather it is active and evolutionary. The parents need to be monitoring the child as does the therapist. As one behavior resolves, focus is applied to another.

For example, an initially shy, reticent, and seemingly withdrawn 8-year-old boy, who became more aggressive in the therapy sessions but not at home, presented an assessment dilemma to me. Was the child simply no longer "turning the anger inward" as the classic view of depression would suggest? Why not at home? Were his projective stories and drawings reflecting anger also? If so, was the anger overwhelming to the child, focused appropriately, or what? The observant therapist becomes aware of the change and is eager to sort out its exact nature and consequences. This requires ongoing assessment during the course of therapy.

With Tim, the 8 year old just mentioned, a repeat administration of several projective picture cards demonstrated nicely how much more clearly he could talk about aggressive content in the pictures than he had six months earlier. In addition, his resolutions to the stories were generally appropriate, and he did not show any signs of being overwhelmed by all this new talk of anger. Thus, I concluded that the anger seen in therapy was appropriate and for some reason was not being reported or seen at home.

DETERMINING THE NEED FOR THERAPY

Let us return to the case of the 6-year-old girl, Abby, fondled by her baby-sitter's brother on at least two occasions. Her distraught parents have presented her to you for therapy after the abuse was substantiated by the local social services office. What do you do? What principles should guide your assessment to determine what treatment needs, if any, exist? I would like to discuss several important guidelines.

The Assessment Should Be Therapeutic in Nature

Ways to do this are to:

1. not rush the process
2. establish rapport before interviewing about the abuse
3. empower the child to make some decisions about what and when to discuss.

Queries about the abuse, the child's beliefs regarding it and herself, and helping her to manage the accompanying affect and to reinterpret those mistaken beliefs can all be therapeutic and a marked reduction in level of symptomatology can follow.

In Abby's case, she initially discussed her abuse in a somewhat matter-of-fact, although nonelaborated, manner. However, she did become somewhat anxious, moving about the room, and then came over to me, moving physically too close. Additionally, she touched me on the nose and around the eyes in a silly manner, something I had not witnessed until a discussion of the abuse began early in the second appointment I had with her. I also thought that her concept of number, other than one, some, and lots, was not well developed, and thus the true incidence of her abuse could not be determined. Finally, her beliefs about the abuse, "it was yucky, gross" were in contrast to her overly familiar behavior with me. This divergence suggested that Abby could benefit from some guided discussion about the abuse.

The Assessment Preferably Takes Place Over Several Sessions

This allows for more information, and a pace that is nonpressured and respectful of the child's anxiety and willingness to disclose can be therapeutic, reminding the child that the intrusiveness of the evaluation process can be manageable and not overwhelming. The fact that Abby's behavior and affect were appropriate during the first session and that it was only when I probed into an area of conflict that some distress and inappropriateness were noted clearly supports the need for extended evaluative contacts. It also supports the need to at least begin some discussion of the abuse if you are to truly know the extent of impact.

The "traumatic events interview" developed by Eth and Pynoos (1985) provides both a model and a point of departure. In this interview, described in more detail later, they essentially have the child recount the traumatic event within the first contact, usually within one hour. There is a great deal to be gained from a recounting and subsequent rein-terpretation, but I prefer to make the pace less intrusive with the sexual-ly abused child.

Multimodal and Multisetting Assessments Are Recommended

Essentially, I want to hear from the child and the parent or parent figures. Information from other settings in which the child may spend time—e.g., school—is also important. I am interested not only in overt behavior but also in the child's internal world; in addition to emotional processes, I also believe the assessment of intelligence and achievement is important. The child's social relationships must also be assessed. Not only do they indicate the level of the child's social development and accompanying social skills but close relationships can also buffer the negative impact of the abuse and be curative.

Abby was reported by her parents and teachers to have behavior within normal limits. However, her kindergarten teacher wrote about her sexual behavior in the margin of the teacher's checklist she complet-ed, indicating that it had been present for several months. Her parents completed the Child Sexual Behavior Inventory (Friedrich et al., 1989) and this also documented her interest in her father's genitals, her moth-er's breasts, persistent masturbation in a number of settings, and hug-ging and standing too close to strangers. Abby's drawing of herself reflected some conflict (she drew herself frowning but was vague about the reason for this), and twice she mentioned a small girl being molested in her responses to several projective pictures from the Roberts Apper-ception Test for Children (McArthur & Roberts, 1982). A friend she had had in preschool was no longer spending any time with her because this child's mother was bothered by some exhibitionism she observed be-tween the two girls and her younger son. Intelligence was in the lower half of the average range, as were her preacademic skills.

My interview with the parents revealed some primary vegetative signs of depression in each and a reduction in the father's ability to concentrate. When I watched Abby with them, I saw that their parenting effectiveness was sub par. The mother reported that she felt so guilty about Abby having been fondled that she could not bring herself to discipline her. Thus, a potential breakdown in the parent-child hierarchy threatened. Fortunately, Abby continued to be reasonably well behaved. Further therapy consultation was deemed necessary after this evaluation period, and because of the broad assessment, we could target goals for both parents and Abby.

The next section reviews areas to be assessed in sexually abused children, including overt behavior and the child's internal world.

ASSESSMENT OF THE CHILD VICTIM

Interviewing

As mentioned in the first paragraph of this chapter, I am not focusing on investigative interviewing as part of the assessment process. I believe that there are some excellent materials that provide models for investigative interviewing and refer you to these (Boat & Everson, 1986; MacFarlane, 1986; White, 1987). I do believe that the abuse is a central issue in the therapy and must be discussed with the child. Within the first two or more therapy sessions the child and I negotiate when and how we will talk about what brought the child to therapy. Although in many cases I have done some of the initial interviewing, we usually do talk about the abuse again once we are meeting for therapy purposes.

What can one learn from those first important interviews that lead into therapy? I refer the reader to Chapter 1 in which I talked about coping with adversity. Children will let you know early on whether they are going to move toward you, move against you, or move away from you (Horney, 1950).

This can occur in the waiting room and may reflect the parents' stance toward you, e.g., if they are angry and distressed, the child may reflect their posture. If the child is being brought by a foster parent, you may be just one of a confusing array of adults whom the child is seeing. None of what these adults do is making any sense to the child. At this time, your role really becomes that of a friendly guide to the child: you can identify the various players in the child's life, clarify why the child is talking to you, and explain what you and the child are going to be doing.

Children look to adults for guidance and direction. We frequently have a naive notion that somehow children should know that they need to come into the therapy room and talk about what is important to them. Our adult-centered perspective may get in the way of realizing what the child needs in the way of guidance and direction.

Summit (1983) defined the sexual abuse accommodation syndrome as emerging in the face of a storm of family confusion that accompanies the disclosure of sexual abuse; children frequently will back away from allegations and essentially accommodate themselves to sexual abuse. Their efforts at individuating themselves from the family situation have been met by feedback that effectively alters these efforts. Your job as an evaluator/therapist in these early interviews is to establish rapport and to position yourself as a guide for the child. This will enable the child to use the therapy successfully.

So, beginning with the first contact in the waiting area, you can assess the child's posture toward you and the child's posture toward the caregiver. Is the separation too easy and the connection with you too quickly formed? Does anxious chatter begin quickly as the child deals with the stress of meeting another new person? Is a hand proffered or not? Does the child exhibit anxiety by needing bathroom breaks? Does the child assume a too familiar tone with you or is the behavior intruding on your personal boundaries? This chapter will discuss different ways to organize your thinking about some of the child's initial behaviors that suggest the issues the child is bringing into the therapy.

My interviews with children are usually conducted in a playroom or in a room in which toys are available. This is true even for somewhat older children, who frequently find it easier to talk to a toy that they are manipulating than to talk directly to me. We cover the basics in the first interview that occur in any child interview:

1. their understanding of why they are there
2. their current situation and with whom they are living; their reactions to and feelings about that
3. their perceptions of their relationship with their parents and peers
4. their likes and dislikes.

Finally, we bring up the issue that will be at least an initial focus in therapy — the sexual abuse. At this point we arrange for when that will be discussed.

A useful technique during this first interview is family drawings or some cards from the Roberts Apperception Test that depict family scenes, leave-taking scenes, and closeness scenes. For the issue of sexual abuse, I sometimes bring cards from the Projective Storytelling Task (Caruso, 1987) and use these as a way to bring about some discussion. Use these cards to determine a child's progress in therapy, e.g., better resolutions to the stories, less anxiety.

I borrow heavily for these first sessions from the Traumatic Event Interview Schedule that was developed by Eth and Pynoos (1985). The three stages of the interview are listed in Table 3-1. I follow this format in a broad fashion when we do reach the time in the first several sessions that the sexual abuse is to be discussed.

It is not surprising to find the child minimizing what happened. In one of my clinical studies (Friedrich, 1988a), I found that a subset of children actually elaborated further over the course of therapy about what had happened to them, but a similar size subset minimized what had gone on over time. In response to children's questions about why it

TABLE 3-1
Stages of the Traumatic Events Interview

1. Possible initial interventions
   Obtain information from parents about facts, behavioral reactions, etc.
   Establish the framework
   a) Be with the child
   b) "I've spoken to other children who have gone through what you have"
   c) Create an expectation that the event(s) needs to be described
   d) Provide drawing materials
   e) Instruct the child to tell a story
   f) Identify coping strategies the child is utilizing (if any)

2. Revivification
   a) Move from drawing to more explicit discussion
   b) Deal with child's being overwhelmed by intensity-emotional release
   c) Get child to discuss more fully in words
   d) Review sensory experiences, e.g., smells, feelings
   e) Promote a full description, despite a rising level of anxiety
   f) Identify worst moment
   g) "Make meaning" of why it happened, e.g., issues of responsibility
   h) Inquire about dreams and, if possible, tie them to the assault
   i) Deal with additional revelations

3. Tying up loose ends (initial attempts)
   a) Summarize what you have learned
   b) Emphasize the normalcy and understandability of the child's responses
   c) Do the dialectic between helpless fear and sadness/anger
   d) Compliment child
   e) Inquire about other concerns
   f) Discuss what they learned about themselves in these interviews

is important to talk about something they have already mentioned to the sheriff or social worker, I do paraphrase their concerns and their sense of exposure to them and take their requests seriously.

This is an issue that frequently comes up in my work with adult victims. Some adults have been able to articulate to me some of their fears that accompany a discussion of the abuse. The insight provided by these adults has enabled me to think about the origins of fears in children. For example, some adults fear that simply talking about the abuse will result in revictimization. Or, in other words, talking about the abuse invites me to abuse the child. Another common adult fear is my reaction to their disclosure, e.g., I will view them in a less favorable light. Other adults feel that this is the only part of their life that anybody has been interested in and talking about it further supports this belief.

Finally, the PTSD literature describes how victims avoid stimuli associated with the trauma, leading to a numbing of general responsiveness. This avoidance must be supportively overcome so that therapy can begin.

Even though some of these fears are not articulated by the child, I anticipate them and try to talk to the child directly about them. For example, I might say, "Some children really worry about what I will think about them when they talk about what happened. Part of you thinks that I won't like you when you tell me. Another part knows it's important to talk about this to safe people. Why don't we try to draw a picture of you? Let's make part of your picture worried about what I'll think. Let's make another part feeling brave. We can decide which one wins."

Children respond to requests of this type in many ways, ranging from refusal to compliance. The drawing from one 8 year old included a self-portrait with him wearing a green shirt that depicted doubt and red pants that depicted the part that was brave. When the red pants won, we talked. I find this type of drawing technique, which captures the child's ambivalence, to be useful. It is borrowed from Harter (1977) and I recommend her excellent paper to you. It provides a way to bring conflicting feelings into the room with a child who has difficulty comprehending two feelings simultaneously.

I also feel that it is important for the therapist to allay the child's fears about being further harmed or abused. This is particularly true for the fragile child, who needs to have structure established quickly in the interview, and also for the child who comes in with a false sense of bravado or pseudomaturity. A statement that "I will never touch you in that way" can be reassuring.

Again, I borrow from adults who have been sexually victimized; they have convinced me of the importance of making those types of reassuring statements. Toward the end of about two years of therapy with a mother who had been sexually abused, and whose two daughters had also been abused, she asked, "Do you remember when you told me that therapy was not meant to be sexual and that you would never touch me in a sexual way back when we first started therapy?" I replied that I could remember and that I felt it was an important rule to establish in my therapy with victims. And she stated, "When you said that, I knew you understood how scared I was."

It may seem strange to be offering a child some reassurances before there is even a statement on the child's part that these are actual fears that the child may have. I do not presume to know what the child is thinking in many cases and, thus, I will not offer these reassurances until I know the child better and understand his or her fears more precisely. However, for many children you can be assured that, although these fears have not been verbalized, they are present.

I will not discuss the theoretical and clinical rationale for why I feel that it is important to have the child talk about the abuse experiences until the next chapter, but suffice it to say children need direction in therapy, the abuse is what brings them in, and they are probably not going to volunteer information unless you give them some indication not only that you are able to handle it but also that it is an important part of therapy.

Behavioral Symptoms

There are three broad categories of behavioral symptoms that one can assess: generic behavioral problems, sexual behavior problems, and behaviors that are thought to be specifically related to traumatic events. Assessment of these last behaviors reflects the research that views sexual abuse symptoms as being conceptualized best from a PTSD framework. The most widely researched and validated measures exist in the first category, child generic behavioral problems. The other two areas are far less well researched, and empirically sound measures have only recently been developed.

The research on the behavioral symptoms related to sexual abuse has become more consistent in the last several years. The initial clinical literature identified a "laundry list" of symptoms, such as bedwetting, nightmares, and fear of strangers, that was thought to indicate sexual abuse (Bolton et al., 1989). This list has been tempered by empirical research with comparison groups. The findings indicate that the majority of behavioral symptoms exhibited by sexually abused children are not unique to this group of children (Browne & Finkelhor, 1986; Conte & Schuerman, 1987; Mannarino & Cohen, 1987).

One of the few behaviors that has been consistently linked to sexual abuse is sexualized behavior, and this is not necessarily the case for even the majority of children (Friedrich et al., 1986; 1988a). In addition, many preschoolers who are sexually abused are already somewhat more sexual simply because of their developmental phase. Thus, it is more likely in preschoolers to see increased masturbation and exhibitionism. Parceling out even the symptom of sexualized behavior in a preschooler and determining if it is present at a greater than average rate is difficult. The reader is reminded of the scant developmental literature on sexual behavior, indicating that there are different periods in a child's life when he or she is more likely to be sexual without any history of sexual abuse (Martinson, 1976).

How useful are behavior checklists for identifying those behaviors that are frequently, although not exclusively, seen in sexually abused children, e.g., sudden changes in behavior, bedwetting, increase in fears, sleep problems, and an increase in aggression? Generally checklists do a reasonably adequate job with these specific behaviors, but for the assessment of other, more specific constellations of behavior such as the "damaged goods syndrome" (Porter et al., 1982) or "betrayal" (Finkelhor & Browne, 1985), interviewing and projective assessment are more likely to provide evidence of their existence. In addition, as therapists we know that one temporary "resolution" to sexual abuse is pseudomaturity, presumably the absence of behavioral problems. Obviously, a child presenting in this manner would not be identified as having behavioral problems with any of the measures of which I am aware.

Whether behavior checklists are sensitive enough to detect underlying pathology is another question. Consider a child I saw recently, a 7-year-old girl, who adapted readily to her foster home, exhibited decreased behavioral problems on the Child Behavior Checklist (Achenbach & Edelbrock, 1983), and showed no overt pathology during a play interview. It was observed, however, that she was extremely passive. During a conjoint session she talked about how she never got mad and was always polite. During the follow-up play session, she then massacred a rooster puppet in a disjointed outburst of aggressive play. Practically every object of destruction in the room was used against the rooster. No empathy was shown despite "protests" from the therapist.

Now consider her background. Her extremely passive mother, battered and abused herself, was overwhelmed and unable to protect her five daughters, all of whom exhibited signs of sexual abuse. The 7 year old, despite being the second oldest, acted as the oldest because of the mental handicap of her older sister and her mother's need for assistance. She had had no opportunity to deal with her own abuse, and her projective test data showed an absence of channels of emotional expression, e.g., very constricted stories. The object of this is that assessment going beyond a rating of her behavior was needed to ferret out what was occurring. Usually, two to three appointments are needed. Girls, particularly, may be underidentified regarding behavioral problems.

Generic Behavioral Problems

The utility of a good behavioral assessment is far greater than just identifying whether or not a child exhibits those symptoms commonly thought to be related to sexual abuse. Rather, the well-validated, 113-item Child Behavior Checklist (CBC), developed by Thomas Achenbach and Craig Edelbrock (1983), can be helpful in identifying for the therapist, and documenting for the mother and other involved parties, the true nature and extent of the child's behavioral symptoms. Child competencies can also be assessed on this measure. Using the CBC provides the therapist with some objective data about problems the child is exhibiting and enables him or her to determine which of those behaviors might be related to the sexual abuse and which of those might be part of earlier, premorbid functioning. It is then possible to target certain behaviors for amelioration.

A technique I have found to be somewhat useful, depending on the reliability of the reporter, has been to obtain retrospective reports of behavioral problems that the child was exhibiting prior to my first contact. In this way we can pinpoint those difficulties that seem to be more related to the abuse. In addition, these checklists can be used over time, in a repeated assessment format, so that the therapist, the parents, and the child can be apprised as to whether or not the child is making progress.

It is also useful to identify checklists that one can use with a wide age range of children and to get as familiar as possible with these particular measures. The behaviors that are incorporated into the checklist should be specific and easy to understand, and use of the checklist should involve a minimal amount of subjectivity.

Behavior checklists may be contaminated by parental projections. A large percentage of sexually abused children are not viewed accurately by their parents, with scapegoating being a not uncommon occurrence. The distortions reflected in the checklists may not be projections, however, at least not in the true sense of the word. Many parents, whose child has been sexually abused, may assign greater weight to any behavior that has sexual connotations, whereas these may have been dismissed as normal by other parents. I feel the increase seen in sexual behavior in these children reflects these heightened perceptions to a small degree.

Everson and his colleagues (1989), from the University of North Carolina, recently completed research indicating that the accuracy of maternal report on behavior checklists is directly related to the level of maternal support of the child. The most supportive mothers were the most accurate, as determined by separate ratings of the child on the Child Assessment Schedule (CAS) (Hodges, Kline, Stern, Cytryn, & McKnew, 1982). The nonsupportive mothers' report of their child's behavior was inversely correlated with the data from the CAS. In addition, therapists frequently see another subset of parents who are so emotionally involved with their child that it is hard to determine whether or not the symptoms they are identifying are actually the child's or a function of the child and the parent.

If you evaluate a young child who has a history of sexual abuse, who seems to be reasonably intact, and whose range of behavioral problems as seen in interview appears small, but whose parent reports significant behavioral problems, you can assume that your therapeutic task is more difficult. Not only do the parent's distorted perceptions need to be altered so the child can be supported and viewed more realistically, but also the existing behavioral problems have to be addressed. On the other hand, child rating scales have been used with psychiatrically disturbed parents and their reports have been both reliable and valid (Friedlander, Weiss, & Traylor, 1986; Sameroff et al., 1982).

The children whom you see are frequently involved in other settings such as a school. Another advantage to some behavior checklists, particularly the CBC, is that both parent and teacher versions exist. This is also true for the Conners Parent and Teacher Rating Scale (Goyette, Conners, & Ulrich, 1978). At the first appointment, the parent can complete a behavior checklist and be provided with a checklist to give to the teacher, who can return it at his or her earliest convenience. Some checklists allow the teacher to report the child's school grades and peer relationships—important information to gather.

Because the teacher's version of the CBC does not assess sexual behavior problems directly, I add the following behaviors at the end of the behavioral problem portion for the teacher to rate on the same 3-point scale:

1. plays with sex parts in public
2. sex play with peers
3. sexual problems (described)

This provides a report of the presence of these behaviors in the school setting.

Preschool Age   Preschoolers are always difficult to assess with regard to behavioral symptoms. The range of behavior tends to be narrower and a preschooler who exhibits significant behavioral problems at one moment may look remarkably different and much more mature even as soon as a month or two later. Available for this age range (2 to 5 years of age) is the Behar Preschool Behavior Questionnaire (Behar & String-field, 1974) and also two versions of the Achenbach CBC. One version is specifically for 2- to 3-year-old children, and the other version is for children from 4 to 16 years of age. The version for 2 to 3 year olds overlaps considerably with the version for 4 to 16 year olds, but it is briefer and more developmentally appropriate. A large percentage of children who are sexually abused are within this age range and some-times may be involved in treatment for an extended time. Thus, it would be useful to initially assess these children with a measure that can potentially be adapted for use when they are older. This is another reason why my personal preference is the Achenbach CBC.

School Age   Here the therapist has available the Achenbach CBC (4 to 16 years of age) in parent, teacher, and self-report versions and the Conners Behavior Rating Scale (in both parent and teacher versions). Current research in this area with sexually abused children is primarily with the CBC (Einbender & Friedrich, 1989; Friedrich et al., 1986, 1988a, submitted; Mannarino & Cohen, 1987). In addition, another excellent behavior checklist that has been used in some research on behavioral symptoms in sexually abused children is the Louisville Be-havior Checklist (Adams-Tucker, 1984; Miller, Hampe, Barrett, & No-ble, 1977).

Limitations of Generic Behavior Checklists   To reiterate, behavior checklists should be only part of an overall assessment (although, as discussed earlier, they can be useful in identifying specific behaviors that are present and warrant intervention). They suffer from the fact that each observer will report the child's behavior differently because of the nature of the observer and the nature of the setting. Checklists do not assess sexual behaviors with enough specificity.

In addition, therapists looking for a modal set of behavioral problems in sexually abused children will find a surprising amount of heterogeneity, and the presence of several specific behavioral problems cannot, by itself, be viewed as conclusive evidence of sexual abuse.

Finally, the absence of any behavioral problems cannot rule sexual abuse in or out. There is certainly a subset of sexually abused children who genuinely appear to be intact behaviorally. They may have had an earlier period of behavioral regression, more immediate to the abuse, but that has ceased. They may appear to be overly compliant and pseudomature, but neither of these behaviors will result in increased scores on a profile. Rather, these may be precursors to the disguised presentation seen in some older sexual abuse victims (Gelinas, 1983). It is only later that this may give way to depression, dissociative episodes, and the type of behaviors seen in some adult victims.

Sexual Behavior Problems

The presence of sexual behaviors in the young child you are assessing can create a dilemma, resulting in divergent tendencies to either minimize or maximize its presence. An example of its minimization is the fact that when sexual behavior is seen in young children, it is too often dismissed as something that every child does. This has happened an infuriating number of times in court, when an expert offers a psychodynamic explanation for the sexual nature of preschoolers, viewing it as an intrapsychic process, e.g., "Oedipal urges," rather than the result of trauma or learning via abuse. (See Summit, 1988, for a review of how the psychodynamic approach has been misused in this regard.)

An example of the presence of sexual behaviors being maximized comes from a consultation that I did early in my experience with sexually abused children. I was asked to evaluate a child who had exhibited "sexualized behavior" during an interview with anatomically correct dolls done at another setting. When I queried further about the exact nature of this sexualized behavior, I was informed that the child had undressed the dolls and had seemed to be "put off" by the dolls' nudity.

To me, this seemed to be highly subjective, and it provided scant evidence for sexual abuse. Undressing anatomically correct dolls is not a phenomenon unique to sexually abused children. Usually children are introduced to the dolls with a statement that goes something like "These dolls have all their parts. Their clothes can be removed." In addition, I was not sure how reliably anybody could measure a young child being "put off."

Needless to say, this consultation ended with my being unable to get any type of statement from the child as to what had occurred. The child did not even undress my set of anatomically correct dolls. Clearly, some more objective means of assessing sexual behavior in children is needed, particularly because sexuality is viewed so subjectively.

While I was at the University of Washington, two graduate students and I began the development of the Child Sexual Behavior Inventory (CSBI) (Purcell, Beilke, Friedrich, 1986). It has since undergone several revisions and is now a 36-item checklist that is completed by a caregiver (Friedrich et al., 1989). It was designed to expand on those few items pertaining to sexual behavior that were included in the CBC and the Louisville Behavior Checklist (Miller et al., 1977), e.g., masturbates too much or thinks about sex too much. It also includes the behaviors reported to me by mothers of sexually abused children, e.g., inserting objects in vagina or rectum or both, kissing strangers, simulating intercourse, or touching another person's genitals.

An extensive normative project on this measure was undertaken in the past two years and 880 normal children 2 to 12 years of age, with no history of sexual abuse, have been compared with more than 260 sexually abused children. The clinical samples were derived from several sites, including two in California, two in Minnesota, and two in Canada. The sexually abused children were significantly more sexualized and differed from the normative sample on 27 items ($P < 0.01$ or $P < 0.05$) of an earlier, somewhat longer CSBI version. A full listing of these items, written in an abbreviated format, is included in Table 3-2. The full version of the 36-item CSBI is in the Appendix and can be used clinically.

An examination of Table 3-2 reveals that the discriminating items fall into several groups, including boundary permeability (e.g., "Hugs adults he does not know well"), sexual aggression (e.g., "Tries to undress others," "Touches other people's sex parts"), self-stimulation (e.g., "Masturbates with object"), and gender confusion ("Talks about wanting to be the opposite sex"). Because I had seen an inhibition of sexual behavior in some sexually abused girls, another subset of items pertaining to that was also developed (e.g., "Does not want to undress in front of others," "Asks parents not to show sexual behavior"). However, none of these items proved to have discriminating power.

TABLE 3-2
Items on the Child Sexual Behavior Inventory Endorsed More Frequently for Sexually Abused Children

	F*	P
Touches other people's sex (private) parts	7.48	0.0001
If a girl, overly aggressive; if boy, passive	7.17	0.0001
Tries to undress others	6.70	0.0001
Talks about sex acts	6.13	0.0001
Uses words to describe sex acts	5.98	0.0001
Masturbates with object	5.45	0.0001
Hugs adults he does not know well	4.90	0.0001
Shows sex parts to children	4.89	0.0001
Very interested in the opposite sex	4.65	0.0001
Imitates intercourse	4.50	0.0001
Puts mouth on sex parts	4.46	0.0001
Makes sexual sounds	4.42	0.0001
Inserts objects into vagina or anus	4.34	0.0001
Masturbates with hand	4.33	0.0001
Asks others to engage in sex	4.29	0.0001
Rubs body against people or furniture	4.20	0.0001
Imitates sex behavior with dolls	3.65	0.0003
Talks about wanting to be the opposite sex	3.64	0.0003
Tries to view pictures of nude people	3.62	0.0004
Shows sex parts to adults	3.36	0.0009
Asks to view explicit television	3.23	0.0014
Touches sex parts in private	3.09	0.0022
Touches sex parts in public	2.94	0.0035
Touches women's breasts	2.76	0.0062
French kisses	2.60	0.0100

Discriminating items ($P < 0.05$)

	F	P
Talks flirtatiously	2.11	0.0400
Tries to look at people who are undressing	2.04	0.0400

*Values from multivariate analysis of variance.

Although some support for the first four groupings listed above comes from a factor-analytic study completed on the clinical subjects (Friedrich et al., 1989), our research seems to indicate that summing the items (0, 1, 2, 3) to get a total score is the most useful approach. This total score is presumed to reflect the level of overt sexual behavior exhibited by the child.

How might one use the CSBI clinically? In general, the CSBI is useful because it does provide an assessment of overt sexual behaviors in children who have been sexually abused. Parents have sometimes indicated to me that after completing the CSBI they had a fuller appreciation of the extent of their child's sexual behavior and that it truly was a problem that they had been ignoring. Thus, it sensitizes the parents and reveals specific behaviors that can be focused on in the therapy, usually by using a contingency management program (described in more detail in Chapters 5 and 6).

However, simply for assessment purposes, it is useful to know that beginning at 2 years of age and continuing to 12 years of age there is a steady decrease at every age in overall sexual behavior, as measured by the CSBI, in the normative sample. For example, at 2 years of age the average child obtains a mean total score of approximately 10, and this decreases steadily so that by 12 years of age, the average score is slightly over 3. A score of 10, for example, may be obtained by a child because the parent endorses four items at a level of 2 or 3—e.g., masturbates with hand, scratches crotch, touches sex parts at home, and kisses other children not in the family.

Actually, there are eight items endorsed by parents of both normal males and females, 2 to 6 years of age, at a 40% level or more. These include:

1. scratches anal or crotch area, or both
2. touches or tries to touch the mother's or other women's breasts
3. touches sex parts when at home
4. kisses adults not in the family
5. undresses self in front of others
6. sits with crotch or underwear exposed
7. kisses other children not in the family
8. if a boy, plays with girls' toys, and if a girl, plays with boys' toys.

Originally, numbers 4 and 7 above were designed to assess indiscriminate affection-seeking behavior. Interviewing the mothers of these normal children led us to the realization that children are frequently expected to kiss various adults not related to them, and they also may kiss children in their day-care and preschool settings. Thus, the items would need to be reworded to make them more sensitive to sexually abused children—e.g., "kisses children the child does not know." Several of these items were endorsed frequently by parents of children who had not been sexually abused.

Taking this into consideration, we feel that if you have a caregiver who knows the child well and can report reliably, an endorsement of an additional five of the items that discriminate at the $P < 0.01$ or better level would be a conservative determination that this child has probably been sexually abused. A preliminary discriminant analysis has confirmed this. Although this will miss the sexually abused children who are not sexualized, it can identify those sexually abused children who *are* sexualized and who may or may not be disclosing the abuse. Again, it is important to have a caregiver who can report reliably. A day-care provider who has extensive contact with the child may also need to be enlisted in reporting the child's behavior.

It is only logical that sexual behavior discriminates sexually abused children from nonabused children. The experience is likely to be the child's first introduction to the meaning of sexuality, and the sexualization inherent in most sexual abuse is frequently perceived by the child as traumatic in nature, i.e., traumatic sexualization (Finkelhor & Browne, 1985). Not only is the behavior modeled to the child but it is also accompanied by anxiety and confusion, both of which fuel a repetition of the sexual behavior, at least for a brief period. Sexual abuse may shape the child's sexualization in a developmentally inappropriate and dysfunctional fashion. Sexual behavior may persist, depending on the nature of the abuse, the nature of the child, and his or her context. Although no exclusive markers of sexual abuse exist, sexual behavior is a frequent indicator.

In a related vein, a behavioral observation study completed with my colleague, Barbara Lui, rated sexually abused children on discrete behaviors they exhibited during the first interview (Friedrich & Lui, unpublished). They exhibited greater problems with boundary permeability (e.g., standing too close to the interviewer, touching the interviewer) and sexualization (e.g., making sexual comments) than did a group of children being seen for outpatient therapy appointments. Pilot research indicated the utility of these behaviors for discriminating abused children from a group of child outpatients with no history of sexual abuse. Ten of the items from the longer measure are in Table 3-3.

Behavior of Traumatic Onset

Another type of behavioral assessment is derived from the PTSD literature. Although essentially a behavior checklist, the types of behaviors the Children's Impact of Traumatic Events Scale (CITES) (Wolfe et al., 1986) assesses are germane to traumatic events, and they do not include the broad range of behaviors that can be present in children with psychological problems. It was modeled after the Impact of Events

TABLE 3-3
Behaviors to Rate During Initial Interview

	Rating	
	Yes	No
Boundary variables		
1. Child physically touches you	___	___
2. Child is physically destructive of objects in office	___	___
3. Child moves about office without permission	___	___
4. Child hits, kicks, bites, or shoves you	___	___
5. Child touches objects in office without asking	___	___
Sexual variables		
1. Child kisses or hugs you	___	___
2. Child sits with underwear exposed	___	___
3. Child touches his or her own sexual body parts	___	___
4. Child lifts clothing or begins to remove clothing in office	___	___
5. Child spontaneously talks about sexual acts or sexual body parts	___	___

Note. These ten items are taken from a longer, unpublished measure developed by W. N. Friedrich and Barbara Lui.

Scale (Veronen & Kilpatrick, 1986) designed to assess the intrusive thoughts adult rape victims experienced. The CITES includes not only items related to intrusive thoughts ("I think about what happened even when I don't want to") but also items assessing the child's perception of blame, guilt, betrayal, stigmatization, and helplessness.

Pynoos and colleagues (1987) developed a PTSD Reaction Index that is patterned after criteria for PTSD as described in the DSM-III-R. For example, the child indicates to what degree he or she is affected by intrusive thoughts or images that are specific to the traumatic event. These would include flashbacks and revivification. The child is also assessed as to the degree to which he or she avoids situations similar to that in which the trauma occurred. Avoidance of time alone with males might be germane to sexually abused children. A version allowing the parents to report their perceptions of the child's PTSD-like behavior also exists (Nader & Pynoos, n.d.).

Frank Putnam (1987) at the National Institute of Mental Health also developed a preliminary version of the Child Dissociative Checklist. This reflects the fact that dissociation has been identified as a not uncommon response to severe traumatization.

Hartman and Burgess (in press) viewed dissociation as a defensive mechanism used by the child to deal with the strong affect invoked by the abuse. They defined it as a process that allows the person to disengage from the trauma — e.g., the experience of being somewhere else. The child may learn to use this process when reminded of the stressful event.

Putnam's 16-item measure includes such items as "Child goes into a daze or trance-like state," "Child is unusually forgetful or confused about things that she should know," and "Child shows rapid regressions in age-level of behavior." In the Friedrich and Lui (unpublished) behavior rating scale (Table 3–3), with which the therapist rates the child's behavior in an initial interview, only one item from the longer version of the measure, "stares blankly," was thought to be somewhat related to dissociative phenomena. However, in a pilot study, it was endorsed at a significantly more frequent rate in children who were sexually abused than in those who were not, even though it was endorsed only for a small subset of the abused children.

Projective Assessment

Projective assessment, both in general and specifically in an assessment of children, is criticized by a number of people and may not be available as a technique to many of the practitioners reading this book. As a clinician who uses this form of assessment regularly, I have come to appreciate its utility when evaluating child victims of sexual abuse. There also continue to be empirically sound papers supporting its utility (Tuber, 1983).

Broadly speaking, there are three types of projective assessments that I use. These include drawings, stories in response to pictures, and inkblots. I will not discuss the available literature on each one, but rather I will direct my comments to how these tests have been clinically useful with sexually abused children.

Projective Drawings

Despite the repeated failure of projective drawings to be empirically diagnostic for almost any disorder, several papers have been written about their clinical utility with sexually abused children (Burgess, McCausland, & Wolbert, 1981; Cohen & Phelps, 1985; Hibbard, Roghmann, & Hoekelman, 1987; Johnston, 1979; Miller, Veltkamp, & Janson, 1987).

The CSBI normative study also found that sexually abused children drew genitals in their human figure drawings more often in the previous six months than the children in the normative sample. However, contrary to Machover's (1948) contention that genitals are almost never drawn by normal children, a larger than expected percentage of normal children were reported to have drawn them at least once.

Included in the possible drawing techniques are the Kinetic-Family-Drawing (K-F-D), a drawing of family activity, and the Draw-A-Person (DAP), a human figure drawing. During the past several years, as part of the interview schedule described earlier in this chapter, I have more frequently asked the child to draw pictures of the act of abuse and also of the perpetrator. These two are solicited usually when we are discussing the abuse, but drawings of the perpetrator have sometimes been requested when he or she comes up as a focus in therapy, particularly in those cases in which the child harbors ambivalent feelings toward the perpetrator, e.g., desire for contact but fear of further abuse. At this time, I may ask the child to draw the perpetrator when he or she is being nice and when he or she is being mean. Because this request usually parallels the child's mixed feelings about the perpetrator, these issues now become open for discussion in therapy.

I urge you to use drawings primarily for building rapport, storytelling, and soliciting possible conflictual themes. Self-drawings may also reflect the growing health of the child over the course of therapy. It is always too easy to overinterpret drawings. The overinterpretation that I have seen seems to have created in me a reserve against interpretation. But when genitals are included in the family drawings, and breasts and mouths are amplified, the child is certainly suggesting that that is an issue of concern and preoccupation. The following captures an interaction I had with a 5-year-old girl in our second interview. She was drawing a picture of one of three different men who had molested her in the preceding 2¹/₂ years.

Therapist: So you think you'll first draw me a picture of Tom?
Child: Yeah. He has a head.
Therapist: It looks like a head and two eyes.
Child: And a body (laughs).
Therapist: That too. I see you're drawing two legs.
Child: And a belly button and a wiener. They gots hair on them.
Therapist: Uh huh.
Child: A big wiener.
Therapist: It looks big to me. Too big for a little girl.
Child: Not a nice picture. Let's do something else — like that over there. What's that?

Therapist: You did great to draw this and show me how Tom scared
         you with his big wiener. I think you are brave — a brave girl.
Child: No, I'm not!
Therapist: Part of you thinks you were a scaredy-cat and part of you
         knows you were very brave.
Child: I'm going to throw this at you (raises a ball).
Therapist: Let's play with that and come back and be brave again
         later, okay?
Child: Okay.

The presence of genitals on human figure drawings done in a clinical
setting is probably appropriately viewed as pathognomonic (Friedrich &
Luecke, 1988). Hibbard et al. (1987) reported that children known to
have been sexually abused were 6.8 times more likely to draw genitals
than were comparison children. There are other telling symptoms that
may be reflected in human figure drawings, including powerlessness,
depicted in isolated and smaller damaged drawings of the child's self,
and also aggression, depicted by an overly large drawing of a boy hitting
his mother whom he blamed for the abuse.

Another telling indicator is the presence of barriers, e.g., walls or
furniture between individuals in the drawing, suggestive of "less likely
or less easily attempted communication" (Spinetta & Deasy-Spinetta,
1981).

Use of the child's drawings of the perpetrator and of the actual act of
abuse are based on my belief that assessment should be both active and
reparative; at the same time it should engender therapeutic movement
in the child. A further rationale comes from the Traumatic Events Interview (Eth & Pynoos, 1985), in which the child is asked to draw the
traumatic event in addition to discussing it. A child may be more able to
draw the perpetrator than to actually talk about the person, and the
same is true for the act of abuse. Again, during the drawing, supportive
comments can be made to the child about the child's bravery, tenacity,
and perseverance in the face of the abuse.

Projective Stories

Both the Thematic Apperception Test (TAT) (Bellak, 1975) and the
Children's Apperception Test (CAT) (Bellak, 1975) are widely used with
children. Initially, I used the TAT almost exclusively and only rarely the
CAT. Increasingly, I am using two measures, the Roberts Apperception

Test for Children (RATC) (McArthur and Roberts, 1982) and the Projective Storytelling Test (Caruso, 1987).

I use the Roberts test because the drawings are more active, realistic, and contemporary. They include drawings of family activities and mother-child affection; they also have several drawings in which fathers are present alone with their children. One of the Roberts Apperception Test cards (card no. 15) specifically does pull for sexual content. It depicts a young boy looking through a partially open bathroom door at the partial side-view of a woman bathing. Consider the following two responses to that card, and the response by the boy with sexual preoccupation (and a history of abuse) is quite evident. Both boys are 10 years old.

Boy 1:   He had to go to the bathroom real bad and so he ran into it without knocking. His older sister was in there taking a bath and he got all nervous and turned and ran out to go to the bathroom downstairs. He apologized to her and she wasn't too mad at him because, after all, it was an accident.

Boy 2:   This is pretty cool. He's looking at a naked woman. You can see her boobs. He's a peeking Tom. I'd like to do that. He keeps looking at her put soap all over her body. She never knows he's watching her. He feels happy.

The second response is clearly characterized both by the boy being drawn to the sexual content and by the absence of an organized story.

The Projective Storytelling Test was developed much more recently than the Roberts test and was designed to assess abused children. It includes pictures that pull for stories related to physical or sexual abuse, or both. Some of the pictures include adults and children, and others include older and younger children. A child who is preoccupied by sexual issues is much more likely to project these issues onto these cards than in response to either the CAT or the TAT.

What the child says in response to the picture is important, but so is the child's demeanor in the telling. A child who seems agitated by the pictures, or who becomes increasingly agitated during the presentation of the pictures, or who begins to tell you a story that has an extremely divergent or bizarre ending is presenting useful cues regarding his or her psychological makeup. The child is indicating to you that he or she is having difficulty regulating affective arousal to cards that are reminders of the abuse experience. Just because a child does not react in this way does not mean that the child was not similarly abused. It may mean simply that the child is better able to regulate this affect.

A clearly needed research study would be to determine whether sexually abused children do provide greater sexual content in their responses to either the RATC or the Projective Storytelling Test.

Apart from the sexual content, which may reflect the child's degree of traumatic sexualization, the impact of the remaining three traumagenic factors can also be assessed via projective stories. Whether or not stories have appropriate and positive resolutions may reflect powerlessness; stigmatization may be reflected in children reporting shame and embarrassment; and betrayal issues may be present in those stories that ignore father figures, describe ambivalent mother-child relations, or more openly recount betrayal and deception. Each of these can actually be operationalized and reliably determined, and I recommend it to any practitioner in this field.

I recall one series of Roberts stories provided to me by an 8-year-old sexually abused child. She had been molested by a female friend of her mother's and also by this woman's teenage son. The mother had not been protective of the child, and the child spent six weeks in a psychiatric hospital after a suicide attempt. Her responses to the 10 cards that I gave to her included absolutely no mention of her mother. Even those pictures that directly pulled for mention of mothers in a supportive setting did not do so. The mother had made appointments at the hospital and professed her concern for her daughter, but it was with these stories that I had a picture of the level of disconnection between those two people and the probable lack of support of the daughter by her mother. This was then borne out when the daughter went home and again engaged in self-injurious behavior. She was removed and placed in a foster-care setting and improved markedly during the course of the foster placement. Interestingly, she could not talk about the abuse while she was in the care of her mother, but she could begin to talk about the abuse when she was in a supportive environment.

The Family Relations Test (Bene & Anthony, 1976) is also a useful, but underutilized, test in this area. Essentially, the examiner, with the help of the child, creates the child's family with cardboard figures. The child then sends messages to each of these family members from a list of standard messages. These messages are both positive and negative, and the child's distribution of messages can reflect the child's perception of and relationship to various family members. It is not surprising that mothers in incestuous families are often perceived as unsupportive and punitive. When this emerges, an important focus for therapy has been suggested.

I have also developed a subset of messages that have sexual abuse material in them that I use with sexually abused children. These messages are then included with the other messages that the child "sends" to the various cardboard figures. This is another vehicle to use in therapy to gently enable the child to begin to talk about the abuse. Physically abused children do report more aggression from the abuser than do comparison children on the Family Relations Test (Einbender & Friedrich, unpublished), but no similar comparison has been done with sexually abused children.

Rorschach Test

This measure is probably the least understood by the average therapist for sexually abused children, but it can be quite useful. The child is asked to provide responses to a series of 10 inkblots, and these responses are thought to reflect how the child perceives emotional stimuli. Given the number of children I see in whom PTSD is suspected, including intrusive thoughts and dissociative phenomena, the Rorschach has been invaluable not only for identifying those particular types of issues but also for providing a broad and rich picture of the child.

When scored with the Exner (1974) system, the Rorschach responses provide information about the child's ability to cope and how the child tends to cope, i.e., by processing things internally, by avoiding affect completely, or by being more affective. Their ability to modulate impulses, the quality and extent of their interpersonal relationships, and their sense of violation and sexualization are also provided to me by the Rorschach responses. Other information on emotional resources, self-esteem, judgment, and depression are also provided. Although a study I recently collaborated on failed to find group differences on Rorschach variables (Einbender & Friedrich, 1989), the problem with the study was that the variables we used were composite variables, thus obscuring some of the explanatory variance. I believe projective testing is more useful on a case-by-case basis than via the examination of group differences.

The Rorschach test can be invaluable, particularly with the diagnostic issue of dissociative phenomena, which present difficult treatment issues and can make a therapist initially believe that everything is all right when in actuality it is not. The Rorschach results can inform me, in several ways, whether a child uses dissociative phenomena. The first is when I notice increasing regression across the series of 10 cards. The child usually begins quite adequately with the first card or so but then may deteriorate as the cards become more colorful and complex. A second indicator is seen when the child provides a response, particularly a mutilated or sexual response, and then denies this response when you ask her what about the inkblot made it look like that. This is a standard process of inquiry on the Rorschach test that enables one to score the test.

For instance, a 12-year-old girl who told me "a bleeding vagina" in response to the center portion of card no. 2 and then on inquiry denied that she had ever said that also denied two other later responses to the Rorschach, both involving mutilated body parts. She was described by her teachers as overly polite but sometimes "not there." I was unaware of the fact that she was molesting a child whom she was baby-sitting during the first few months of therapy. The girl became extremely depressed when this was discovered, and initially she denied the fact. We struggled for a few months while she grappled with the issue "How could I be doing something I wasn't aware of?" Interestingly, this girl also had several earlier reported episodes of shoplifting, and she denied awareness of those, although her mother confronted her about them. Her abuse history included being raped at 7 years of age by an older stepbrother and then, from 9 to 11 years of age, having repeated vaginal sexual intercourse with another stepbrother. She had been threatened with death if she made any attempt to report it.

A recent study (Tuber & Coates, 1989) used the Rorschach with boys with Gender Identity Disorder of Childhood, a syndrome seen occasionally in sexually abused boys. Results indicated greater deviance overall, suggesting disturbance in aspects of functioning other than simply gender symptomatology.

Finally, the Rorschach is also useful at documenting a child's being in touch with reality. Sometimes attorneys for the offender will talk about a child's fabrication of events, and the Rorschach is an excellent tool for the psychometric assessment of reality testing.

Child Self-Report Measures

Despite the plethora of measures designed to elicit the child's report on everything from fears, anxieties, depression, self-esteem, and general behavior, they have often been disappointing to me clinically and in terms of research. The chapter by Wolfe and Wolfe (1988) mentioned earlier is dominated by a discussion of child self-report measures and I encourage any reader interested in these measures to review their chapter.

Four different studies have used self-report measures with sexually abused children (Einbender & Friedrich, 1989; Friedrich et al., submitted; Gomes-Schwartz et al., 1985; Wolfe et al., in press). These measures were designed to assess variables ranging from self-esteem to depression and anxiety. From my reading of each of these studies, none of the child self-report measures from sexually abused children differed from those of normative samples or showed significant elevations when contrasted with those of smaller comparison samples.

For example, in the Friedrich paper, we assessed more than 40 young boys who had been sexually abused and who were being referred to a special treatment program for boys who continued to exhibit behavioral problems after having completed a brief course of initial therapy for the sexual abuse. Thus, by design, the majority of these boys should show significant behavioral problems. We could not identify those problems on our self-report measures, with the boys reporting themselves to be completely intact on two measures of self-esteem and one measure of depression. Yet they were seen as having significant behavioral problems by their parents and their therapists.

A recent study examined the discrepancy between adult and child reports about child problems with competence and self-esteem (Zimet & Farley, 1986). Although the adult ratings were highly correlated for these children, all beginning day treatment and presumably disturbed, the authors stated that the children's "highly inflated positive self-ratings may simply be a well-constructed defense against the painful self-disclosure of their current status." In a similar vein, children in a social skills training group conducted at the Mayo Clinic actually got significantly "worse," by self-report of self-esteem, by the end of 16 weeks of therapy (Rasmussen, 1989). They were viewed as having become more self-aware and also less defensive as a function of the treatment.

The reason for this dilemma is probably the design of the self-report measures. Although I do believe that a measure such as the CITES (Wolfe et al., 1986) can be useful because it is specific to sexual abuse, younger children will respond in a socially desirable fashion; they have trouble making generalizations, knowing their own psychological processes (particularly when they have been traumatized), and may not be used to self-disclosure in general. Harter's Perceived Competence Scale for Children (1982), designed to assess the child's sense of self, including self-concept and self-esteem, is a more successful measure because it reduces the tendency to give socially desirable responses. This area of child self-report research clearly shows promise.

Cognitive and Achievement Testing

Initially, some therapists whom I have supervised are under the assumption that children are quite similar intellectually and have equal verbal facility in the therapy room. That is not the case. Children vary widely and the level of their variation is not fully known unless a careful cognitive and school achievement assessment is done. This allows you to know what the child's verbal abilities are, whether or not school achievement is up to par, and whether or not intervention is needed in the school setting. It also can make for convincing testimony when you are testifying about a 4-year-old child with an IQ of 110 who has reported to you that she was abused. It is hard for a perpetrator's attorney to counter the fact that this child is performing at a cognitive level higher than 75% of her peers.

I have been involved in several cases in which false allegations have been the issue. I recall one in particular in which the child was said to have made a detailed report that included several technical words and to have appropriately used sophisticated language. When I met her, I was struck by her lack of verbal skills and the fact that she did not understand such concepts as above-below, in-out, and between-next to. At 6 years old, her measured intelligence was in the low 60s on the Stanford-Binet, a widely used intelligence test. Her perceptual-motor skills were at the 3-year level. Thus, I could decide based on some convincing evidence that, at the very least, this child had not generated the initial report nor the detailed drawing provided to me by a caregiver depicting "how daddy had put his thing in her." She had neither the intelligence nor the verbal or drawing skills to make such a statement. This enabled us to be more critical about that first report and to make a better determination of what actually was going on in her life.

Academic Assessment

The use of a careful academic assessment concurrent with the beginning of therapy can add information that is helpful to more than just overall treatment planning. A significant percentage of abused children come from disadvantaged families and, for that reason alone, are likely to have learning difficulties. Their parents may be overwhelmed and not able to advocate getting appropriate help. There is also evidence that suggests that children who have been physically abused, and that certainly would include a subset of sexually abused children, have language difficulties that can be documented early on (Friedrich, Einbender, & Luecke, 1983).

Two recent studies (Einbender & Friedrich, 1989; Koverola, 1989) showed that sexually abused girls, in contrast to nonabused girls, have significantly lower cognitive abilities and academic achievement. No one can determine the origins of this lowered intelligence, whether it is situation-related or, probably, multifactorial in nature, but the problem does exist. If the child's school success is ignored in your treatment of the child, an opportunity for her to have personal success and the opportunity to make friends may be excluded from this child's life.

We also know that some sexually abused girls are going to exhibit pseudomature behavior. This precocious socially appropriate behavior may keep them from coming to the attention of an overworked school psychologist who could detect a possible learning difficulty. Truancy and running away from home were identified as two behaviors in teenage girls who have been sexually abused (Goldston, Turnquist, & Knutson, in press), which differentiated them from nonabused adolescents, and school difficulties probably played a role in precipitating some of this behavior.

Now consider the case of Hilary, an 8-year-old third grader, living with her mother and allegedly sexually abused by her father on weekend visitations. These visits had been indefinitely stopped via court order after a local mental health professional had stated in court, "The child's sudden onset of school difficulties and school phobia are classic markers of sexual abuse." The professional went on to state that the child became agitated and upset when discussing her father, and although no specific allegations were mentioned, long-term therapy was deemed necessary to uncover what had actually happened. Adding to all of the confusion was the hostile nature of the parents' continuing relationship. The mother's belief that her former husband had molested her daughter was supported, for her, by her belief that he was still subscribing to *Playboy*.

The child was referred to me and she did indeed present as a fearful child, who spoke little and seemed afraid of me (and presumably other men). My academic assessment revealed a child who had done average work in both first and second grade, by maternal report, but who had a WISC-R Full-Scale IQ of 86 and significant problems in reading comprehension and perceptual-motor skills. Her handwriting was quite poor and done laboriously. These test results presented an alternative, but equally viable, explanation for the school difficulties. The transition from second to third grade is marked by a much heavier academic burden, and it seemed reasonable that her adequate early work would not preclude a sudden drop, given evidence for some perceptual-motor and possible language problems. My therapy focused on relaying these results to the mother and school, obtaining extra assistance in school for the child, and helping resolve the school phobia with conjoint interventions designed to help the mother parent more effectively and set clearer expectations for her daughter.

After almost three months had passed, Hilary's symptoms had improved and she had given no indication of sexual abuse, despite two separate attempts by myself to use the Boat and Everson (1986) interview model, allowing for more and specific questioning. In fact, at the second interview, she had gone beyond her initial passivity and staring into space and denied that abuse had occurred. During this period Hilary had had no contact with her father.

Given her improvement, a reasonable explanation for her school difficulties, and her denial of sexual abuse, her mother and I began to move in the direction of resuming visitation. However, the post-divorce marital conflict continued as a factor in this family.

This case illustrates the fact that assessment can illuminate tough cases in a more objective manner that I hope results in better decision-making conducive to the continued growth of the child. The disruption of the parent-child relationship and, as importantly, the academic pressure on Hilary, were clearly not helpful and, in fact, were harmful to her ongoing growth and development.

How Assessment Is Useful in the Planning of Treatment

Even at this point in the chapter, you may wonder "What can I learn from assessment to guide treatment that I could not learn simply from some repeated exposure to the child and the family?" At least three broad reasons for assessment can be stated.

1. Behavioral assessment, more than any technique, enables the therapist to (a) identify quickly the nature and scope of behavioral problems in a child, (b) pinpoint those that lend themselves best to treatment given that particular family, (c) get the family focused on positive change, and then (d) document improvement over time. This is particularly important in those families that are skeptical about therapy and tentative with the therapist. Some return on their investment is needed for them to stay with therapy.

2. Children who are significantly traumatized may have assumed a veneer of propriety and superficial maturity. The therapist who simply uses nondirective play therapy may decide little is wrong and terminate therapy prematurely. What do therapists do when they have a shy, sweet, 9 year old in their office who claims everything is fine, has a few minor somatic complaints, works too hard in school, and gets better grades than expected given her intelligence? The therapists know full well that this child is not fine, because the abuse that she experienced was so horrendous. In my practice, I use a thorough assessment and the material that is generated in the course of the assessment is brought back directly to the therapy. When this child responds with mutilation on the Rorschach test and has themes of abandonment on the Roberts test, those are issues that we now know must be a focus in the therapy.

3. These children, particularly the females, often have unidentified school achievement problems. They are quiet, get along adequately with their peers, do not bother their teachers, and thus, do not come to the attention of school officials. But, as mentioned before, therapeutic intervention should occur on many levels and across many modalities. In addition to the weekly therapy that you are providing and the occasional groups the child is attending, if this child is now receiving Title I assistance in the school setting and improving her reading so that she is no longer in danger of failing third grade, you have aided her for her lifetime.

ASSESSMENT OF PARENT FIGURES

Probably it is in this area that the term ecological is most accurately used. It is critical to know what is going on with the non-offending parent in terms of psychological status; I have worked hard to be an informed consumer and producer of evaluations on offenders. This enables me to know what type of incestuous father this child has lived with and whether or not this man has the proclivity and resources to make the changes that are needed.

I also feel that by knowing what makes a good evaluation of a sex offender, I can also be a good advocate for my child client. If a local mental health professional has given the child's father only a brief interview and an MMPI, stating that this man "doesn't fit the profile of an incestuous father," it is essential to know at the very least that there is no such profile (Friedrich, 1988b). I want to know enough about what constitutes a valid evaluation in these circumstances and be of assistance to the county or state's attorney as he or she pushes for a more thorough evaluation.

At the very least, an offender evaluation must be done by someone who has a specialty interest and expertise in this area. A generic mental health professional will not suffice. After this important criterion is met, the evaluation must consist of extensive interviewing, including thorough sex, legal, and chemical-use histories; objective personality assessment, e.g., MMPI, Millon Clinical Multiaxial Inventory (MCMI); and projective personality assessment, e.g., Rorschach, TAT, or Incomplete Sentences. Psychophysiologic assessment, e.g., penile plethysmograph or polygraph, can be useful but has a technologic seductivity about it that can muddle the usually clear thinking of some experts. Finally, the expert must be open to police reports and social service interviews with the children and put the burden of proof onto the person being evaluated to rationalize those reports away. Salter (1988) includes an excellent guide to offender evaluations.

For non-offending mothers, I also routinely ask for an MMPI evaluation. Although some people have suggested that this is an extra burden to an already overburdened individual, I do not think that this request is too burdensome as long as I explain that it helps me to understand her and to plan better for her daughter's or son's treatment. I explain the fact that one way for me to help her daughter is to get to know her and any problems that she might have. The abuse of the child can provide an opportunity for the entire family to make changes that are necessary and long overdue, and knowing her in a better way can bring that about. I routinely provide feedback from objective testing and use this session to help identify treatment goals.

It is critical to know about the mother's level of depression, passive-aggressiveness (which tells me the likelihood not only of her going along with treatment but also of her parenting consistency), and also her own reality testing. If I see certain profiles that suggest that she may also have been sexually abused and may not have resolved that herself, I want to be able to support her in getting personal therapy for those issues. Other shorter screening measures that may also be used are the SCL-90 or a depression measure, such as the Beck Depression Inventory. However, I find both of these provide too little information.

One of the more commonly found MMPI profiles in mothers of sexually abused children is a 4-3 profile, which has been identified in 18% of these mothers in two separate studies (Friedrich, 1988b). It suggests the strong likelihood of anger, family conflict, and a tendency to ignore the obvious. A parent with this profile frequently has children who act out aggressively, and the parent benefits more from structured, goal-setting parent training programs than from something more flexible or unstructured. When planning for treatment, this is useful information to have.

EVALUATION OF CIVIL DAMAGES

It is appropriate that a chapter on assessment include at least some mention of assessment in those cases involving civil damages. These cases are increasing and I am generally supportive of them for several reasons:

1. The long-term psychological damage can be great.
2. The remuneration obtained may go for much needed therapy expenses.
3. The formal act of assigning blame and demanding restitution may be a naturally therapeutic event.

However, the process of gathering evidence, providing depositions and testimony, and the limbo status many of these cases acquire can be negative and undermine the good that could be obtained under ideal circumstances (Berliner, 1989).

Regardless, mental health professionals are frequently being requested to make determinations about long-term consequences of sexual abuse in children as part of legal cases demanding civil damages. Similar issues that apply to other civil damage cases are present here, namely the difficult task of determining the specific impact of an event or series of events on a person at a point in time and projecting into the future. Given that child sexual abuse is for the most part a new field and few of us have followed child cases into adulthood, the task may be educated guesswork in some cases.

Sexual abuse presents several other difficulties beyond determining impact. One of these is the fact that the families in which sexual abuse occurs are frequently disturbed prior to the fact, and for a long time they may not have provided the type of nurturing environment needed by the child.

For example, in a large civil damage case involving many children who were sexually abused in a day-care setting, the task of sorting out psychological impact of abuse, over and above the fact that their parents had previous psychiatric histories, were undereducated, and were predominantly lower class and that the children may have been physically abused, neglected, or sexually abused in other settings besides day-care, presented a nightmare of an assessment task for me.

One of the professionals in the case, on the side of the plaintiffs, wanted to attribute every deviation from the norm to the sexual abuse. Although I could argue that a 12-point deviation from an IQ of 100 could be attributable to the child's parents' low average intelligence and the unstimulating home environment, I wanted to consider the fact that this may have made the child more vulnerable to sexual abuse and less able to report reliably and also that it could be a function of the abuse, because learning problems in abused children have been documented (Einbender & Friedrich, 1989; Hewitt & McNaught, 1987).

It is important to heed the advice of Gary Melton (1987), who made the obvious case for professionals to stick to the facts in these cases or to lead with their heads rather than their hearts. The invitation to choose sides, lose objectivity, and distort evidence is powerful.

I would like to provide a list of those few things about which we can have some reasonable certainty regarding long-term impact.

1. A frequently noted impact is the impairment of sexuality and the capacity for intimate relationships.
2. Long-term effects may not emerge until much later and Gelinas' (1983) finding that many female victims maintain, as adults, a disguised presentation must be taken into consideration. When a child appears intact, despite documented abuse of some severity, a careful assessment is all the more necessary for determining impact.
3. Family variables must be considered. It helps nobody to ignore them or to elevate them as the sole source of any variance.
4. Civil damage suits are frequently stressful to victims and may prolong the therapy process and make it aversive. Although these reasons should not deny pursuit of damages, these facts should be considered.
5. Present the facts as a psychologist or other mental health professional, not as the judge and jury. Do not try the case in your evaluation. That is the task of the court and should be left to the court. You do yourself and your profession a disservice to step out of your role.

The best evaluation can be done when premorbid data exist, a comprehensive psychological evaluation of the child's or adolescent's current status can be done, and some trajectory can be charted between those two points and some point in adult life that is expected to be diminished, at least to some degree, by the abuse. Here again, a psychologist must maintain objectivity in the face of the spoken or unspoken request to help this child through the awarding of a large amount of damages. This can be hard to manage. Not only is the client compelling, if solely because of the victim status, but attorneys may also be compelling and are good at shopping for the opinion that best enables due process for their clients. This sets up the evaluator to be engaged in a triangle, with the three members of the triangle being the psychologist, the attorney, and those bad people who did this terrible thing to the child. When a triangle is set up with these members, it is difficult for the psychologist not to ally himself or herself with the attorney for the child.

4

Treatment Issues and Case Management

Canst thou not minister to a mind diseased,
Pluck from the memory a rooted sorrow,
Raze out the written troubles of the brain
Shakespeare, Macbeth

Therapists who "lead with their hearts" emphasize the relational elements at the expense of the analytic; the reverse is true of those who "lead with their heads." Neither extreme is sufficient. This is particularly so when faced with the complex and emotionally exhausting situations presented by children and families in which sexual abuse is a primary feature.

The immediacy of the trauma; the personal, emotional activation that occurs on meeting a child; and the frequent presence of social and legal services, each with its own agenda, create ample opportunity to lose perspective. Some of the problems that can emerge quite rapidly are:

1. failing to fully involve all necessary participants
2. losing therapeutic leverage if a relationship congruent to the family's needs is not begun
3. not knowing all of the issues facing the child and the family
4. losing objectivity and dispassion.

In our eagerness to help the child, we may not pay as much attention to the details of the case as we should. Therapists must modulate their concern and interest in helping the child by also reminding themselves to proceed carefully and systematically. I have met therapists who remain uncertain, after months of therapy, about the actual nature of the abuse, who the caseworker is, the full range of symptoms the child is exhibiting, and whether the mother is significantly depressed or keeping contact with the perpetrator, or both. Sibling behavioral problems are another area of ignorance, as is the child's school functioning.

These often are therapists who are well-meaning and exude care and compassion. They cannot be faulted for that. But it is not appropriate to do a poor job of evaluating the full panoply of problems just because the child has been traumatized. You do not inflict further trauma by being analytic and evaluative. But you do run the significant risk of making mistakes and jeopardizing the child's progress by not engaging your analytic self.

I learned this lesson as a result of my own mistakes. For example, a family that was hard to engage could probably have been kept in therapy longer, to the benefit of the child, if I had known earlier that the boy was dyslexic and a bed wetter in addition to having been sodomized. School consultation could have been initiated and an enuresis plan with a high level of success could have been put into place. This might have solidified my relationship with this family if they could have received some "benefits" from therapy much sooner. I learned all of this later when they reappeared at the office of another therapist who obtained a release to speak with me. In the meantime, the child's behavior at school had gotten him suspended, six months had elapsed, and the abuse was harder to access.

It is for the reasons mentioned above and the need to keep in balance both the therapeutic attitude (heart) and the analytic attitude (head) that this chapter on therapy issues was written. It is a reminder that there are objective targets for treatment and that the therapist should make a determination of what these are when the child and family present for treatment. This allows the family to be treated in a comprehensive and yet an individualistic manner. Canned treatment programs have some utility, but I am deeply concerned about the programs that have limited flexibility and creativity, e.g., the use of groups for young children as their only therapy modality, without an appreciation of the other individual and developmental issues that may be operative. This type of treatment decision-making was not designed for the child.

DECISION-MAKING IN THE TREATMENT
OF CHILD SEXUAL ABUSE

Assessing the Therapist's Belief Systems

Planning for treatment involves first an assessment of the beliefs that you bring to the therapy process. Each of us distills clinical knowledge through filters that reflect personal biases and experiences. I mentioned earlier in this chapter individuals who emphasize the relational aspects of the therapy and other therapists who emphasize the more analytic or goal-setting aspects. That is just one dimension, albeit an important one, along which therapists can differ.

Impact of Sexual Abuse

Another essential belief system that we should think about is one's belief about the impact of sexual abuse. In Chapter 1, I developed a theoretical model that argues that sexual abuse and its impact should be seen along a continuum ranging from neutral to very negative. Sometimes when we see only one type of child or family, we may believe that abuse is either much more discrete in its impact or primarily very negative. It is important to recognize this variability because it reminds us again of the hopefulness that can be present even in traumatic events and that the possibility for positive change always exists. It also forces us to realize that there are strengths and sources of resilience in the individuals whom we see that exceed any of the curative powers that we might be able to bring to these dysfunctional systems.

Just as we think about abuse impact as being continuous rather than discrete, we should also think about therapy as a continuum. Is this child going to need to be in therapy for a long time? Is the goal character change or symptom management? A good case could be made for the therapist's need to capitalize on different events or transformations that occur in the child's life and to apply therapy judiciously at that time. Of course the dilemma that we find ourselves in when we work with these families is that we can only count on the child to be available to us at certain times or for certain reasons, e.g., they are in foster care. Thus, in order to maximize our time with them, we sometimes tend to see them longer than we need to—at least for that particular period in their lives. I believe that the goal of symptom management is much more defensible than character change in these children; it leads to a much more focused and accountable type of therapy.

I was asked to provide a second opinion to a family whose son, almost 3 years old, had been molested in a day-care setting, and it became clear that my opinion about the goals of therapy clashed with the opinion of the first therapist. The first therapist, traditionally trained, felt that because of the young age at which the abuse began (age 2½ years), the effects were more likely to be profound, and twice-weekly play therapy for a minimum of a one-year period was recommended. Reassessment would be done after one year and some decision would be made at that time about the need for further therapy.

Given some of the case examples I presented earlier, the reader may have the impression that I do not see the need for long-term therapy. That is not true, and many of the children and families I see remain in therapy with me for several years. In this particular case, I was not inclined to view the young age at onset as a negative. Rather, I viewed it as providing a type of protective resource for the young boy. He was not aware of the true nature of the abuse, and he appeared to me to be looking to his parents' reaction for a guide for his own reaction. They had responded appropriately to the disclosure, which had occurred fairly early after the abuse began, and their pursuit of a second opinion did not mean that they were shirking their duties as parents, but rather they were drawn up short by the other therapist's pronouncement. Oftentimes in this initial crisis stage, after abuse has been discovered and the family is struggling with what it all means to them and the child, an important therapeutic posture to take is one that tempers their anxiety with some realistic optimism.

Role of the Therapist

My second belief has to do with our perception of our role as therapists. Like many therapists in the past five to eight years, for a while I thought my role was to also be a magician. I was enamored with paradoxical techniques and the use of strategic psychotherapy in bringing about rapid change. I applied these techniques to any and all people who came through my door. But I am not immune to reality and I began to see that "magical" acts in the therapy room oftentimes did more to confuse and frustrate my families and clients and to drive a wedge between us than it did to facilitate change. I realized again that the essence of therapy is still within the relationship, and it is that developing mutuality that provides the framework and workplace for change.

For example, reframing the child's behavior in a manner that helps the family to see the child more positively can be a valuable technique. However, Alexander, Waldron, Barton, and Mas (1989) provided some important cautions in their study of psychotherapy with delinquents and their families. These types of negativistic and chaotic families are similar to some of the sexually abusive families that we see. What they noted was that angry families have a hard time accepting therapeutic pronouncements about the child's more positive aspects.

We frequently hear warnings about being swallowed up by the family's belief systems and losing our therapeutic leverage. But we do not have any leverage unless we are at least within shouting distance of families and they see that we can appreciate their dilemma. Families frequently must be educated about the process of therapy, and they want and need concrete results. Psychoeducational approaches probably have much more utility with chaotic families and families with long-standing pathologic features than do more strategic interventions. Simply taking the time to explain to the child the rationale for why he or she is going to be seeing you can do much to guide and focus the therapy in the manner in which it needs to move. To ignore this simple need of the child or family, or both, is not going to be helpful.

Formality of the Therapy Process

A third belief concerns how formal the therapy process should be. Those who conduct therapy for any period with these families — and these are both intrafamilial and extrafamilial sexual abuse families — are going to find themselves doing things in a clinical setting that they have never done before. Part of this is going to be for the purpose of augmenting and developing the relationship with the family and the child, but some of it may simply be due to clinical necessity or expedience, or both. Weekly sessions that last an hour may not be what the family needs. Longer sessions that are somewhat more widely spaced, sessions in the home, and sessions involving different subgroupings of the family are all options that must be considered. More about planning and timing of these family sessions will be discussed in later chapters, particularly Chapter 6.

Issue of Sexuality

I also believe that these families challenge our very core when it comes to the issue of sexuality. Taking a careful personal inventory about our own sexuality and sexual experiences is an important prerequisite for doing therapy and planning appropriate therapy in this arena.

We need to ask ourselves how we learned about sexuality, what our family attitudes were, whether negative sexual experiences in our past cloud our ability to relate maturely, what we feel about child sexuality, and more. If we are seeing sexually abused children and their families and have never discussed these questions with other adults, preferably a therapist, it is more likely than not that we cannot do as good a job in therapy as we would like.

Choice of Therapeutic Modality

Do we focus too much on the sexual aspects of the abuse and the child's subsequent behavior or do we not focus enough? Can we perceive the individuals in the family accurately? Or have our own personal issues created blind spots that result in misperceptions? Our choice of therapeutic modality will also be reflected in our belief system. The degree of emphasis we put on individual versus family versus group approaches must be for reasons other than simply an unexamined belief that one or the other is more important. We should remind ourselves regularly that there is no empirical evidence to support the efficacy of any of these three primary modalities (Berliner & Wheeler, 1987). Certainly there is no evidence that supports the utility of one over the other. Seeing a child individually may be less demanding than seeing the child with the family or observing the child's regressive behavior in a group setting. But has the decision to see the child individually been made carefully and with some degree of objectivity?

These beliefs are our cognitions about what works and does not work, and they must be examined for us to be able to do the type of therapy that is most efficacious and most personally sustaining for the therapist. A preliminary review of one's beliefs must occur at the beginning of the therapy process. However, burnout is a big issue and this will be discussed in more detail in Chapter 10.

Untreatable Families

Jones (1987) has brought a dispassionate and needed clinical wisdom to the treatment of sexually abused children. His paper on false accusations (Jones & McGraw, 1987) is just one example. The popular literature and defense attorneys would have us believe that children routinely make false accusations. His careful study of this matter not only found a low percentage of false accusations but also identified several reasons for their occurrence, e.g., adults were more likely to make the report for the child, and adolescent females who made these reports had been molested earlier.

Jones has also reminded us that the task that we have created for ourselves is sometimes an impossible one. We are familiar with families that seem untreatable. They are part of everyone's caseload. I am not sure what to recommend about impossible families. I know that my usual reaction to them is to throw myself into further efforts and not accept the inevitable, believing that by sheer willpower and energy I can circumvent it. When reality finally hits home, I probably react in a passive-aggressive fashion and my withdrawal from the family only satisfies their world view that nothing can be done and everybody is out to get them.

Knowing ahead of time those characteristics that make for untreatable families can help us focus our energies in different areas. We may have to think about termination of parental rights much more quickly than we usually do. We have to work to prepare the child for the iatrogenic effects of long-term involvement in the social services system, e.g., frequent foster-care placements, school disruptions, and growing frustration with those people who were supposed to help. Table 4-1 provides a listing of those factors whose absence characterizes untreatable families (Jones, 1987).

Included in these characteristics are 10 variables, each of which is probably weighted differently. Jones does not talk about what combination of these variables is most important. Certainly, in some of the families that we have worked with, all of these have been rated negatively; i.e., these families were high on the untreatable list. The first on his list, and possibly in terms of importance, is simply the acknowledgment that the abuse occurred. This should come from both the child and the parents, but particularly from the parents. A breakdown at that particular point would make a powerful statement about the estrangement between the parent and the child. Maddock (1988) wrote about the child who is reporting incest.

> The child who is involved in the reconstruction of incest without the developmental advantages of an adult faces a major challenge to her map of reality — indeed, to her sense of survival and selfhood. . . . She is . . . to render the "truth" about her experience in a consistent and convincing manner, despite the fact that this is likely to result in substantial disruption of her family life and possible imprisonment of her father or other perpetrating family member.

TABLE 4-1
Untreatable Family Checklist

_____Abuse acknowledged
_____No maternal involvement
_____No history of mother having experienced incest
_____Abuse begins when child is older
_____Absence of force or sadism
_____No intercourse
_____Child and sexual abuse perceived accurately
_____Mother-daughter closeness
_____Abuse is reactive to major family stress
_____Adequate functioning in the child

Note. Higher score indicates better functioning. Modified from "The Untreatable Family" by D.P.H. Jones, 1987, Child Abuse and Neglect, 11, 409–420.

The absence of maternal involvement in the incest is also critical and suggests that the family is more likely to be successfully treated. A history of maternal incest probably creates blinders for the mother; thus, the absence of maternal incest would be important and help the family move toward treatment. When the mother has been an incest victim, not only does that present another difficult therapeutic issue but it also may render the mother unable to acknowledge incest in her own child.

Also facilitating the likelihood of successful family treatment is the onset of abuse at an older age. What Jones (1987) appears to mean here is that the older the child at the time of victimization, the less regressed the offending parent, e.g., molesting an early adolescent rather than an 18 month old. A related variable is the absence of force or sadism accompanying the abuse and the absence of intercourse or penetration.

It is also essential that the child is perceived accurately in the family and that there is an absence of scapegoating. In the same way, the sexual abuse must be perceived accurately as something that is wrong, cannot happen again, and is the responsibility of the offending parent. Related to this accurate perception of a child is the greater likelihood of mother-daughter closeness. When one recalls Finkelhor's (1984) risk factor of mother-daughter estrangement, one realizes the importance of this variable.

Jones' (1987) last two variables that make a family treatable or untreatable include abuse being a reaction to a major family stress, something akin to Groth's (1979) regressed sexual offender, who offends as a reaction to a major stressor, e.g., loss, and the presence of generally adequate functioning in the child. Although it is true that adequate functioning in the child can be a smoke screen for underlying pathologic factors, particularly in females, adequate social skills, peer relationships, and generally adequate academic functioning can go a long way toward reflecting not only a healthy family but also a child who has the resources to deal with the demands of therapy.

When a family has few or none of the variables on the checklist in Table 4-1, the therapist should think seriously about the feasibility of seeing this family. The therapist should also think seriously about the viability of this family as a unit and, if a child is still in that setting, whether there might not be a better out-of-home setting that one could provide for this child.

Goal Setting

Part of my increasingly pragmatic focus with these children and families is my ever-increasing need to involve the family and the child in setting goals. I mentioned earlier that the families who come in are usually unfamiliar with the therapy process, and a pragmatic approach is usually best. The most concrete way to enact that is through the setting of specific goals. Usually these are multiple goals covering several different areas and behaviors (Gries, 1986). It takes some cooperation from the family and the child to arrive at goals for treatment, but this can usually be done in the first several interviews.

I use a version of the Goal Attainment Scale method of goal setting described in detail by Justice and Justice (1979). Five to six goals are developed and three levels of attainment are established. The first level of attainment is essentially where the family and child are now with respect to a specific behavior. The second level is the acceptable outcome for a particular goal, and the third level is the optimal outcome.

The process of setting goals focuses the family and frequently brings about some therapeutic movement. In addition, specific goals can correspond with the goals of the agencies that are helping the family. You stand a chance of being believed and understood if you talk about specific movement in specific areas. Because we frequently are an arm of the court and social services system in our roles with sexually abusive families, despite our wishes for greater autonomy a better coordination of goals can only help the family. The goals can be altered or refined as time goes on. Table 4-2 shows some examples of goal-attainment scaling with a family and a child. Although each of the goals can be weighted and actual change scores calculated, for the majority of families I see the goal setting and monitoring process suffice.

The mother-child pair depicted in Table 4-2 was highly conflicted. Tara was 10 years old and had been molested by two different boyfriends of her mother at two separate times in her life—at 5 and 9 years of age. She presented alternately as a young, dependent child with a mild reading disability and as a pseudomature, angry adolescent, complete with bra, makeup, hose, and extremely short skirts. She was the only child of her 46-year-old, former schoolteacher, alcoholic mother, Claire; her biologic father could not be determined. Claire's one area of competence was steady employment as a hotel maid (16 years at the same hotel). Tara had attended every session of a 12-week group for sexually abused preteens, and she valued that experience.

We began weekly family therapy just as the group was ending. Tara had a continuing need to talk about the different men who had abused her and why they had done so; she was beginning to be more direct in her resentment toward her mother. On the other hand, she seemed extremely interested in her mother obtaining a new boyfriend. No con-

TABLE 4-2
Sample Goal-Attainment Scale

Goal	Child discipline	Claire's isolation	Schoolwork	Open to Tara's talking about abuse	Going to AA	Regular eating/bedtime
Status quo	No consequences No expectations	Stays at home Sees sister once in 4 months; does not go out with co-workers	Does not read with Tara; does not check for homework	Tells Tara to shut up when abuse is mentioned	Does not attend AA; does not call sponsor	Do not eat together; do not have bedtime
Adequate change	Two chores earn an allowance	Visits or calls sister twice per month; has coffee with friend once per month	Reads to Tara once per week; asks about homework each night*	Does not tell Tara to shut up and attempts to listen	Calls sponsor for coffee once per month; attends AA twice per month*	Eat breakfast together 4 times per week; 10 p.m. set as bedtime; one night/ week with friend
Optimal change	Three chores earn an allowance*; use loss of privilege as consequence for misbehavior*	Visits weekly with sister*; has coffee with one or more friends weekly	Reads to Tara 3 nights per week*; helps with homework 3 nights per week	When Tara talks, mother listens, then shares own feelings*	Attends AA weekly; sees sponsor twice per month*	8 meals together each week*; 9 p.m. set as bedtime*; one night/ week with friend

*Status at termination of therapy   AA = Alcoholics Anonymous sistent discipline was used by Claire, who spent her off-hours at home, doing little with other adults and occasionally binge drinking. Tara needed help with her schoolwork, particularly reading. Further examples of Claire and Tara's estranged and irregular life-style were that neither could remember eating together over the previous two years and that Tara's sleep habits were irregular: she would spend the night, unannounced to Claire, with a neighbor or cousin, and her chronic fatigue interfered further with her schoolwork.

Each of these issues emerged in the first two sessions, and goals were developed in the third and fourth sessions. Family and individual sessions totaled 37 during the next 6 months, and Claire and Tara were seen primarily as a family for an additional 15 sessions during the next 8 months. Treatment was successful and was aided by Claire's intelligence, Tara's primary neediness versus her secondary oppositionality, transportation for Tara funded by social services, and the rapport between Claire and myself, which was fostered by my willingness to discuss some of her favorite books with her in some sessions. A final goal was added to our original six goals toward the end of therapy and involved Tara's clothing and makeup. The actual therapy process will be discussed in more detail in Chapter 6.

Presence of Overt Behavioral Problems

An important initial guide to treatment is the presence of behavioral problems. These can take any of several forms, and they can be observable at home and in any of several settings. The ubiquity of the behavioral problems is some indication of the need for treatment; if behavioral problems occur in every setting the child is in, then this is much more problematic than if the problems occur only in one setting. These behavioral problems can be quite generic or they can be more specific to the abuse. Probably the most specific to the abuse would be either sexually reactive behavior or post-traumatic behaviors, such as the onset of phobias and fear reactions around men or during separation from the non-offending parent and recurrent images.

Guiding the treatment further would be the presence of an oppositional or conduct disorder, particularly one that is long-standing and that predates the abuse. If it is of relatively recent occurrence, it is important to determine whether this follows a breakdown in parenting with the disruption of the family, or what the cause might be. Again, social-skill deficits in the child increase the need for treatment and suggest that the problems in the child are much more long-standing.

Researchers are becoming increasingly aware that stressors can have a delayed as well as an immediate impact on a person. Hetherington (1984), who has written about children's reaction to divorce and not sexual abuse, stated that the point at which researchers tap into the coping process of children and families will affect their view of the responses of the parents and children to stress.

> Certain consequences of stress emerge rapidly, some increase over time and then abate, and still others show a delayed emergence. . . . The research evidence suggests that most children can cope and adapt to the short-term crisis of divorce within a few years; however, if the crisis is compounded by multiple stresses and continued adversity, developmental disruptions may occur.

I believe that a behavioral reaction in victims that is not discussed enough is the fact that because they have been used in a nonempathic manner, their own sense of empathy may frequently be impaired (Troy & Sroufe, 1987). Their sensitivity toward another person's distress can be blunted and diminished. We sometimes have the erroneous notion, or the hopeful wish, that because someone has been a victim, this knowledge will prevent that individual from revictimizing. That is not the case. The defect in empathy shows up in how these victims parent, being unable to protect their own children, or parenting their male children differently than their female children. Empathy is not easy to teach or to develop in therapy sessions, but it should not be ignored as a treatment issue.

Behavioral Symptoms Related to Traumagenic Factors

It would be possible in this chapter to talk about the numerous varieties of symptoms that might be shown in sexually abused children that warrant further treatment. However, as a way of organizing a discussion of some of these symptoms, I would like to begin by talking about those behaviors that seem to be related directly to the intensity of the traumagenic factors described by Finkelhor and Browne (1985). Although not the final word with regard to the wide extent of symptoms that could be exhibited, these behaviors do make for an excellent starting point.

Traumatic Sexualization

The first traumagenic factor that we will discuss is traumatic sexualization and its accompanying behavioral manifestations. The impact can be both immediate and more long-term. For example, the initial sexual activation which might be shown in a young child may disappear because it is not being reinforced, but then it could reappear in another form as the child moves into adolescence and is reintroduced to sexuality. A recent paper by Goldston et al. (1989) reported a study of a group of sexually abused girls and noted that the behavioral symptoms that distinguished sexually abused adolescents from nonabused adolescents involve sexual acting out and running away from home.

Briefly stated, traumatic sexualization is the precocious introduction of the child to sexual behavior that is out of the child's realm of knowledge or map of relationships. The behavioral problems that emerge can range across any of the categories that were mentioned in our discussion of the Child Sexual Behavior Inventory. These include:

1. self-stimulatory behavior such as masturbation
2. sexual aggression, as seen in those children who initially were victims and have become victimizers
3. a more subtle type of impact related to a disregard for personal boundaries (e.g., boundary permeability)
4. a less frequent and less well understood disruption of gender identity and resulting gender confusion
5. overinhibition and even aversion to sexual behavior of any type.

The context in which this behavior occurs is always important. A separation of families along a continuum with erotophobic on one end and erotophilic on the other has been suggested (Boat, 1987). Families that are more erotophobic could be quite punitive and overreact to the exhibition of sexual behavior after abuse. This could bring a further sense of shame, doubt, and guilt to a child and the resulting confusion can be a difficult treatment issue. Erotophilic families may not see the behavior as problematic despite the fact that it is becoming more frequent and the child is developing a pattern of peer relationships that is increasingly inappropriate. Parents who are in either of these extreme camps are much more likely to have had a history of victimization themselves, and thus their objectivity regarding the child will be distorted and based primarily on their own issues, rather than respectful of the child's needs.

What is then brought into the therapy setting are such issues as sexual preoccupation, precocious sexual activity, acting out with peers, and aggressive sexual behavior. On a more personal level this is shown by sexual behavior, even overt behavior, being manifested in the therapy room by the child. It can result in inappropriate behavior on the part of the therapist as Adams (1982) mentioned in his book *A Primer of Child*

Psychotherapy. He recounts a vignette in which a child psychiatry fellow seemingly felt compelled to show his penis to a sexually provocative young child.

In my discussions with therapists, it appears that the overt manifestation of traumatic sexualization in the therapy hour is more common in female children seen by male therapists or male children seen by male therapists. This is thought to be true because this more closely approximates the child's abuse experience. However, it is not limited to the match between sex of therapist and sex of child. Younger children, in particular, are not that differentiated with regard to sexuality, and they may appear to be pan-sexual. They have been activated and aroused by whichever adult is in their presence and when accompanied by anxiety, sexuality is going to be part of their acting-out behavior.

The intensity of this behavior can be very disconcerting and unsettling to the therapist. Kay Hodges, the developer of the Child Assessment Schedule (Hodges et al., 1982), described a girl of latency age who was in her practice. The child told her in the middle of a therapy session, "What I need right now is a man" (Hodges, 1988). On a more personal note, over an eight-month period, after which we finally had a successful resolution, I was nervously playing a "boyfriend-girlfriend" game with a 6-year-old girl. This consisted of writing notes to each other, occasionally sitting in chairs parallel to each other, pretending to be driving a car, and allowing her to pretend that she was "16 or 30" when she was interacting with me. You can imagine the distress that her behavior caused in the fundamental Christian foster family in which she was living.

It is the outside context, school and family, where the impetus for behavioral change really becomes most noticed. In the same way that it is hard for much of society to realize that sexual abuse occurs with the frequency that it does, it is also hard for most people in society to tolerate overt sexual behavior in children. In a recent study which surveyed child psychiatric inpatient units (Kohan, Pothier, & Norbeck, 1987), it was noted that sexual behavior by children in the unit was a difficult behavior for staff to manage and prompted many inappropriate reactions.

Stigmatization

The second source of trauma that we will discuss is stigmatization. The dynamics operating here are similar to those described by Porter et al. (1982) in their discussion of "the damaged goods syndrome." The

victim is denigrated and left with a sense of shame, and the reaction of
the family may be "Oh my God, how can it have happened to you?" Or
"Why did you let it happen?" The child can be blamed, and Finkelhor
and Browne (1985) describe the psychological impact as including everything from guilt, shame, and lowered self-esteem to a profound sense
of differentness.

In some ways, the younger the child the less the sense of stigmatization. It is true that younger children will blame themselves and readily
assume responsibility for what has happened. There are at least two
reasons for this. The first reflects the fact that for children to feel like
damaged goods, they will usually need to have some sense of time perspective. They need to be able to see where they have been and what
options are now lost or less attainable as a result of the abuse. A second
reason is the egocentricity described by Elkind (1979) that makes adolescents so vulnerable to what they perceive to be other people's perceptions of them. There is also a transparency of self that seems to come
about with adolescence and makes the stigma of being a sexual-abuse
victim even more difficult to manage personally.

An interesting point was made by Lamb (1986), who discussed the
seemingly impossible task of the therapist to counter this insidious and
frequently not discussed sense of shame and stigma. The therapist sometimes deludes himself or herself into thinking that simple assurances of
"it's not your fault" will be enough with these children. Lamb wrote,
"The caring therapist . . . intends to relieve the child of feelings of
guilt." She made the point that these assurances are not going to be what
brings about change.

In fact, the platitudes that therapists say to children frequently distance children and therapists because the children become convinced
that the therapists truly do not understand them. For example, some
"victims . . . do not necessarily feel like victims" and to impart this
status to them may be disempowering. Another child will think that it is
her fault because the perpetrator has told her that and the family in
either overt or covert ways makes her continue to feel that way. Again,
simple platitudes will not be helpful for correcting these feelings.

Sometimes the management of the case, e.g., removing the child
from the home and leaving the father in the home, is unspoken testimony to the child's belief that he or she is at fault. And now the child is not
only at fault for the sexual abuse but also responsible for the later
breakup of the family and the loss of income to the mother.

Damon and several of her colleagues have taken issue with Lamb's
therapeutic strategy of avoiding telling victims the abuse was not their

fault (Damon, Todd, & Crespo, 1989). They propose several ways that therapists can actually explore the issue of self-blame and counter its influence on the child, including talking directly about the self-blame the child is doing.

One can see why the treatment issues that appear related to stigmatization include isolation, maybe an overidentification as a victim to the point of being a victimizer, involvement in self-defeating peer groups, self-mutilation, and even revictimization. A sexually abused adolescent explained to me that she became a punker in school because "None of us knew what we were doing. We all felt sort of lost. To be with the nice girls just made me feel shitty."

Sometimes the poignancy of the stigmatization comes only from adolescents or adults who have the verbal capacity to talk about it and have a little perspective on the situation. Another mother stated, "I could have forgiven myself for all of the sexual abuse that occurred before the age of 14. But I knew what was going on after I turned 14 and I still let it happen. I don't think I can ever forgive myself for any of it." The therapist can feel quite ineffective when countering that solidly entrenched belief system with "I really want you to believe that it's not your fault." As Lamb (1986) pointed out, the therapist can get farther if the confrontation is moved from the area of blame to the area of decision-making. The younger child made some faulty decisions that led to abuse. This is a function of faulty decision-making and ignorance about the range of appropriate decisions. At the very least, there is now room for new and more appropriate decisions.

Finkelhor and Browne (1985) reported that another psychological manifestation of stigmatization is self-mutilation. Long-term incest survivors are frequently misdiagnosed as having borderline personality disorders because one of the features that is seen is self-mutilation (Gelinas, 1983). In her excellent paper, Gelinas discussed how this misdiagnosis might occur, and she urged effectively that unless the full constellation of borderline symptomatology is present, the diagnosis is all too frequently inappropriately applied.

It is much more appropriate to view self-mutilation, in the absence of other borderline symptomatology, as reflecting the individual's attempts at understanding and mastering the abuse experience. From the words of one adult incest victim, "I am not sure why I do it. He was always messing with my body, and sometimes I think if I mess with it I am safe from him. Even though he's not around anymore and wouldn't do it, I guess I still feel safer." Suicidal ideation and behavior are related to self-mutilation. Now that I ask more frequently about this with child victims, I am hearing more suicidal ideation from these children than I had before. Its presence seems more related to their perception of hopelessness in their lives than to overt depression.

Betrayal

The third source of trauma that we will discuss, along with its psychological manifestations and treatment implications, is betrayal. Here the child's trust and vulnerability are manipulated and the child's well-being is disregarded.

Children should be raised with the expectation that others will provide care and protection. This expectation is violated when parents do not provide support and protection. Basic trust cannot be established or persist (Erikson, 1963). Empirical data come primarily from studies of physically abused children (George and Main, 1979). For abused children, the history of interpersonal relationships with caregivers is characterized by a sense that the caregiver will manipulate them or disappoint them by not providing consistent support. Thus, their attachment is impaired, resulting in ambivalent and avoidant-detachment relationships.

This ambivalence is probably related to the ambivalence that we see in our office. We work hard with the children and expect them to join with us against the "bad people who did such terrible things to you." Then we find out that they may share that perception but they are also simultaneously sharing a perception that that person is important to them.

Betrayal represents the loss of a relationship. The psychological impact will obviously be seen in depression and unresolved grief. In addition, because dependency needs have been frustrated, you will see an increase in dependency coupled with an increase in mistrust, particularly of men. In the treatment room, probably because I am a man, I do see the ambivalence manifested by the child vacillating from some anxiety on seeing me, to overt clinging behavior, and frequently mixed in with a fair amount of rejection. One child demonstrated her ambivalence by hiding from me in the waiting room before each session. I was required to prove my interest in her by playing this game each time we were to meet. Only gradually did her need to hide and have me pursue disappear from our relationship.

Powerlessness

Clearly, another traumagenic factor related to depression and grief is Finkelhor and Browne's (1985) factor of powerlessness. The child's body territory has been invaded. Although young children are frequently in a relatively powerless relationship with adults, sexual abuse is more pervasive and focused. This violation of personal boundaries has as a natural result the boundary permeability that we discussed earlier. The process of the victim becoming the victimizer may in some ways undo that sense of powerlessness. The fact that boys are usually the ones who become victimizers speaks to how important power is to them, and consequently how this powerlessness factor may be even more salient for them. Themes of power and dominance seem to be more common in my therapy with boys than with girls.

Coupled with revictimization might be specific psychological issues, including anxiety, fear, sense of lowered self-efficacy, and need to be in control in interpersonal relationships as a way of guarding against further powerlessness. Thus, you can see that the behavioral manifestations range from passivity to overt aggression. A single traumagenic factor has a wide variety of behavioral manifestations, reflecting the diversity of the children being abused, the nature of the abuse, and the context that they are in. The therapist with these children must expect a large number of behavioral presentations, and these presentations will vary over time. We need to pay close attention as therapists to what these children come into our office with, and not place our own experience on them.

Table 4-3 is an attempt to highlight the different developmental impacts of each of these traumagenic factors. As you can see, not all cells are filled at this time.

As I mentioned before, these traumagenic factors are largely the child's perception of the abuse, and this constitutes the individual level of victimization (McCarthy, 1986). However, there are two other levels of victimization: the family and the larger sociolegal area. For example, in the area of traumatic sexualization, the child learns early, due to repeated interviews that focus solely on the abuse, that the abuse has become the child's "sexual ticket of admission" (Schoettle, 1980).

The repeated placements in foster care and the drawn-out court proceedings that do not offer enough protection to the child add to a sense of powerlessness. An adult victim whom I worked with would not go to her 30-year class reunion, despite the fact that she had successfully resolved many of the issues related to her sexual abuse. This was because, when she was 15 years of age and in high school with these classmates, her father's name was published in the paper as having been picked up by the police while molesting a minor daughter. She was the only daughter in the family. Her mother did not allow her to transfer

TABLE 4-3
Traumagenic Factors and Developmental Level

Age at onset of abuse (in years)	Traumagenic Factors			
	Sexualization	Powerlessness	Betrayal	Stigmatization
0–1.5			Trust violated; disrupts normal attachment	Child has little sense of self/other relations, so impact in this domain is small
1.5–3	Accelerated onset of normal heightened interest			Parental reaction most critical here to the degree of stigmatization
3–5	Normal increased interest in sexuality is heightened	Issues of autonomy are central, possibly even more salient for boys		Child can do own stigmatization
6–12	Normal inhibition may either increase or not be allowed to decrease	Issues of industry and productivity are central		
13–18	Adolescent sexuality issues heightened—e.g., homosexuality			

high schools, and she was forced to deal with her own anguish about what her classmates knew.

Discussion of the Sexual Abuse

By now, the reader is aware that I believe strongly in the importance of helping the child to discuss, as much as is possible and through whatever medium is workable, the various instances of sexual victimization that resulted in the treatment. There are a number of children whom I have seen whose neglect and physical abuse experiences far surpassed in number and impact their sexual abuse experiences. With these children, I find it useful to discuss as many of the discrete instances of abuse as is possible, hearing from the child which of the various insults appear to be the most damaging. In addition, I realize that children will vary widely in terms of the degree to which they will discuss the abuse and the relative importance that they attach to the abuse.

Although I believe that it is important to negotiate early on with the child how and when this discussion will take place, and I may be more directive about this than the average therapist, I also meet resistance and amnesia for the events and find that a subset of children is going to be reluctant to disclose. For example, I have kept careful clinical notes about the disclosure process on the past 43 children and adolescents whom I have seen for therapy purposes. The child and I were able to have a discussion of the abuse, and its accompanying affect and cognitions, at a level that appeared to be clearly helpful to the child in 31 of these cases. The remaining 12 were along a continuum ranging from absolutely no disclosure to a rote disclosure and a subsequent refusal to talk further about anything related to the abuse. What is particularly disappointing is that the majority of these 12 had been seriously abused, e.g., penetration with force over a 5- to 23-month period.

This underscores your need, as a therapist, to "meet" children where they are and work with what they provide. When they provide resistance, you discuss verbally, use drawings, and even role-play the resistance. This can foster the relationship to the point where resistance can be overcome. I am reminded of a pearl of wisdom from Sheldon Kopp (1977) that is applicable here. In his discussion of resistance, he says that the degree to which the client becomes free matches the degree to which the therapist is free to hear what the client has to say.

There are many reasons why the child is reluctant to talk about the abuse, including individual and contextual variables. Individual variables include:

1. amnesia for the events
2. the child's inability to verbalize exactly what happened due to immaturity or intellectual limitations
3. the child's perception of his or her role with you.

Contextual variables include:

1. the lack of rapport with the child
2. the child not being oriented to the therapy process
3. the child fearing consequences of telling about the abuse
4. presence of caregivers who have warned directly or indirectly about these consequences.

For the contextual variables, I attempt to create a supportive context, utilizing foster parents and caseworkers — even parents who are relatively neutral, but not truly supportive of the child, can be used over time. For example, sometimes conjoint sessions with the parental figure or caseworker can empower the child to talk and to feel doubly supported through the process. The presence of another person also counters the belief that some children have that "If I talk about it, it's going to happen again." With some children, I have found that the real discussion of the abuse takes place only in a group setting, usually with older latency or adolescent victims, in which a less inhibited group member begins to share experiences and this paves the way for the child to discuss his or her experiences. It is important to appreciate the range of variables that can influence disclosure and discussion and to create a therapeutic context that allows for this process of uncovering to occur.

There are at least two points of view about the role of uncovering the abuse instances. Some individuals feel that the child's powerlessness is magnified in a therapy setting in which the child cannot have complete control. Nondirective therapists feel that the work in therapy should focus only on what the child presents within the therapy session. This is believed to be more respectful and more natural to the child. On the other hand, I know that children struggle to derive meaning out of their experiences, look to adults for direction, and feel more confused if the adult is not clear about the purposes of therapy. To be overly conciliatory and reassuring to the child is only one element of therapy.

In many ways, good therapy reflects the elements of good parenting. Baumrind (1982), in her discussion of authoritative parents, whom she sees as superior to authoritarian and laissez-faire parents, wrote that in addition to unconditional regard for the child, parents need also to make maturity demands on the child. Facilitating the child's discussion of the sexual abuse experiences is part of making appropriate maturity demands on the child.

Let us now turn to more specific arguments for and against uncovering. Table 4-4 is a synopsis of these arguments. Regarding arguments for uncovering, the therapy context can create numerous opportunities for the child to understand the abuse experience that are not available outside of therapy. If the child does not have the opportunity to get answers to such unasked questions as "Why did he do it?" the child leaves therapy without having this essential bit of appropriate meaning. Affect is frequently activated at those times when abuse is discussed. This includes anxiety, depression, and anger. Too few of the sexually abused children whom we see have the opportunity to be in a context where these are allowed and modulated and understanding of the feelings is facilitated. If a previously overly inhibited child now has the opportunity for the display of affect that is neither punished nor creates too much internal anxiety, the opportunity for growth has been enhanced.

Werner (1948) suggested a theory that reconciles the two simultaneous forces of integration and differentiation in the development of children. Sexual abuse heightens the likelihood of fragmentation of self or an extreme and unhealthy variant of differentiation. Areas of the child's

TABLE 4-4
Arguments For and Against Uncovering

Arguments for uncovering
1. Creates opportunities for the child to understand the experience
2. Affect is available for therapeutic change
3. Fragmentation is circumvented in favor of integration
4. Safe context allows for restoration of a more appropriate functional map of relationships
5. Child is allowed a change to view self in a more positive light; inappropriate cognitions are now exposed and can be challenged
6. Trauma is frequently secretive; to disclose makes it no longer a secret

Arguments against uncovering
1. Family conspiracy exists against talking; to uncover creates further stress
2. May lead to behavioral regression
3. Further reinforces child being out-of-control
4. In the proper treatment context, everything eventually emerges anyway
5. Goes counter to the child's coping style; ignores the fact that repression and denial can be useful at times

life are cut off from discussion and amelioration. Accessing the sexual abuse begins the process of integrating these elements into the child's life in a new and positive way, rather than allowing them to remain unchanged and to emerge at different critical transition points as the individual grows older.

Another argument for this uncovering process is that your interaction with the child is helping the child to create a healthier internalized map of relationships. Your office can be safe, and although I have seen several instances in which for brief periods I have become aversive for the child because the child associated me with painful feelings, we have always been able to work these through and our relationship has been subsequently strengthened.

Before some angry children will respond to kindness and regard from the therapist, which may be a completely unfamiliar set of experiences to them, they need to experience the therapist as someone whom they can "bump up against," and whose kindness and regard for them are not simply a function of personal weakness. In some ways, by focusing the therapy on this important element, this subset of children does have an opportunity to react against me in a way that does not lead to their destruction but that does lead to a furthering of the relationship. To do good therapy, we have to create a goodness-of-fit between ourselves and the child and be comfortable with a wide variety of roles that we may need to adopt at different times. Thus, through approximations, we help to alter our client's interpersonal style and internal map.

Uncovering allows the child a chance to view himself or herself in a more positive light. We know the child may be at a developmental level, e.g., egocentric, whose cognitions will interfere with future adaptation. It is impossible to get at these inappropriate cognitions in the way that the child truly thinks and feels about them unless we hear them emerge in the context of the uncovering process. As Lamb (1986) wrote, the therapists' need to feel helpful in the face of their own powerlessness over preventing the child's abuse experience can get us into a lot of difficulty, can create barriers between us and the child, and can keep many important issues from being discussed. We may offer assurances prematurely, thus disrupting the uncovering process.

Finally, sexual trauma is frequently a secretive event or set of events. For many, it will remain a secret and be discussed fully for the first time only when an adult, victimized as a child, seeks psychotherapy.

There are also several arguments raised against this uncovering process. Several of the reasons listed in Table 4-4 speak to the fear that the uncovering process will lead to excessive anxiety, fearfulness, and being out of control. In addition, it may create intense loyalty conflicts. Another set of arguments arises more from the basic tenets of traditional, nondirective child therapy. It is true that for many children an implied or overt set of rules exists against talking about the abuse. Uncovering can create unpleasant tension and conflict about family loyalty. The therapist runs the risk of becoming the odd person out in the triangle consisting of family, child, and therapist. However, the management of the intensity of affect and internal distress in the therapy session is something that can be done through skill and personal presence.

A useful recent paper has given suggestions about how to find and keep clients in the "therapeutic window" between the extremes of denial on the one hand and feeling intruded on by their memories on the other (Cole & Barney, 1987). Although the client is moderately distressed even when in this more tolerable range of affect, working through can be accomplished. The authors described several techniques, developed for adults, that can also be used with children. For example, one technique is grounding, which helps the client orient himself or herself to day-to-day reality and counters the fear of getting "stuck" in the past.

It is true that some children will regress behaviorally in the initial course of therapy and that parental figures need to be apprised of that. However, this now gives the family an opportunity to use more adaptive ways of dealing with the child, to create a new appreciation in the family that the child is working on important issues, and to allow for an emergence of more appropriate behavior. The child does not have to feel out of control during the course of uncovering. The utilization of less direct methods of talking about the abuse, such as drawing or talking about "as-if" memories, can be the starting point for many children.

An example would be useful here. A 7-year-old boy, Seth, was molested by his 16-year-old stepbrother, Scott, in a tree house. He would not talk about it at first, but he did agree to draw a picture. The picture depicted Seth standing on a tree branch, with his mouth on what appeared to be a stick floating in the air, and only later was the stick defined as Scott's penis. Still reluctant to speak directly, our session went as follows.

Therapist: Well, how about if we do this. You know lots about tree houses, don't you?
Seth: Yeah. I do. I could even build one. All by myself.
Therapist: I bet you could. I'd like to see the one you build.
Seth: There's lots of good trees to build it in.
Therapist: Lots of good trees. Yeah. But what would you tell another

7-year-old boy to do? Let's call him Tim. He wants to build a tree house, but he's worried about his older brother coming in and doing things to him.

Seth: You mean, like making him suck on him?

Therapist: Yeah. What should Tim do?

Seth: Well, his brother's a lot bigger than he is. He can get him up there with some candy. Or to show him his new pocket knife. That's what Scott did.

Therapist: Okay. What name should we give Tim's brother? We want to make this as real as we can.

Seth: Scotty?

Therapist: Okay. And what does Scotty make Timmy do?

Seth: Well, he says, "I want to show you something cool." And he shows him his knife, but only up in the tree house. And then he — I don't know.

Therapist: We're just talking about Timmy now. Something happened to him like it happened to you. Okay?

Seth: Okay. Just to him?

Therapist: Yeah. To Timmy. Maybe it's sorta like to you, too.

Seth: Well, then he shows me his dinger and how it gets bigger, and he wants me to show him my dinger too.

And with this process of talking "as if" he were another boy, Seth continued a discussion of the abuse.

For another child, who was anxious from the moment I met him, and who became increasingly anxious as he talked about his father, we built into our sessions opportunities for him to use deep breathing as a way to calm himself. He told me, with some pride, about a later instance at school in which he got quite upset because something had happened on the playground, and he remembered what we did in the therapy room and his deep breathing brought about a greater sense of control.

Another argument against uncovering is that good therapists create good therapy contexts in which the child is allowed to dictate the important issues. If the sexual abuse is an important issue, it will emerge. Maddock (1988) reminded us of the overwhelming set of family inhibitions and loyalties the child has to overcome before the sexual abuse can be discussed. There is frequently an attachment to the offender; role reversal is common in these children and frequently they are role-typed as being overprotective and seen as putting other individuals' needs before their own.

I am not naive enough to think that in the short time I frequently have with these children I am going to become a more important person to them than other people in their lives who have had a wider range of experiences with them. Usually our therapy efforts are not ideal, and the child does not have support from family or time to work through the many issues in a leisurely manner. Even when that is the case, I still feel that uncovering early in the therapy is important.

Finally, an argument against uncovering is that there are some children who cope by the overuse of denial and repression. It is true that uncovering is more difficult for some children than for others. However, the dominant use of less healthy defenses is something that the therapy process should help to alter. A child denies the existence of something because to acknowledge it would create both internal distress and possible interpersonal difficulties. Frequently, these children have too few opportunities to learn how to deal with internal distress other than to deny it or to act it out in an unmodulated manner. Part of our duty as therapists is to help the child learn a wider range of coping styles and behaviors. We want to facilitate the child who moves away from us (Horney, 1950) to be able to also move toward us. This greater sense of mutuality in connection can emerge through the discussion of the various traumatic events that led the child to your office.

These arguments for and against uncovering are not inclusive, and others can be raised on either side. The child looks to the therapist for direction and we miss valuable opportunities for therapeutic intervention when we fail to supply that direction and create an environment in which the child learns about a wide range of feelings and the appropriate ways to express them.

MANAGEMENT OF UNSUBSTANTIATED
SEXUAL ABUSE CASES

A fairly common problem, particularly when the child is younger, although it could actually occur at any age, is when the abuse is impossible to substantiate clearly and the likelihood of the child continuing in a potentially abusive situation is high. Cases like this, and I will focus primarily on the younger child, usually come about because the child has not provided a clear statement about what has occurred. I usually feel that contributing to this is the subtle message "not to talk." The format that I have tried to use in these cases borrows from Hewitt (in press), who has greatly influenced my thinking.

Sometimes these cases come to you from another party and it is important to determine whether or not the initial evaluation was thorough and adequate. Everson and Boat (1989) examined a large number of sexual abuse cases to determine the criteria used by protective service workers in judging the validity of allegations. They cited several examples in which the worker was more skeptical of the claim than either the research warranted or a rereading of the case suggested. If the evaluation is deemed inadequate, it may be difficult for you to rectify that, given the time elapsed or the number of interviews the child has already been through. However, it is important to make that determination and to see if it is possible to bring out more information.

Sometimes the inadequacy is the result of the father's evaluation; i.e., he is being perceived as a nonrisk when he actually may be a high risk. It is important to know what constitutes a quality evaluation of a man accused of inappropriate sexual behavior with a child. More often, particularly when the child is young, someone has not interviewed the child adequately or known what to do with the behavior that the child has exhibited. Whatever the case, if this child is coming to you from another party, a thorough assessment of the initial evaluation needs to be made.

If the evaluation were done adequately, before any visitation by the father of the child were resumed I would establish a baseline period in which the child's behavior in other settings and my interaction with the child could be established. This usually is a several-month period that allows for some cooling down. It is important at that time to identify people who can be reliable behavioral observers of the child. Part of what is going to guide your advocacy of these children will be their behavioral responses to a resumption of visits.

At least one extended interview, and possibly another, needs to be conducted with the non-offending mother and the child, and the overall quality of the relationship must be ascertained. Does the mother show appropriate empathy toward the child? Is there appropriate dependency between the child and the mother? What can be determined about their attachment history? In addition to evaluating the overall quality of the relationship, it is important to find out what is appropriate behavior in the family regarding sexuality, nudity, and touching. Careful determination needs to be made of that, frequently in a playful manner (e.g., "Is it okay for people to kiss you on your bottom?").

Finally, it is important for the mother and the child to identify who can be told and how they can be told if further abuse occurs. Sometimes you will find in this interview that the subtle command to the child not to tell has come from the mother. In one case with a 4-year-old child, our interview ended when the child began to talk about what actually had occurred now that he had heard overtly from the mother that it would be okay to talk.

The father also needs to be interviewed separately and then with the child if you have already made a determination that the initial evaluation was thorough and that you are going to continue to proceed with managing this case. The same issues and the same format need to be used during the father-child interview. It is hoped that a bind against further acting-out is created, at least temporarily, in the father by talking about what is appropriate and who could be told and how they can be told.

This is followed by a conjoint meeting with the parents and the child. Again, the quality of the parent relationship (usually these are contested custody cases) needs to be determined, along with a rediscussion of what is appropriate in the family and who can be told and how. At this time a moratorium is also established on further evaluations, other than the behavioral ratings that will be obtained from the various neutral observers in the child's life. This also allows the therapist to continue to exercise some neutralizing effect in the situation by continuing to receive behavioral ratings and by completing subsequent firsthand observations of the parent-child relationships at different times during the course of the resumption of contact.

In the several successful cases in which I have used this format, I have been pleased with the fact that the child's behavior has generally become much more adequate over time. There have been several cases, of course, in which the parents have not been able to back off and the visitation has become too hotly contested. Then you do see continued disturbance in the child or behavioral regression, or both, and frequently some further court intervention is necessary.

It is difficult to determine what the child's initial regression at the resumption of contact with a parent or after return from foster care to a non-offending mother actually represents. Regrettably, the decision usually cannot be made until enough time has elapsed that habituation and a return to more appropriate behavior have either occurred or not occurred. In the meantime, the unsettling experiences are harmful, and the reexperience of loss if the reunification process needs to be interrupted is also another issue with which to cope.

CASE MANAGEMENT

The case management considerations that will be described in this section are different from the larger case management responsibilities that are held by the statutory child protection agency that is mandated by the state to handle investigation and management needs. In this section, the case management issues that will be described are more specifically germane to therapists who are working independently or in small coordinated groups within mental health centers or outpatient agencies. In these settings, most cases of child sexual abuse are managed poorly. Problems with case management arise in four separate areas (Sgroi, 1982):

1. a lack of willingness to accept responsibility for the cases
2. incomplete knowledge of the dynamics of sexual abuse and the legal statutes that dictate its management
3. the absence of a well-trained professional staff who have investigative and clinical skills
4. the failure to use in a coordinated manner the various services available within the community.

When the therapist is treating only a small part of the system, there is a built-in invitation to ignore the responsibility that comes with treatment of sexual abuse. There may be a lack of communication with the other therapists and caseworkers, and a failure to know who the individuals are in the child's life. This unwillingness to assume responsibility comes from therapists' lack of follow-through when cases threaten to get lost between the cracks.

Case management suffers also when therapists start to second guess their own treatment processes. This happens when you are faced with repeated discouragement because of poor case management and this gradually evolves into a belief system in which intervention of any sort is thought to be abusive. It is true that we get discouraged, but intervention becomes abusive because it is poorly managed and not enough individuals are willing to assume an active role in managing it.

It is necessary to be aware of the dynamics and mechanics of child sexual abuse, the families within which it occurs, and the potential treatment issues. This requires a therapist to be well-read and to treat each new case as something that can be learned from to help both that child and subsequent children and families.

A therapist also needs to be aware of the legal justice system. Failure to know the civil and criminal statutes related to child sexual abuse may prevent the therapist from utilizing legal leverage to begin and continue the treatment process. It is not enough to make a determination that sexual abuse has occurred and to be engaged in a therapy process.

Our duties as therapists also include creating as protected an environment for the child as is possible. Does the child feel safe about having disclosed the abuse? Has the offender used force and threats against the child previously and are these likely to occur in the future? Who is available to the child in a supportive role? Each of these areas needs to be assessed so that abuse does not continue and negate our therapeutic efforts.

I have had cases in which there was no movement in therapy until safety and protection could be concretely established. With one family, the mother and her phobic 3 year old used a "cleansing" ritual I suggested to "reclaim" each room of their house from the abusing stepfather. In one session, the mother referred to him as a rat. Probably because it was the end of a long day, I suggested that she and her daughter purchase rat poison and put a piece in each room. The mother laughed, but did so with her daughter's help, while stating to her, "Daddy's a rat for what he did to you. Now he won't come back to bother us anymore." The child's sleep disturbance was eliminated, and her separation anxiety ceased, both within a day or two of the "cleansing ritual." Other tangibles, like restraining orders, changing locks, removing the offender's possessions, and getting an answering machine or an unlisted telephone number, can create a sense of greater safety and support for the child victim.

In addition to assessing the child's protection needs, it is imperative that we know who are the current and potential professionals in this child's life. This adds to our case management difficulties in that it is important to have working communication with these various individuals. Rarely do we get paid for time on the telephone or letter writing. Yet child abuse cases carry with them a large amount of time spent with collateral contacts. The tough cases present huge time demands but there is no reimbursement.

Agencies are also frequently reluctant to enhance their therapists' overall case management skills by allowing for time in which the therapist is able to do the necessary networking. Stanton and Todd (1981) wrote extensively about managing difficult families. The families about which they wrote included a heroin-addicted member. Early in their family therapy work with these individuals they found that the networking responsibilities were adding another 50% to 100% time per week on each case. Therapists could not be expected to adequately handle these cases if they were not being paid for this time. In the age of budget cuts, inequities can be difficult to correct. If they cannot be corrected, we run the risk of increasingly poor case management.

In addition to coordinating the overall treatment program and being involved with the various treatments by social service professionals, case management also involves taking a pragmatic and responsible approach to the case. This is not the arena for the fainthearted. As I have written in Chapter 10, therapists in these cases must know how to balance the issues of control and affiliation. We have to feel comfortable with the appropriate use of authority to push many of these families along, but we cannot lose sight of the fact that a therapeutic relationship is essential. We do not have to lose leverage with these families when we exert appropriate control or when they are ordered to treatment by the court. Forcing ourselves to become more pragmatic and concrete about setting goals, developing a list of problems that need to be corrected, and designing specific treatment programs are essential.

Another case management responsibility is the ongoing need for monitoring and assessing the impact of our intervention. The use of the goal-attainment scaling described earlier with each family makes a determination of our impact much more quantifiable. In addition, the assessment strategies outlined in Chapter 3 must be brought into the treatment arena.

Cases must be monitored not only for a recurrence of abuse but also because as professionals we should be continually interested in the long-term outcome of these families. When these families leave therapy, we too rarely know whether or not our interventions made a difference. Sometimes we prefer not to know because we want to have as little to do with some of these families as possible. However, this type of countertransference negates our therapeutic effectiveness, and maintaining an active and long-term interest can be one way to demonstrate our personal interest and responsibility to these families. This comes with the territory of a therapist for sexually abused children and their families. We need to assume this responsibility.

Finally, case management involves working with the legal profession. This activates much approach-avoidance in me personally and I do not have very many answers. Yet, these cases often have legal components that are complex, difficult to negotiate, and directly counter to good therapy. Conte (1989) discussed the increased legalism that has entered our practice. How are the therapist-investigator roles defined? How do we deal with an attorney's recommendation that the child not have therapy until after the trial for fear of losing the case due to the child having now been "contaminated" by the therapy? To be an impassioned supporter of children and their needs often conflicts with the dispassion we must also have in order to be viewed as objective experts lobbying on the child's behalf.

5

Individual Treatment

I will always be a stranger who never feels at home,
who does not really want and is not really wanted, who
can never belong, who must always be a little in love
with death.
Eugene O'Neill, Long Day's Journey Into Night

Individual therapy has a definite role in resolving both the immediate
and long-term impact of sexual abuse in children. Individual psychotherapy with children has a long and rich clinical history; a recent
meta-analysis of child psychotherapy outcome studies concluded that
the overall positive impact of therapy was greater than that seen in the
nontreatment comparison groups (Weisz, Weiss, Alicke, & Klotz, 1987).
Interestingly, the average number of sessions across the studies included
in the review was fewer than 18. This is briefer than the frequently
recommended long-term therapy that is prescribed for children by more
traditional therapists. Although they are rich in theory, I believe that
there is little reason, other than tradition, to recommend traditional
psychoanalytic approaches for working with sexually abused children.
Insight requires looking backward, a task difficult and inherently unin-
teresting to most children who are focused on the present. Harter (1983)
asserted that developmental limitations of children in the understanding
of multiple and conflicting emotions, intentionality of behavior, locus of
control, perspective-taking, metacognition, and self-concept can render
even some play-therapy techniques inappropriate (e.g., interpretations), especially for younger children. Play-therapy techniques must be
adapted to the social-cognitive limitations of the child (Harter, 1977).

The review by Weisz et al. (1987) noted also that behavioral methods
were significantly more effective than nonbehavioral methods, a further
argument for a more direct approach. This was true for all ages studied,
from preschool to adolescence. There were few well-designed studies of

131

group treatment outcome of children, but they did demonstrate an overall significantly positive treatment effect (Weisz et al., 1987).

However, no studies exist that document the success of individual therapy with sexually abused children. Many of these children are from families with multiple problems, including intrafamilial and extrafamilial abuse, which decreases the likelihood of success of individual therapy in these cases, particularly when this disruption persists during treatment. Thus our optimism about therapy's potential positive impact with sexually abused children must be tempered by some appreciation of how complex the treatment needs may be.

Think, for example, about a young girl removed from home, who is in a foster home that provides only basic needs, and then only perfunctorily, and whose infrequent interactions with the non-offending parent leave her confused and distressed due to "messages" of no support and the importance of "keeping her mouth shut." She will not want to talk about what happened, and her internal distress is likely to persist and not be easily reached by either individual therapy or the behavioral training offered to the foster parents. Her basic needs of safety and trust have not even been met and thus the likelihood of her being open to the demands of therapy is poor.

Individual therapy is most likely to be effective when the following criteria are met:

1. Ongoing support of the child is provided by a primary parent figure.
2. A sense of safety has been or is being established for the child to protect against future victimization.
3. The therapy with the child is occurring concurrently with therapy that is creating systems change and the nonabusing parent is having regular contact with the therapist.
4. The therapist is skillful, goal-oriented, conceptually clear, and willing to be directive in a supportive context.
5. The child is able to communicate regarding the abuse and can tolerate the intensity of the therapy process.

ONGOING SUPPORT

I would like to elaborate on the importance of each of these five points. The first states my belief that the child must be experiencing ongoing support from a primary parent figure. Preferably, this would be the natural or adoptive parent of the child, who not only has reacted supportively to the child's report of abuse but also can appreciate the need for therapy. A modicum of support may be present, indicated simply by the fact that the child is in therapy.

Support also implies emotional availability, an entity more difficult to assess. The parents may be unavailable for various reasons, e.g., depression at the combined losses of a child abused and a relationship with a significant person (the offender) or coping with the ghosts of their own abuse. Sometimes, this support is slow in coming and may develop only as the parent becomes involved in group or individual counseling.

In the worst case, the parent is actively nonsupportive and rejecting, or parental rights are slowly being terminated. Because the child is maintaining hope for the relationship with the family-of-origin and the child's status in life is ambiguous, the child is unable to truly feel much connection to alternative providers, e.g., foster parents. With time, the surrogate parent-child bond can develop to the point where the child can invest in therapy despite occasional lapses when conflicted visits occur.

Benedek (1989) recently stated, with regard to juveniles who had committed homicide, "While the child is in the throes of court issues, supportive therapy is all that can truly be done. Psychodynamic therapy, with its emphasis on insight and exploration of earlier issues and traumas, is contraindicated and may be dangerous." This has definite applicability to individual therapy with sexually abused children. Although court involvement is required for a minority of these children, its prospect can be quite threatening. Until court issues are resolved, the child is left without a sense of closure. Recent data demonstrate that court involvement can be helpful to the child in the long run (Runyan, Everson, Edelsohn, Hunter, & Coulter, 1988).

SENSE OF SAFETY

The second issue reflects my belief that the child must feel safe from further victimization. Graphically illustrating this is a case reported to me by Sandra Hewitt, a psychologist in St. Paul, Minnesota (Hewitt, 1988). She was working with a family consisting of a mother and her several young children, each of whom had been molested by their father. He was in jail and awaiting sentencing. However, week after week, little improvement was noted in the children's level of disorganization and regression. Dr. Hewitt's clinical sense was that more progress should have been made, given that the mother-child relationship was reasonably adequate and the children were generally supported by the mother.

She queried the mother during one session about what remained in the home that could remind the children of the father. It emerged that the father's collection of large snakes, which had been used to intimidate the children against disclosure, remained in a cage in the house, and the mother had to regularly feed them live mice. The mother felt powerless about removing them, fearing her ex-husband's rage when he found out. Dr. Hewitt worked out an agreement with the mother to find another home for the snakes. This literal, and also symbolic, removal of the father's presence was accompanied by a steady improvement in the children's functioning.

If you are carefully assessing therapy movement, via checklists and specific goals, you can see clearly if the child is progressing or not. You can then determine whether the context is safe, particularly if you now have something, other than intuition, to inform you if therapy is progressing.

We also see safety being threatened when visitation with the perpetrator occurs. Untreated fathers all too often are allowed contact with their children because of a naive and mistaken notion that this can be helpful to the child and that the "bond" must be maintained. There are situations in which this relationship should be supported, but not in those cases in which the abuse continues to be denied, treatment is not progressing, and the nature of the previous relationship is not also considered.

Attachment behaviors by the child do not mean that attachment exists; attachment is far more complex than simply a child voicing happiness at seeing his or her father. Recall the paper by Parker and Parker (1986) cited in Chapter 1, in which incestuous fathers appeared to be predisposed to incest due to their relative noninvolvement in the early socialization of the child. Thus, from the very beginning, the attachment was suspect for a large percentage of these fathers, and to bow to an argument that this attachment should be preserved does little to help the child.

In addition, this creates confusion in the mind of a child, whose literal beliefs about good and bad have already been distorted. Their unspoken question is, "If he did something wrong, why didn't something happen to him because of it?"

Finally, it is extremely important to eventual outcome for the child to talk about the abuse in a supportive and empowering environment. If this is prevented or derailed to allow for a relationship that arguably has less influence on final outcome, a sad event has occurred. Frequently the pursuit of visitation by the offending person serves a defensive function, e.g., to deny the abuse or its impact. Rarely is it going to be pursued for appropriate reasons in the untreated person.

CONTEXTUAL CHANGES

The third point articulates the need for contextual change to support the individual change that is occurring. The deterioration of individuals returning home after psychiatric hospitalization was the impetus for the development of family therapy (Hoffman, 1981). The younger the child, the more embedded the child is in the family context and reactive to the affect and stresses that are present (Kegan, 1982).

Again, Maddock (1988) offers some useful perspectives on this matter. Families construct reality together over time, and the child's view of self, what is right and wrong, and view of self in the family will be shared by the child as well as each of the other family members. Therapists do not share this view, and until a relationship can be established, they have little hope of altering this special reality. If other family members can be moving to a new family reality, the child's movement will be facilitated. The tasks of therapy require much affective energy; when loyalties are divided, there is even less energy to bring to therapy (Boszormenyi-Nagy & Spark, 1973).

APPROACH TO THERAPY

The task of the counselor in these cases is formidable enough to be compromised by inexperience or a poorly formulated plan of therapy that moves along in a directionless manner. This fourth point from the above list addresses the task of the therapist. If we believe that individual therapy is a necessary part of the child's treatment, lessening the likelihood of its effectiveness by using an inexperienced therapist who does not work well with children is not what the child needs. Actually, few child therapists are formally trained, and the majority of us learn by necessity and experience, adding training sporadically during our careers. The admonition to "play with the child" is all the supervision some ever obtain (Brady & Friedrich, 1982).

The nondirective model suggested by Axline (1969) was not designed with the sexually abused child in mind. As lovely a model as it is, it is applicable to the same people who are thought to benefit from psychoanalytic therapy, i.e., those who are verbal, neurotic, and have lots of time and money. These four characteristics do not fit even a large minority of the children I see. For example, many of these children come from families that rarely talk, and the child has no vocabulary for feelings. The child may never be oriented to the purpose of the therapy and what is expected, adding to the child's confusion and frustration. Failing to orient the child to the purpose of the therapy and intervening too rapidly or too slowly are the most common mistakes made with these children.

TOLERANCE FOR THERAPY

Finally, a necessary condition for successful therapy relates directly to the child. The child must, over the course of therapy, discuss the abuse. Children who are severely traumatized or have poor verbal abilities will have difficulties with this task. The traumatized child may have dissociated the events, or the child may literally fear that to talk about the abuse is to invite revictimization. Talking is almost the equivalent of doing, in their minds.

Verbal skills have, since the beginning of psychotherapy, been one of the criteria for successful therapy. Adequate language functioning is related to the greater likelihood of learning to successfully modulate one's behavior (Richman & Lindgren, 1981). Good language abilities ease the therapy process, but I hope that child therapists do not limit themselves only to verbal production in the playroom. Abuse and other elements in the child's life are accessible via drawings, role playing, and storytelling techniques (Russell & van den Broek, 1988).

An important question pertains to highly resistant children and whether therapy is contraindicated. Should you refuse to be the therapist in these cases? Aren't you just being another coercive, insensitive adult? To reiterate, resistance in children arises from the children's context, most centrally their relationships to parents. It does not help to view resistance in children primarily as intrapsychic. If their behavior warrants intervention, you need to determine how to change the context so that resistance diminishes; if this cannot be done, your role changes to behavioral consultant to foster parents, teachers, and parents.

The child also must be able to tolerate the therapy process. Some children are not ready for therapy, and this must be appreciated. To others, the abuse per se is not the most painful aspect of therapy. I remember, quite clearly, the comment of a 14-year-old boy, Tom, who had been abused by a camp director. He actually discussed appropriately, on several occasions, the abuse and what he perceived to be the personal implications. But when we would talk about his mother, whom he was not living with at the time, Tom would get very uncomfortable. He once stated, "I don't want to talk about her. I can like her when I don't talk about her. When I talk about her, I remember her hitting me. I don't want to remember any of that." If I had not backed off, supported his request, and, in essence, titrated the negative presence of his mother, he would have found therapy too aversive and the integrity of our relationship would have been seriously threatened. We were able to talk about the pain in their relationship only much later, and then only in a third-person manner.

Therapist: When do you think teenagers, who feel so many mixed-up things about their mothers, can talk about her without seeing red?

Tom: They have to be able to do it bit by bit.

Therapist: That means. . . .

Tom: Well, like if I was you, I'd just have them talk about a few bad things and then some stuff that's okay. But not for long.

Therapist: Like a few minutes for each and then go on to something else.

Tom: Yeah.

Therapist: Maybe I'll try that with a kid I know next time I see him.

Tom: You could try it with me.

Therapist: I think I will. Thanks for the idea. I think you just taught me something.

Tom: Thin ice.

Therapist: Like skating on thin ice. Let's see. I see some ice skates over there for us.

Tom: Slow, now.

Therapist: If I'm too slow, I go through the ice.

Tom: That's the only way I can talk about her, slow.

Therapist: Sort of a little at a time, and real slow.

Tom: Yeah.

Therapist: What if we agreed that 5 minutes was maximum? All the talking we'd ever do at a time about her was 5 minutes. We'd be real strict about it.

Tom: Two minutes.

Therapist: Then 2 minutes it is. When should we use up our 2 minutes?

Tom: Next time.

Therapist: I'll be waiting. And probably so will you.

Tom: Yeah, sure.

If the above criteria cannot be met, alternatives to individual therapy must be relied on, such as helping foster placement be as therapeutic as possible via consultation to parent figures and teachers regarding behavioral management.

Individual therapy for children is too often begun with no direction, by poorly trained therapists, and with a failure to appreciate the importance of context in making it successful. Nothing done in an hour a week with these children can resolve the abuse if it is not done as part of a larger therapeutic context being created for the child in which safety, stability, and support are being provided. What individual therapy can do, quite well, under these circumstances, is to maximize the child's ability to benefit from the context and to aid the child in making sense of the abuse before it gets suppressed, denied, or repressed and not resolved.

In addition, behavioral programs at home can be coordinated and developed in the therapy hour. I have a bias toward briefer periods of therapy that are sensitive to the child's overt improvement and current developmental level. For example, if a child presented with numerous problems that are essentially absent after 12 to 15 weeks and the child seems to be not very forthcoming in the sessions, I would discontinue the individual therapy and provide guidelines to the parents to direct them as to when I may need to see the child again (recurrence of symptoms). I would do this even if I believed that we had not had the opportunity to fully discuss issues that come up with more verbally productive children. Individual child therapy is done for other reasons than to focus on child issues. For example, sometimes the individual therapy is continued because it helps to manage the mother-daughter relationship, e.g., "She does better when she is seeing you than when she is not."

For example, I saw a 9-year-old girl for approximately 60 sessions, over a 4-year period, with the last session coming when she was 13½ years of age, and she and her mother and younger brother were moving to another state. Molested over several months by her stepfather, Kathy was never very verbal, family sessions were never easy, and our usual mode of interaction, during the individual portion of our sessions, was a few brief verbal exchanges that caught me up on a few areas in her life, and these were then followed by several games of "Sorry." Board games are frequently overused in therapy, but with Kathy I had to work with what little she brought into the room. The board games allowed us to have a regularly rewarding time together.

Early in the therapy some interactive puppet play was a high point therapeutically and allowed for some disclosure about the abuse. A few tears were also seen at that time. I also consulted with her rural school and provided cognitive and achievement testing that she had never received from school personnel. This enabled her to get some Title I help with language-based classes. The longest period of consecutive appointments we had during those 4 years was for an 8-week period at the beginning of therapy. Typically, we would have four to six sessions, about half of them family-oriented, that would begin when the mother would call about a new problem, e.g., low grades, Kathy's exaggerated interest in boys, shoplifting, or deterioration after testifying in court. The mother had a long history of episodic relationships with men. Her distrust of men continued with me. Yet Kathy was eager for every appointment, seemed visibly to like me, and her mother attributed much status to me and would usually alter her parenting temporarily. Never during the course of therapy did I feel that optimal treatment was occurring, but I had let them reach a compromise with me that met their needs. I believe that this example is actually representative of a significant portion of the children seen in individual therapy.

Let us turn now to a discussion of different phases of the therapy process, and the therapeutic elements within each phase. The concept of phases in therapy with abused children is not new. For example, Jones (1986) also has described a three-part model: the starting phase comprises the first 4 to 6 weeks; the closing phase, the last 6 weeks; and the middle phase, the intervening period.

FORMING THE RELATIONSHIP

Despite the plethora of approaches to therapy, relationship variables still seem to reflect more of what is curative about therapy than do specific techniques. Thus, developing a working relationship is essential. How does one do that with children who often have impaired attachment histories? All therapists need considerable flexibility in adapting to the clients they see. I do not deny that personal autonomy in the therapist is important, but too much is made of "not getting swallowed by the system." We do lose objectivity as a matter of course. If we did not we would probably not be doing therapy. Finding a middle ground between creating a good fit with the child and maintaining individual objectivity is what needs to happen.

The importance of *sameness* and *stability* cannot be minimized in the process of forming and maintaining relationships. Because of the abuse and the concurrent chaotic home environments of many of these children, they have not had the opportunity to internalize ways of modulating affect and inhibiting internal distress. Thus, external structure in the form of sameness, predictability, and stability can be useful.

If the child's time with you is not marked by rapid swings in affect or tempo, the child can be focused on the therapy. Possible avenues toward this are the use of the same way of greeting and leave-taking, developing rituals to do together, even structuring the session (e.g., "We always do this first," said a 6 year old to me in our third session, when I bypassed the "drawing of something that happened to you" that we had done twice before).

An example of a ritual that I had with a young boy was "high 5s" at the beginning and end of each session. He would usually "lose it" and try to turn it into wrestling, at least during the earlier sessions. But the ritual provided a vehicle for regular, natural, and appropriate physical connection, and was circumscribed enough so that it had a natural ending to it.

Horney's (1950) concept of *interpersonal styles* suggests, at the very least, that the child therapist must learn how to form relationships with children presenting in each of these three broad interpersonal categories: moving toward, moving away, and moving against. Try to take stock of yourself at this time. Which children do you work with best? Are these children the same ones with whom you relate most easily? I ask that question because children who are needy and dependent (moving toward) may attach to you indiscriminately (easy), but their compliance with therapy may not reflect true work. It may only reflect that they will do anything to continue the relationship. Change is not at the top of their list of needs; getting their dependency needs met is.

Let us consider some of the ways to approach each of these children. Obviously, there will be combinations of styles possible, particularly since setting can make a significant difference in how children present, but in this next section we will discuss only the extremes. Some children may initially present in an aggressive or *moving against* style, but this then abates readily. More persistently aggressive and contrary children make therapy a difficult process. A key to remember is that this relational style developed only after initial, natural attempts at attachment when they were younger were thwarted, frustrated, or met punitively. Unpredictability is also the most common parenting style they have seen (Patterson, 1986). Thus, they do want to relate, but they do it inappropriately, and your task is not to thwart or meet punitively these interpersonal needs. Predictability is also important.

I was asked to see a 12-year-old boy who had been involved in the viewing and making of pornography by his parents. Extremely defiant, he oozed hostility at all of our early appointments. My instinct was that to adopt a gentle, nurturing posture with him was to invite further abuse and anger from him. He was looking for victims. We began to connect with each other via mutual swearing. He swore at me a great deal and I complimented him on his expertise, challenging him to come up with new and more creative terms for me, his group home leaders, the caseworker, my office, and his teachers. I would add a few choice words to his long string, and he genuinely liked that. It jarred his image of me and demonstrated my acceptance of him in the only way he understood. I certainly had some explaining to do to his caseworker, who brought him to one of his appointments, and I greeted the boy, "How's my favorite asshole doing today?" and he replied, "Not bad, dickhead." He worked productively with me for more than a year before he was placed in long-term foster care with his minister's family.

For these *moving against* children, I contract for times when they are more cooperative and ask them to demonstrate to me that they know how to do something other than show me how mad they are. Nevertheless, maintaining a nonpunitive therapeutic posture can be difficult. These children can activate negative, punitive reactions in the most nonreactive therapists. What do you do, for example, when a 5-year-old girl, during a role play in the seventh session, has you lie down on the floor, pretend to sleep, and then instead of "watching TV" as she said she would, hits you on the head with a mop handle? This child, Vanna, will be discussed at different places in this chapter because she was difficult to manage. One of the angriest 5 year olds I have seen, she could not be trusted with the infant foster child in her foster home, and she was in a class for children with emotional and developmental difficulties. About the only thing going for me early in therapy was that I was a man. She seemed both more fearful and yet more drawn to men, and she had reason to be; she was anally raped at 2½ years of age and molested by a second perpetrator for the next 1½ years.

Returning to the incident described in the previous paragraph, when I jerked to a sitting position her expression was a mixture of being startled and pleased. I was glad to see some surprise on her face — I wanted to believe that part of her was not simply malicious. I told her that she had hurt me, that hitting was never allowed in the room, and then pushing my luck, added that she needed to go into time-out for three minutes. She then launched herself at me in a rage, refusing to go into time-out.

I am not sure where the inspiration for my next move came from. I was holding her from me, so I would not get hit further, and I said, "We both have to go into time-out, me for five minutes because I'm bigger and you for just three minutes, because you are littler." She could not argue with this logic, and after telling me, "You're stupid," she sat in one corner and I sat in another. I used this mutual time-out with Vanna a number of times, each successfully. It seemed to work because it was not punitive, it was egalitarian, and it ended with each of us laughing because "You look silly in time-out. A big man in time-out."

Interestingly, Vanna's older brother, also molested and seen by me in therapy, used primarily *moving away* as his interpersonal style. Again the need for connection is present in these children as it is for those in the moving-against pattern. I believe that the neglect has been more profound in children who are avoidant. These also tend to be children who are more likely to have an innate tendency for inhibition of affect.

Several things have become evident about how to work successfully with this group of children. The first is that you have to provide the emotional investment in the relationship, usually for some time, before it begins to be more mutual. Do not schedule these children when you are tired, because they are used to low-energy, emotionally absent parents. At the same time, they do not know what to do with too much enthusiasm and turn that off also. Track the child closely, using your physical and verbal presence. These are the children for whom I try to take Polaroid pictures of the two of us together; I give them a copy to provide a visual reminder of the possibility of our connectedness.

The second component of successful work is to make yourself desirable to the child. With other children I might announce some limits early in the therapy, e.g., no hitting. With this group, I do not do that— it simply provides another reason not to make the effort to connect. Small food treats and simple gifts, such as stickers, at each session are some other ways to make yourself desirable. Words of praise usually are not even heard by these children until much later. They simply do not have a framework for it, or else to acknowledge the praise is to go counter to their detached, noninvested style.

The following is an interchange between Vanna's brother Jeff and me, at the end of a session, after two months of weekly contact.

Jeff: You give stickers to my sister too. She said that.
Therapist: I give them to my favorite kids.
Jeff: I'm not a favorite kid.
Therapist: You bet!
Jeff: You say that to all the kids you see. And don't say you don't.
Therapist: Well, you're the best kid at not taking a compliment.

I did not want to let Jeff escape without something positive. Frequently, it is at the connecting and leaving times that the child's true anxiety emerges. We were beginning to connect, and his particularly distancing comment at the end of this session, after some warmer and seemingly mutual interaction just earlier in the session, may have been his style emerging then in a protective way. However, over the course of our work together, even though he was less distancing with me, other people whom he met always described him as aloof and unfriendly. I am uncertain whether we made significant changes during our time together. This group of children seems so "sealed-off."

The final interpersonal style we will discuss here is *moving toward*. Some of this style is good; too much makes for difficult therapy. If the child is sexualized in his or her interactions, this behavior is likely to emerge with the therapist, particularly with an opposite-sex therapist if that is the same as the abuse configuration. The countertransference issues that can then emerge for the therapist can be difficult to manage. I have reserved more discussion of these issues for the final chapter. It suffices to say that the child's behavior toward you may result in your making subtle distancing moves that deinvest you from the therapy process (Berlin, 1987).

I also have difficulty with these children because I am not sure when we have a true working relationship as opposed to their simply being extremely compliant and cooperative in a dependent way. This is akin to the indiscriminate affection-seeking seen in physically abused children (Friedrich & Einbender, 1983). Some of these children are extremely talented at smoothing out conflict and conforming to the therapist's input and requests. It is nice to see some resistance at times because it suggests the emergence of personal autonomy.

It is not useful to frustrate these children's dependency needs, however, by simply becoming increasingly passive-aggressive in response to their needs. Rather, an approach I use a great deal is to divide the sessions into segments, and contract with the child when we will work, when we will sit quietly, and when we will simply "play," and for a small subset of children who seem to both need it and can manage it, when we will "cuddle" or sit close.

Therapists reflexively avoid physical contact with sexually abused children. To do so effectively removes from the therapy several dimensions of the abuse. A child learns by contrasts, e.g., your behavior vs. the behavior of the offender. Talking with the child about the meaning of a supportive pat or a hug, and processing the experiences afterward, can be a corrective emotional experience. However, it must be entered into with care.

An essential component of therapy with children is to develop a capacity for "being" with them. This requires removing the usual adult, formal operations manner of thinking and accessing much more primitive ways of thinking, feeling, and responding to events. I have listed seven different potential vehicles enabling therapists to be with a child and will discuss each of them briefly. These are not designed to be gimmicks, but to further the relationship at times when you and the child are at odds, or tension is getting intolerable, or more "juice" is needed in the relationship.

Be an Animal

When in doubt, make growling noises or assume the mannerisms of an animal. Children share a special kinship with animals and for you to take on that persona is to be part of that special kinship. Meowing, barking, or wiggling your nose like a rabbit is frequently useful. Over a series of sessions with a young boy who had been sexually abused by his mother, I realized that I was involved in an increasingly commanding style with him. He was becoming less compliant, and we were recreating the coercive cycle he and his mother and other adults used. Yet, his behavior was such that he was off task and needed structuring a great deal. The entire tenor of our relationship changed when I pretended to "bark" at him when he needed to be reminded of something and to make other, more pleasant, dog sounds in praise of more appropriate behavior. Over several sessions, our relationship became much more positive and far less coercive.

By being an animal, you also elicit behavior in which the child is clearly one up with regard to you. The child may respond in a gentle caretaking manner or may get aggressive and punitive. Either one of these reactions can tell you a great deal about the child.

Anthropomorphize

Young children, particularly very young children, imagine that everything around them not only has a life of its own but also has the capacity to feel, perceive, and take action. Even objects that we have long thought to be inanimate can become animate and can adopt a human self. Assuming that the carpet has feelings when you fall onto it and then apologizing to it or talking about how the carpet likes to be next to someone is one simple example of anthropomorphizing. Telling the child that "even the walls were crying" when she was telling you some painful event makes a lot of sense to the younger child and is a way to enlist the room in providing social support.

Be Conspiratorial

I am a firm believer in solidifying a dyadic relationship by pitting it against a third party. This is simply the concept of triangulation (Hoffman, 1981) but used in a more therapeutic manner. Speaking in whispers or into the child's ear about different matters is one way to be conspiratorial. There is usually no reason for you to talk like that to the child. It just helps develop and move the relationship along. Sharing secrets and whispering interventions into the child's ear clearly strengthens the relationship and allows the child to feel as if he or she has a special bond with you.

For example, I perceived that I was not connected to a rather skittish 5-year-old boy, who was hyperreactive to sounds and sudden movements, but who seemed to ignore me. Yet when he commented about an occasional sound in the hall, he enjoyed our peering under the crack in the door together to see what was going on. For a few sessions, that seemed to be the only mutual thing we did. However, it led to greater rapport.

Secret-sharing and conspiracy can imitate the child's role with the abuser. Contrasts between yourself and the abuser, however, can be drawn, and the child can learn to see you more accurately and as clearly different from adults who have been inappropriate.

Show Wide-Eyed Fascination

An example of this technique comes from an interview I did with a 5-year-old child, Caroline, whom I was interviewing so as to provide input to her therapist regarding her need for additional treatment. Shortly into the interview she indicated to me that she had lost her two front teeth. In as good a 5-year-old way as I could, I asked her to show me, told her she was a "lucky duck," and opened my mouth to show her that I had not lost any teeth but wished that I could. All of these new phenomena — e.g., losing teeth, hearing an ambulance, riding an elevator — are magical to children and need to be magical to the adult with whom they are relating.

Activate the Primary Process

By primary process, I am referring loosely to the term by the same name defined in the psychoanalytic literature as those immediate and important needs defined by the id and driven by the pleasure principle (Schwartz & Johnson, 1985). One of the quickest ways to create a sense of mutuality and relationship is to activate this primary process. I do this frequently with bodily functions, e.g., burping, passing gas, sneezing, and hiccuping. These processes are still looked upon with a great deal of amusement by most children, although the sufficiently socialized children pretend that they are grown-up and do not see any humor involved. Exaggerating one's response, e.g., "That was the smelliest fart!" or talking about bodily functions with great glee can be really useful in enhancing your relationship with a child.

It was quite useful in my work with Jeff, for example, mentioned earlier, who seemed to epitomize the *moving away* interpersonal style. I am reminded of another example, in this case a 12-year-old boy whom I saw for an extended period of therapy. He came into my office at the first appointment with his aunt and it was obvious that the relationship between them was strained. He was living with his maternal aunt and uncle after a six-year history of incest with his father had been discovered. His mother had died two years earlier. I could see that we would have a great deal of work to do in resolving not only his incestuous experience with his father but also the loss of his mother and the family he knew.

Early in the course of our individual contacts, however, he came in and talked about how he had temporarily lost his TV video game because of swearing in school. His use of the game was part of a behavior management system we had worked out with his aunt, and he seemed to be blaming me and "my stupid ideas about kids" for the loss of the game. When he was done with his indictment of me, he belched very loudly. Rather than argue with him, or even reflect his distress verbally, I stated, "That burp tells me what you think of me and my crazy ideas. Can you do another one?" He told me that he could "do hundreds" of them, and he proceeded to. I counted them, timed their speed with my stopwatch, and we turned a contentious instant into something far more positive and facilitative of our relationship. A further opportunity provided by this is that it allows you to respond positively and affirmatively to anything a child might "produce."

When children need to interrupt the session to use the bathroom, it often is a reflection of their need to back away from intensity or to deal with the by-product of anxiety. These bodily signals from the child should be noted and possibly some supportive comments could be useful as they head to the bathroom, e.g., "I think we needed to take a break from all that we were talking about."

Use Concrete Operations

Children think in a more concrete manner than adults, and what makes sense to them does not necessarily make sense to us. Concrete thinking also underscores the need for rituals in these children. Some children demonstrate their anxiety by hiding from you, either in the therapy room or in the waiting area. If you act as if you cannot see young children, they believe you actually cannot. I sometimes use a playroom on a lower floor, and a little girl loved to push the elevator button twice because there were two of us. I suggested she do that because it seemed to create a sense of mutuality.

Trance logic or trance language also fits here. Anxious children believe your statement to them that they "will talk about what they need to talk about," or that we will spend "just the right amount of time together," or "once we take the splinter out, you can get better" (referring obliquely to the need for a discussion of the abuse). Other techniques derived from hypnosis will be discussed in a later chapter.

Mirroring

This is an essential skill and probably captures best what I mean by "being with" a child. Reflecting the child's behavior through words and actions is nonintrusive, noncoercive, and respectful. Hypnotherapists utilize mirroring of the client's words and physical actions as an important prelude to trance induction, because it enhances the relationship. Brady and Friedrich's (1982) first level of intervention with children describes physical mirroring as the therapist's way of creating structure and safety for children. This of course can then lead to a rather remarkable sense of connection with the children, leading to your being as vulnerable to all of their feelings as they are.

An example of this comes from a session with Vanna, a child mentioned earlier in this chapter. She chose to play a game that was frustrating for her, a magnetic fishing game. The "fish tank" would go round and round and she would try to "capture" the fish with a magnetic pole when their mouths would open. She tolerated frustration poorly and began to threaten to break the game. All the while I mirrored her frustration, groaning when she did, yelling at other times when she would, and imitating her frustration as closely as possible. After several minutes had passed, in which she exhibited greater self-control than I had expected, probably because I was actively supporting her via my mirroring, I moved a step past mirroring when I suggested that we scream loudly at the next failure. We did, and the several instances of mutual screaming and subsequent laughing at each other because it was silly did more to cement our relationship than anything in the previous 11 sessions.

Because of her impulsivity at school and home, we later turned that and several other exercises into vehicles where she could learn to "think before she acted." At our termination session, 19 months later, Vanna reminisced about different events in our time together, and that particular instance "with the fishies" was one she spoke about with a great deal of pleasure.

The techniques described above are, I hope, more than simply techniques; they reflect my belief that "being with" and adapting ourselves to how the child thinks and relates can be enormously facilitative of the relationship — the central element in the change process.

DOING THE WORK OF THERAPY

The phases of therapy are not distinct. I hope that they are seamless. Several caveats should be repeated. The change you are looking for will not be achieved unless the child (a) feels safe and connected, (b) is able to talk about the abuse, and (c) the child's context is both reasonably supportive and changing in a positive and more supportive direction. I find it difficult to justify individual therapy, particularly with younger sexually abused children, unless at least these three factors are operative. The work of therapy cannot be done unless the child's caregivers are also prepared for whatever behavioral disorganization may accompany this phase. You have to be meeting with them also.

The several foci in this component of therapy include:

1. making "meaning" of the abuse experience
2. helping the children to view themselves more accurately
3. decreasing the likelihood of further abuse
4. providing the children with an experience that they view as both positive and meaningful in the future if the need arises
5. addressing specific behavioral goals.

These are ambitious goals, and subgoals exist within each. How does one accomplish them, particularly when the three preconditions mentioned above are suspect, time is against you and the child, and social and legal systems are moving in ways counterproductive to therapy? Often you cannot, and some decisions need to be made about what can realistically be done with the resources available. I will discuss each of the five principal foci, as I see them, in the next section and attempt to make suggestions about what is more or less realistic under different circumstances.

Making Meaning of the Abuse Experience

The phrase "meaning-making" comes from Kegan (1982), a child-clinical/developmental psychologist whose writing has had a profound impact on how I conceptualize children and their developmental and therapeutic tasks. Children actively engage their world, and from the beginning they are developing a model of relationships, or personal constructs, as Kelly (Monte, 1980) would have labeled them. They are also learning how or how not to modulate their behavior and affect.

The child attempts to make meaning of new events, applying increasingly sophisticated cognitive processes and previous experiences to the process. The fact that victims so frequently see themselves as "bad" reflects a common pathway the meaning-making process takes. Not only might the child be naturally egocentric but also something unexplainable, out of the child's realm of understanding, is being done to the child furtively or coercively, or both, so it must mean that the child is bad. In addition, often that message is coming with varying intensity from the family.

The first step in understanding and changing this child's conceptualization is to begin to share the child's frame of reference, to hear from the child what happened. I hope that the material in Chapter 4 has convinced you of the necessity of this, and that the traumatic events interview process has provided one of several appropriate means to this end.

Early in the therapy process, the child is oriented to the therapy and some agreement is reached allowing for discussion(s), verbally or nonverbally, about the abuse. Brevity is frequently the order of the day. It can be confusing to the therapist because a brief retelling of the abuse is characteristic, at least initially, of both the healthier child and the child who feels least safe or able to talk. The few children I have seen who have been from the onset relatively explicit and detailed have all been more disturbed, and, as a rule, less able to back off from the retelling and more likely to be reactive and regressed as a result.

An early discussion of the purpose of therapy and the need to talk about the abuse is presented for an 8 year old, Lynn, abused by her aunt's fiance. An earlier conjoint interview with Lynn and her mom had actually ended with the mother explicitly giving Lynn permission to talk to me about "you know, whatever happened between you and Bob." Although vague, it was some measure of support to Lynn, by her mother, to work in therapy.

Therapist: Do you know why we are sitting in here and talking?
Lynn: Not really, no.
Therapist: No one told you even a word?
Lynn: My mom?
Therapist: What did your mom say to you about why you and I would be meeting and talking?
Lynn: I don't know.
Therapist: Well, maybe she didn't say very much, or maybe she said something that sounded like you weren't sure about it?
Lynn: Yeah.
Therapist: Or something that's hard to talk about.
Lynn: Yeah.
Therapist: Well, I talk to kids a lot—especially kids who have had things happen to them that make them feel different or bad.
Lynn: You do?
Therapist: Yeah, even to other 8-year-old girls. Sometimes they say it's hard to talk to a grown-up they don't know, especially a man, but then they learn that it actually helps.
Lynn: Uh-huh.
Therapist: Like you may talk to me about your feelings about school, or your mom, or about things that happened that made you feel bad—like just a few weeks ago.
Lynn: You mean Uncle Bob? I mean Bob. He's not my uncle anymore. He never was, but I used to call him that.
Therapist: I see. You used to call him Uncle Bob, but now you don't because of something that happened.
Lynn: Uh-huh. I hate him now. Karen does too.
Therapist: Karen's your aunt?
Lynn: Yeah. She was going to marry him before he did that—what he did.
Therapist: So you told her what happened?

Lynn: My mom did. I couldn't.

Therapist: Who all have you told?

Lynn: Just my mom. And the lady cop.

Therapist: And that's a big part of why you and I are talking today. I talk to kids who have had these things happen to them. It helps them get over it and go on feeling good about themselves.

Lynn: Uh-huh.

Therapist: So sometime soon we will talk about Uncle Bob — I mean Bob. When do you think we can?

Lynn: Do I see you another time?

Therapist: Yeah. As long as we need. Do . . .

Lynn: Next time. I'll talk about it next time.

Therapist: That's a good idea. I think kids should wait till they get to know me better before they share all this stuff. Should I remind you next time or will you do it on your own?

Lynn: You remind me.

Therapist: Okay. I'm a good reminder. And you know what?

Lynn: What?

Therapist: When you finish telling me about it, you will actually start to feel yourself beginning to feel like, to feel better again.

Lynn: I will?

Therapist: That's the nice part about our talking together like this. Whenever you talk about something, it helps because I listen real hard and help to understand it.

What can be derived from this brief segment are several reminders. Talking is difficult, even with parental support. Allowing the child the ability to have some leverage and choice in the matter is both respectful and necessary, and the child needs to hear both support and a rationale for why it is an important part of the process. This often has to happen any number of times. The next segment comes from the middle of the following session.

Therapist: You wanted me to remind you today — to be reminded to talk about Bob. I am ready to listen, I mean if you are ready to talk.

Lynn: Oh. Yeah. I guess I can.

Therapist: I know keeping private about this sometimes seems the best, like it would make it go away. But actually, and you'll find this out, talking about it is the only way, the best way for it.

Lynn: Should I tell you everything?

Therapist: Talk as much as you can and if you want to stop at any point let me know.

Lynn: Well, he used to come over with Aunt Karen. That's when he'd mess with me.

Therapist: So at your house, I see.

Lynn: Well, Karen and mom would go shopping and he'd watch us kids, me and Joshie.

Therapist: Oh, so he was the only grown-up around, and he was with two little kids, you and Joshie.

Lynn: He never did nothing to Joshie—just me.

Therapist: Well, you kept Joshie safe, at least.

Lynn: Yeah. He'd put Joshie in the crib and do this tickling game. I hated it.

Therapist: You hated it.

Lynn: Uh-huh. He'd touch me all over, even inside my clothes. I told the time he made me take off my clothes—all of them—yuk!

Therapist: Yuk!

Lynn: He was gross. He smelled.

Therapist: He sounds very gross. And smelly.

Lynn: Uh-huh.

Therapist: You've done real good. I guess I'm wondering. Did he do other yukky things to you?

Lynn: Yes. He made me touch his pee—Joshie has one but his was bigger. Lots bigger. Gross!

Therapist: So he touched you and wanted you to touch his penis. He just wouldn't stop.

Lynn: No. Do you want to hear something even grosser?

Therapist: If you can tell me it, okay.

Lynn: He wanted me to kiss his pee!

Therapist: Gosh, he just wouldn't stop, would he? Making you kiss his pee. He really smelled then.

Lynn: Yeah. He kept making me and making me and making me.

Therapist: And he's so big—so much bigger than you.

Lynn: He said he'd hurt me and Joshie.

Therapist: So he didn't want you to tell on him, but you were brave enough to. How are you feeling? You've told me a lot of things that are hard to talk about.

Lynn: I'm glad my aunt got divorced from him.

Therapist: So you're glad she believed you.

Lynn: My mom kept saying, "What's wrong, what's wrong," so I told her.

Therapist: So your mom knew something bad had happened and wanted you to tell her and you did. Even though he was so big. You surprised him. He thought he had you scared.

Lynn: I only told because mommie kept asking.

Therapist: Well, your mom helped you to start talking about it, but you still were the one who went through it and had to talk about it.

Lynn: He said I was lying, I wasn't!

Therapist: He wouldn't take responsibility for being bad to you. A real creepo.

Lynn: I know. He even lied to the police and everybody.

Therapist: Sometimes when kids tell about someone doing this, touching them where they shouldn't, making the child touch or kiss them when the kid doesn't want to, sometimes kids feel sort of mixed up, good about telling someone and making it stop, but bad because it's hard to talk about that stuff. Do you think part of you felt good about telling your mom but part of you didn't?

Lynn: Yeah. She said, she said, "Why didn't you tell me sooner?" I felt bad.

Therapist: Almost like you were being blamed, even by your mom.

Lynn: Yeah.

Therapist: As if you were bad. Do you think you are? Bad, I mean.

Lynn: No. I don't know.

Therapist: It's like most of you really knows you weren't bad—you aren't bad because of what Bob did. But a part of you worries you might be bad.

Lynn: Yeah.

Therapist: You even look sad now—thinking that a part of you might be bad.

Lynn: Uh-huh.

Therapist: Should we work together to change that? To help you believe you aren't bad?

Lynn: Okay.

Therapist: Maybe one way to do this would be to talk about how brave you actually were. Have you ever thought about the big part of you that did something brave?

Lynn: No. I did?

Therapist: Well, this is how I think about it. Bob was sneaky. He started out tickling you. Then he tickled you in your private places. Then he made you kiss his pee. No one was home to help you.

You were protecting Joshie. And you still told, even though he told you not to and you were scared. That sounds brave to me.

Lynn: Uh. But when I think, I feel bad.

Therapist: It really made you feel bad inside. Like you're a bad person?

Lynn: Uh-huh.

Therapist: I see. So deep inside there are still some real bad feelings. If we were going to draw a picture of you, how much would we call brave and how much would we call bad?

Lynn: I don't know.

Therapist: It's sort of hard to think about.

Lynn: Yeah.

Therapist: Sort of hard to even talk about.

Lynn: Yeah.

Therapist: Should we come back to this later? Figuring out how much is brave and how much is bad?

Lynn: Yeah.

We then moved on to talking about more benign topics. I sensed a growing anxiety in Lynn about continuing in this vein, because of the subject matter of the abuse, and because we were talking about this issue of badness. She alluded to perceiving some blame for not reporting this sooner, and that seemed to be critical in her judgment of herself. In a manner similar to a cognitive-behavioral approach to depression (Beck, Rush, Shaw, & Emery, 1979), Lynn and I discussed blame and responsibility, and the balance between brave and bad. Lynn clearly was assuming responsibility for the behavior of Bob, and this needed to be corrected.

Her sense of shame was also a focus, and we looked at other things about which she had been ashamed, but no longer was. She had a history as an above-average student, although her classroom performance had recently suffered from about the time the abuse started, and her "goodness" in class was used as a counterbalance to the "badness" she was feeling. For several sessions, we kept a focus on this as part of each session with Lynn, drawing pictures of her as brave and bad.

I also planted seeds of expectation that she would eventually see herself more positively, "as another 8-year-old girl I used to talk to was able to." This "bringing in" another person is akin to the "my friend John" technique of Milton Erickson (Haley, 1973), and it will be discussed in more detail in Chapter 9. Finally, we used portions of a few sessions to help Lynn explicate her growing sense of anger at Bob, e.g., listing all the things he ever did that made her dislike him and deciding on appropriate and not so appropriate punishments. When we terminated after 11 individual sessions, 5 conjoint sessions with her mother, and 4 individual sessions with her mother, Lynn had decided she was brave, Bob was bad, and her behavior and schoolwork were back to previous levels. No further problems had emerged at an informal 18-month follow-up.

The exact extent of her abuse was somewhat more severe than she reported to me in the transcript above. According to the police, Lynn had reported one incident of oral copulation and digital penetration in addition to the fondling. The duration was approximately three months and Bob had been with Lynn five to six times with no supervision.

My use of the dichotomy of brave and bad is based on the dialectics that exist in all feelings one has (Kegan, 1982). Particularly with children, the either-or, good-bad, black-white extreme is to be expected. Most of us know that, but we sometimes fail to remember that the dialectics are always present. For every thesis, there is an antithesis. Thus, expect that even for children who put up a brave front and state that they are "feeling fine," their true affective world is likely to be more complex.

Some examples are needed here to illustrate this more fully. Referring back to Lynn, if I had talked only about her being brave, without anticipating there were other feelings present, we would not have gotten into the much needed discussion of her perception of herself as bad. Likewise, if I had immediately stated, "You are not bad. It's not your fault," Lynn would not have heard me. Rather, I met her where she was, but then introduced a new possibility to her about bravery also being part of her feelings and perceptions.

Over the years, I have sometimes thought about therapy as a complex "dance," and my description of what I do with these children is "doing the dialectic." Essentially, this means that I help the child appreciate the two sides inherent in any feeling or thought — the ambivalence present in their relationships. By doing this, therapeutic movement can occur and the child can move to a more complex and mature perspective.

An example of this comes from Harter (1977), who presented a detailed case in which, over time, she helped a young child integrate a more mature picture of herself as a student. A 6-year-old girl perceived that she was very dumb and could not see that she was also quite intelligent. Through the use of a drawing, a therapy move Harter describes as intuitive, she introduced to the child the notion that the dumb part was for math, but a smart part also existed. Eventually, these drawings were utilized to help the girl elaborate on other feelings that seemed either-or. The entire paper by Harter is worth a careful reading and helps us to further realize that "one important source of the difficulty in simultaneously acknowledging conflicting emotions involves certain cognitive limitations of the young child."

Another example comes from an older adolescent, molested by her grandfather, who also molested her mother. The mother-daughter relationship had long been stormy and physically abusive, and as the girl got older, truancy, delinquency, and running away were an increasing part of her behavior. Over a three-year period, I saw Martha sporadically, usually two to three sessions at a time followed by a long separation, sometimes with her mother, more often individually. Meanwhile, her mother had finally found a therapist to help her with her own significant problems and, over the same time span, had shown marked improvement regarding employment and in a more positive and consistent relationship to her daughter. When I would see the mother in family sessions with Martha, I was struck by the contrast. Her gains were evident on her MMPI, with significantly less depression, anger, and alienation and significantly more resilience. However, these gains were confusing to the daughter. She called to see me after her last attempt to run away, and partway through the session she said something very close to the following.

Martha: I don't know my mom anymore.
Therapist: She seems like someone you've not met.
Martha: Yeah. You know, sometimes I would run because I knew she was going to hit me. But these last times, she was being nice. I ran because she was being nice. That's dumb.
Therapist: (doing the dialectic) Part of you feels more comfortable with the old mom, the mean one, but another part of you wants this new mom so bad, you run because you're afraid.
Martha: That's it! Isn't that crazy?
Therapist: No. The old is comfortable and predictable. You knew to a "T" when you'd get hit. Now you don't have a clue.
Martha: You said it. I'm so confused.

The process of making meaning out of sexual abuse experience preferably occurs via more direct discussions between the therapist and the child, but it also occurs in more indirect ways. The child may be quite young, may not know the full extent of the abuse, may have blocked some from recall, or may be extremely inhibited.

Elements of the therapeutic relationship may also contribute to one child being more indirect than another. If you find that children are routinely reluctant to talk to you, it would be useful to get feedback from co-workers about their perception of why children may have problems talking to you. Conditions in the larger environment, including parent-child relationships, the threat of not seeing a father again, or the threats that were used against the child, may also contribute to the absence of discussion of the abuse experience. Some of these reasons are more difficult to manage than others.

The children I have the most difficulty working with in this specific area are clearly those who do not feel safe about talking. Younger children can be engaged with drawings, anatomically correct dolls, or other similar techniques to guide a discussion. My therapeutic relationship with children can be developed, and children come to feel more comfortable with me over time. But it is the implicit or explicit threat of harm to the child, to family members, or to the family's integrity that is the most difficult to counter. In these cases, I believe that you need to think clearly about what realistic goals can be established for this child.

At the beginning of this chapter, I mentioned several preconditions for successful individual therapy with sexually abused children. If a child already is feeling beleaguered at home and also by you as the therapist, you are obviously not going to succeed. My suggestion is to focus on realistic, behavioral goals in the foster home and at school. Being coercive in the therapy process, which can result from attempting to have the child discuss the abuse, is counterproductive.

For some of these children, who are in a dilemma about talking to you because of the context, there is little you can do to get them to discuss the abuse. Children learn quickly what happens as a consequence of their actions. A 7-year-old boy who desperately wanted to return home to a very unfit and unsafe family successfully stonewalled any discussion of abuse, even though an older sister was quite explicit. Conjoint meetings between the sister and the brother did not erode his position. Other children, facing a similar dilemma, may be more open after conjoint meetings with a sibling or a trusted relative.

Storytelling that is initially vague and does not implicate either the child or any adult, and then progressively becomes more and more explicit, is an example of another approach that I have used successfully with some children.

Another child and I engaged in a discussion, over several sessions, about "the absolutely worst things that could ever happen to a kid." As we moved slowly from third person to first person, he finally was able to discuss the abuse. The experience that we had over those several sessions was very therapeutic for this young child.

Another child agreed with my offer that he "tell me one bad thing about it each time he saw me." As each week went by, another detail of the abuse emerged. Luckily, we had sufficient time for the entire story to emerge, and it actually emerged much more rapidly once the recounting of it began.

Lindahl (1988) described a case in which a young child, who denied abuse, was engaged in writing "therapeutic letters" to another young girl who had been abused. This indirect technique was apparently successful at allowing for later disclosure and accompanying symptom improvement.

For some of these children, the abuse experience is going to be secondary in importance. Other life experiences may be far more distressing to them. With these children, you help them process the abuse experience along with the other salient issues in their lives. What you are providing to the child is a cognitive framework around which previous events and future experiences can be organized. For children who frequently are provided few models for thinking about feelings and behavior and who have a map of interpersonal relationships that has little room for the presence of supportive relationships, this combination can be healing.

Enhancing the Child's Accurate Perception of Self

We began a discussion of this when we briefly reviewed the case of Lynn, the young girl who was struggling with feelings of guilt and shame after the abuse by Bob. The therapist not only wants to help children view themselves more accurately with regard to issues of guilt, shame, and responsibility for the abuse but also wants to help children view themselves more accurately and positively around issues of potency and hope for the future and to have a perception of themselves as valued.

These are often difficult to achieve. Not only do cognitive limitations exist but also the abuse experience itself frequently causes children to present in a more socially immature manner, and they are frequently in a family in which they have learned to perceive themselves negatively. How does a therapist go about altering these types of entrenched personal perceptions?

Initially, the therapist needs to actively help children talk about how they perceive themselves in different contexts. Using Harter's (1977) technique, introduce the child to the task of self-exploration by drawing a circle and having the child divide it into pieces that indicate the extent to which the child views himself or herself as having smart-dumb, good-bad, and happy-sad dimensions. Then, borrowing heavily from cognitive-behavioral therapy, examine the origins of these different cognitions and their realistic and unrealistic aspects.

The wonderful thing about play therapy is that role-play opportunities can be developed and the child can become the parent or teacher and have an opportunity to project negative beliefs about self onto you, allowing you to then respond in a manner that can teach the child a more adaptive way of functioning.

During the time away from therapy, the child is encouraged to look for those experiences that confirm or disconfirm the belief system, and then talk about them with you. I capitalized on a 15-year-old boy's developing obsessive-compulsive style by having him monitor a range of thoughts and feelings, including sexual thoughts, for me each week and then using that as a focus of discussion in the therapy. This type of responsibility is not well assumed by younger children, but there are instances in which it can be useful.

In my attempts to correct negative self-perceptions, I point out examples of those instances in which these children have behaved more appropriately in the session. These are markers of progress. I routinely point out to children when they have talked about an issue in a more adaptive style. A young child who exhibited apprehensiveness at visits with Dad, and who heard his mother routinely describe him as a "scaredy-cat," was praised by me for being appropriately watchful and quite smart for being wary when around his father. I believe that well-managed group therapy for these children can contribute nicely to the children's developing more accurate perceptions of themselves, particularly because it gives them a sense of not being alone in having been abused and in having such negative feelings about themselves in relationship to the abuse.

CREATING SAFETY

A logical therapeutic goal is to empower the child to do whatever is possible to decrease the likelihood of being victimized further. School-based sexual abuse prevention programs have existed for the past 10 years, but empirical validation of these programs has been minimal (Wurtele, 1987). This has not seemed to hinder continued development and implementation, probably because subjective evaluations are gen-

erally positive. However, school-based prevention programs are target-
ing a different set of children than we see clinically. Abuse has already
occurred, and unless the predisposing conditions and risk factors have
been altered considerably, the likelihood for further abuse remains dis-
tressingly high (Cohn & Daro, 1987).

In order to help children manage their future safety more appropriately, a decision-making perspective is helpful (Lamb, 1986). This
moves away from the perspective of the child as the helpless victim. It is
also far more useful because it allows the therapist and the child to
develop a careful analysis of future situations, to develop a list of potential decisions, and to role-play the enactment of those decisions. For
example, helping the child understand that the offender's threats
against disclosure can be circumvented by telling the appropriate person
can add a necessary input of realism.

However, I feel that an even more important mechanism for creating
future safety exists within the family sessions that are a routine part of
my work with these families. I know from listening to victims that the
best prevention efforts do not always work. The trance-inducing quality
of families can be difficult to break. If the mother cannot be overtly
supportive of the child's future safety, the child is not going to take his or
her own safety mechanisms very seriously either. If the father is the
perpetrator and the family is moving toward reunification, issues of
safety need to be a critical part of that therapy.

Therapy as the Creation of a New Map of
Interpersonal Relationships

A critical part of the work you do with these children includes those
elements that go into building and maintaining the therapeutic relationship. These include such things as respect for others, the give and
take of a relationship, learning that comfort can be derived from being
viewed in a nonjudgmental and fully accepting manner, and also that
scary and overly stimulating affect can be made manageable.

It is hoped that the therapeutic process helps the child in correcting
each of the four traumagenic factors identified by Finkelhor and Browne
(1985). The sense of betrayal is a difficult one to counter, because the
impact can be so profoundly negative and disruptive to the child's world
view. If the abuse is never discussed, the offender's actions and motivations can also never be discussed. However, part of the child's learning
how to manage the sense of betrayal is to discuss the offender, his motivations, and why his behavior was so negative. Here also is the opportunity

to discuss the ambivalence that many children feel about the perpetrator, with betrayal being only one part of the potential set of feelings.

Powerlessness can be addressed by the empowering actions of the therapist, assisting the child in gaining mastery in several different areas and helping the child see that progress is a function of one's own personal efficacy. This allows children to plan new behaviors and to think about themselves in a different manner. An appropriate sense of power comes about through the interaction of two healthy people. It is not fostered by a therapist who does not help children to openly discuss those instances in their lives that make them feel powerless.

The impact of traumatic sexualization is seen in the therapist's office in several ways, including overt sexual behavior and boundary permeability. The therapist is able to give the child feedback regarding sexual behavior in the therapy and those instances that are brought into the therapy by the child. Again, unless the sexual aspects of the abuse have been discussed, this is a difficult area for the child to correct. Finally, the stigmatization that the child experiences can be corrected in a relationship that fosters the child's learning how to view himself or herself more accurately, confronting the shame and guilt with fostering a more realistic self-perception.

Too often, these children are seen only briefly and therapeutic issues emerge at later dates. Child therapists need to have a future perspective, knowing that the work they help the child complete at this time may simply be preparing the child to seek out the opportunity to do further work later on. The data on invulnerable children, who overcome enormous adversity and continue to maintain adequate levels of functioning, continue to implicate positive social figures in the child's life as critical to the child's remaining confident (Garmezy, 1983).

When I ask the parents of sexually abused children about their own upbringing and who gave them a sense that they were valued, the ones with the best prognosis are able to talk about parents, teachers, and even the occasional group home house parent or counselor who reflected back to them a sense of themselves that they could hold on to and value. These individuals gave that person a sense of their own personal capacity as well as a sense that adversity could be overcome through working together.

Specific Behavioral Goals

As part of the child being oriented to therapy, and in keeping with my more pragmatic and direct approach, we develop several goals. For some younger children, this amounts to nothing more than an agreement to discuss several topics over time. For example, I have said, "Well, I think that every time we meet we are going to talk about those mad feelings you have inside that get you into problems at home. We have to work to get you out of all that trouble." It can be more specific than that, as with Michael, only 5 years old. In the family session we agreed that Michael and I would spend time talking about his sexual behavior individually, mom would monitor its occurrence at home, and we would discuss this the next week during the conjoint portion and the individual portion. This atmosphere of greater openness, difficult for both Michael and his mother, allowed for more discussion and a more rapid decrease of symptoms.

The integration of individual and family therapy can be difficult. Issues of whose therapist you are may get raised, and the child may not see you as positively. However, the overall leverage you can gain, resulting in less symptomatology, may correct this imbalance.

Specific goals can be identified and made the focus of much of the therapy. There can be several generic behavioral problems present, some directly related to the abuse (e.g., an increase in phobic reactions and anxiety) and others predating the abuse. The finding by Weisz et al. (1987) that a greater effect for individual child therapy was obtained via behavioral, directive approaches as opposed to nondirective approaches adds further impetus to goal development.

The therapist has the option of choosing the most appropriate treatment focus. For example, play therapy would probably not have been successful in the case described by McNeill and Todd (1986). A 5 year old ruminated about her abuse. Her whining and fidgeting at these times reactivated her parents' distress and guilt about the extrafamilial abuse. It became apparent that the behavior was triggered in those interactions she either felt ignored by her mother or was being punished for other misbehavior. An operant procedure that used the mother as the primary change agent was introduced and was quite successful, with results persisting at 12-month follow-up.

Less overt behavioral manifestations may be better dealt with individually. Although we may hope that a child's depression will lift if the child is provided enough successes at a board game played in the therapy room, far more success is likely if the depression is acknowledged, its origins traced, and a cognitive approach used to assist the child.

Jones (1986) described the numerous contributors to depression in the sexually abused child, and the extent to which these can be explored can prove helpful. These contributors include:

1. mourning the loss of family integrity
2. mourning the loss of one or more parents
3. mourning the loss of a special role in the family
4. experiencing a sense of isolation and differentness from other children.

It is also possible that the child's hopelessness is translated into suicidal ideation or attempts, although this is usually in older children. This should not prevent inquiring about this with younger children, who sometimes will surprise us with the graphic nature of their ideation. Not only did a 9 year old acknowledge suicidal ideation, but she also drew a picture for me of how her neck would fit inside a rope, "but you have to tie a special knot and I don't know how."

Externalizing behaviors can also be addressed in child therapy, although a contextual focus is far more appropriate (Alexander & Parsons, 1982). Impulsive children can learn to plan ahead and role-play greater reflectivity (Kendall & Braswell, 1985); socially awkward children can practice social skills; and aggressive children can engage in a discussion of their victim's feelings, an important tool in teaching greater empathy. It is often with these children, who are more aversive to their parents, that I use individual therapy as part of a larger, systemic therapy. An example can help to explain this concept.

Beth, a 10 year old, had an extremely negative relationship with her single mother. She had been molested several years earlier but did not receive therapy until she began to assault her mother. Our therapy contacts were divided into time for a conjoint session and an individual session. I was the therapist for both. One day Beth and I came into the family session after having finished our session and Mary, her mother, said, "I guess she told you I'm a bitch, didn't she?" I countered by telling her that Beth was actually telling me, somewhat indirectly, that she missed and needed her mother; that she had told me about Mary's destructive relationship with her own mother; and that Beth and I agreed that we were going to try to prevent that same thing from happening between the two of them. My "interpretation" of our session, to Mary, had greater weight because it came from the private, individual session with Beth. Mary was less able to challenge it. For the first time ever, we began to talk about Mary's own fears of this same outcome, and we identified what was the same and what was different about their relationship.

I used this technique several more times to add momentum to the therapy. By talking with Beth individually about issues that were important to the family, I could then legitimately introduce this into the family session. Mary began to see Beth more positively because it now appeared to her that Beth cared about her, despite the anger she also exhibited. Mary's view of Beth was becoming more differentiated, in Werner's (1948) term, and she could no longer project negatively on her in such an indiscriminate manner.

The sometimes wrenching task of reintegrating various family members can also be facilitated quite nicely in the individual therapy process. It is occasionally at this time that you first hear ambivalence about the reunion process and fears for future safety. The anxiety of the upcoming process seems to activate greater realism in some of these children. They have now moved from a defensive posture, in which ambivalence and fears for safety were not accessible, to a position in which they are. The child may invest in therapy as never before, because the issues feel very real and present.

There are other specific therapy goals that could also be discussed. The essence of the previous section is that you can facilitate change more rapidly if you utilize the relationship you have to convey the message that important work goes on here—sometimes playfully, sometimes not. Greater specificity can greatly help the child because the child can be more of a full partner with you in a process if the child knows where it is that he or she is headed.

Two final comments are needed here. The first is that behavioral therapy with children can provide the necessary direction and immediate symptom management that nondirective, intrapsychic approaches are less able to do. The second comment is that behavioral approaches (utilized in a family setting where parent-child attachment is suspect, and consequently the parent is viewed more as a coercive than a reinforcing person) may not work until the parent-child relationship can improve in quality. The child can learn best in the context of a supportive relationship.

TERMINATION

Often a luxury in these cases, the formal termination process should actually be planned from the beginning by deciding ahead of time how the child will deal with this process, and what goals need to be achieved during the time you are together. In those instances in which I do not do the job I need to do to identify which goals are necessary and realistic, I know that I am overworked, do not have the time or energy to invest in this essential component, and may also feel defeated about the case and what I see going on that is counterproductive. That is probably true for other therapists; if so, too many of the most needy children are being underserved.

A central therapeutic issue that arises at this time is the child's dealing with rejection and the loss of the attachment to the therapist (Jones, 1986). These issues are all the more salient because of the previous history of loss. The child's reaction to termination will be dictated in part by these previous losses, how well the child has been prepared, and the nature of the therapy relationship. The interpersonal styles described by Horney (1950) may also enter into the leave-taking process, with the *moving-away* child sometimes taking it as further proof of the unreliability or unavailability of people. The separation can be difficult for the therapist also, because the therapist may be reminded that there is further work necessary or may be ambivalent about the child's future safety.

Several techniques can be helpful at this point. The first is to plan approaching the child about termination well in advance of the expected last session. Sometimes this can be done by tapering off the frequency of sessions. A month to six weeks is a useful time frame. With some children whom I see for a limited time, at each session's conclusion we count how many more sessions are remaining. Thus the issue of termination is always present, but I do not believe this adversely affects the strength of the relationship.

It is also possible to gauge how much you have been incorporated into the child's life during those last sessions as you reminisce about your time together. Some children remember events in great detail, others in lesser detail, and others avoid remembering much at all. This last version is possibly a more adaptive way of dismissing you as a therapist than it was for Helen, who refused to see me her last session, saying loudly in the waiting room, "I don't like you." Her five years of life were replete with repeated separations from parents and considerable neglect, over and above her sexual abuse. Helen might have managed far more adaptively if the therapy had not been prematurely stopped after eight sessions, due to a change in geographic residence and a resulting transfer to a new therapist.

Some therapists have clear rules about no contact after termination, but again the uniqueness of this population emerges, in that you may be involved in monitoring the reunification process or see the child again at some later date for other issues. This may engender a different set of reactions.

In summary, a perspective emphasizing the relational and directive aspects of individual therapy has been presented. A developmental perspective has been suggested, along with the importance of working within the context of the child. The constancy of the therapist, the valuing of the child, and the opportunities provided to experience new behaviors and come to some new understandings can be the key to the child's relearning how to modulate the thoughts and emotions that were distorted by the abuse experience.

6

Understanding and Treating the Family

In states of overwhelming anxiety, there is no such
thing as a child: there is only a child in his family.
E.J. Anthony

There are few areas in the conceptualization and treatment of sexual abuse that generate more controversy than the role of the family in incestuous abuse. At the 1988 Hilton Head Conference on Child Sexual Abuse, Lucy Berliner, M.S.W., and Noel Larson, Ph.D., two noted clinicians and theoreticians in the area of sexual abuse, engaged in a 7-hour debate regarding the place of family therapy and theory in understanding and treating incestuous abuse. Those who saw family issues as primary in the etiology and treatment of incest were at odds with clinicians whose primary emphasis was protecting the victim from further abuse and restoring the victim to an adequate level of functioning. There have been many interminable and somewhat awkward discussions among clinicians regarding the role and goals of family therapy in the treatment of sexually abused children.

It is difficult to dispute that the family is critical when considering how stress impacts children. Families are "the central microsystem, the headquarters of human development" (Garbarino, 1982). The review, in Chapter 1, of family variables that predispose a child to sexual abuse also pointed strongly to the need for intervention at a family level. I believe this is true for both intrafamilial and extrafamilial abuse. Put somewhat too simply, a primary reason for the strong differences of opinion that exist between family therapists and victim advocates is the fact that family therapy assumes circular causality within the system.

In other words, every member of the family is viewed as an integral part of the system, and actions of each member of the system influence every other member of the system. This can be thought to imply blame for family members other than the offender. Family therapists also place less value on individual psychopathology in the traditional psychiatric nosology sense. Thus, the belief that a bad father is doing bad things to his child, separate from the mother's or child's actions or the role of multiple generations, is an anathema to a family therapist. However, when you are primarily a victim advocate, it is easy to believe that the bad father is doing bad things to his child, and that the child in particular and the remaining family members in general are not contributing to the incest.

This reflects the polarization of the sexual-abuse treatment field into two nonoverlapping camps. These are the victim-advocacy group and the family-systems group. An overly simplistic definition of the victim-advocacy group involves their emphasis on the rights of the child victim and the non-offending parent victim, usually the mother. If the father has a future role in the family, it is to be severely curtailed. Extreme pessimism exists when thinking about the likelihood of his returning successfully to the family and resuming anything resembling a parental role. Herman (1981), wrote that traditional family therapy is inappropriate for the incestuous offender because of its tendency to attribute a multitude of evils to the combination of a domineering mother and passive father.

Victim-advocacy clinicians clearly reflect a well-developed and justifiable outrage at our cultural system which allows parents, and fathers in particular, to exploit children and, in a broader sense, allows men to sexually and physically exploit women. Incest and all manner of sexual abuse are viewed from a perspective that emphasizes the sociocultural contributors to violence against women and children.

As originally conceptualized, a family-systems approach to treatment emphasizes the interaction of all members of the family. Causality is seen as circular, and all interpersonal linkages are reciprocal in nature. Behavioral problems are not simply a function of bad behavior directed at an individual. Rather, behavioral problems represent the cumulative interaction of all members of a system over one or more generations, and they reflect the difficulties that families have in negotiating various transformations in the life cycle.

There may be some softening of the purely systemic viewpoint for a number of family therapists. Bograd (1986), writing about wife abuse, stated, "Responding to wife abuse challenges family therapists to take unapologetically value-laden stands." The same is true for sexual abuse. Many family therapists who work with families with serious psychological problems have developed an appreciation for the place of individual psychopathology. Systems theory is developing an appreciation for the different levels of system, including family and individual levels.

For example, some incestuous fathers are increasingly seen as having both criminal and compulsive features along with preexisting emotional problems that they bring to the family (Meiselman, 1978; Langevin, 1983). At the same time, the child victim and the non-offending mother are viewed as reflecting roles that have been attributed to them in this nonfunctional family system.

Paul Dell (1989), a previously unrelenting systemic theorist, recently wrote a paper critiquing the purely systemic conceptualization of wife battering, suggesting that power issues may also need to be considered and allowing that systemic theory had been remiss about this. It does seem curious that, despite family therapy's emphasis on the system, it can be accused of ignoring the larger cultural system that victim advocates see all around them.

Another argument is that family therapy may not be effective with these families or a subset of these families. Experienced clinicians have all heard horror stories, of uncertain veracity, about ineffectual family therapists who were naive about the compulsivity of incest perpetrators, and who saw the family weekly while the incest was continuing to occur. However, the clinical treatment literature on child sexual abuse favors no approach over the other, and until evidence of treatment outcome is presented, we will continue to see the need for various therapies, including family-based approaches.

Anecdotal stories are, however, not the type of evidence that is needed to disprove the efficacy of family therapy and a family-systems model in both understanding and treating child sexual abuse. Naive therapists are ubiquitous. There are naive family therapists who do not appreciate that incest does not stop by increasing parental subsystem communication. There are also naive therapists, espousing a victim-advocacy model, who do not appreciate the heterogeneity of incestuous families, and by devaluing the perpetrator and overvaluing the non-offending mother they may fail to address the severely strained mother-daughter dynamics that have long been present. Untreated, these dynamics can have a deleterious impact.

For example, I do not believe the best treatment for a family, even with several instances of reactive abuse, is necessarily to dissolve the family. What may go untreated is the resulting or preceding mother-daughter estrangement, coupled with a decrease in SES. A more effective treatment is a family-systems approach that addresses the individual and systemic issues leading to the abuse, reinforces the parental system, enhances both adults' abilities to get their emotional needs met more appropriately, and holds of paramount importance the safety of the victim. Only if it is feasible and congruent for all parties should the result be to keep the family together. The child is less likely to be blamed and negatively affected by a downward turn in the family's financial status. SES is, after all, one of the few variables that is routinely and negatively correlated with various childhood difficulties, including depression and school problems (Graham, 1979). One does not have to be a mother-blamer or a father-lover to appreciate the utility of the family-systems model for both conceptualization and therapy. When used appropriately, the family-systems model allows for a more accurate and richly developed perspective of each family member.

The question that legitimately gets raised is whether a family-systems approach is also useful in those instances of extrafamilial sexual abuse (Conte, 1986; Finkelhor, 1986). Father-daughter incest represents only a small subset of the larger sexual-abuse problem according to these critics. This remains to be empirically validated, but broadly defined intrafamilial abuse (any relation, close friend) will comprise the majority of sexual abuse cases that present to a treatment program; family variables that contribute to the abuse or potentiate the reaction after the abuse will be present in the vast majority of these cases. In addition, extrafamilial abuse not only activates negative parental reactions but also is often contributed to indirectly by family stress or chaos.

The remainder of this chapter develops several family-related themes. Initially, various theories pertaining to characteristics of incestuous families will be examined, and several key elements will be distilled. Finally, a model for applying family therapy to various incestuous and nonincestuous families will be developed and supplemented with case examples.

Because this chapter focuses on the family issues of both intra-and extrafamilial sexual-abuse cases, some of my comments may be more relevant to one situation than to another. I will attempt to clarify this when I think it is necessary.

FAMILY CHARACTERISTICS

Literature is scant regarding preabuse family functioning in incestuous families. It is also unclear what the preabuse family functioning is in families whose children are sexually abused by individuals outside the immediate family. The current literature on families with a sexually abused child is primarily clinical in nature, with empirical research only recently emerging.

Clinicians have reported frequently in the past 20 years about features that appear common to the small sample of incestuous families they have seen (Lustig et al., 1966). To what extent these variables specifically contributed to the abuse or are features common to a large number of dysfunctional families is an unanswered question. Another problem with this search for common features is the fact that only a small percentage of incestuous families are described by the features mentioned in the literature; incestuous families are heterogeneous.

Herman (1981) identified at least two types of families in her research: incestuous and seductive. They differ in the overtness of the sexual behavior by the father, with more overt behavior seen in the incestuous families. The incestuous experiences may be father-daughter, brother-sister, mother-son, or combinations of these.

Clinical observations have not revealed the existence of any single or essential family variable that explains its etiology or continuation. Mrazek and Kempe (1981) stated, "Of all the contributing factors mentioned in the literature, the most predictive are likely to be the absence of a strong, satisfying marital bond and *prior* incestuous behavior somewhere in the family." Other clinicians describe several common features, which may vary depending on the families seen, the referral sources, and the clinician's biases.

Only recently, however, have clinicians and researchers begun to talk about the differences among incestuous families, which I believe more accurately reflects the underlying heterogeneity of incest (Larson & Maddock, 1986). I recall, for example, the first incestuous family that I saw. My initial perception was of a family that was extremely rigidly controlled and closed off emotionally to each other and to me as the therapist. I was thus surprised when two-thirds of the way through seeing this first family I began to see a second incestuous family, which was extremely chaotic, had child physical abuse and husband-wife battering as secondary referral issues, and appeared to be just the opposite, along a dimension of chaotic-rigid, from the first family that I was seeing. From the beginning, I began to appreciate the fact that incestuous families presented in various shapes and forms, and although there were some underlying common features that clearly deserve mention and discussion, a clinical approach that appreciates the individual differences of each family, and then places the family in the context of larger common features, might be the most advisable.

An Integrative Perspective

An excellent paper that attempted to distill a great deal of theorizing about incestuous families is by Alexander (1985). Although the model she developed fails to incorporate deviant sexual arousal patterns seen in a significant subset of fathers, she describes three features that are seen, to a greater or lesser degree, in a large percentage of families in which incest is an issue.

A first feature reflects the fact that incestuous families are frequently quite *isolated*. Alexander described this as decreased information exchange with the environment. The family is closed off and individual members in the family are not able to experience the types of appropriate socialization processes and naturally curative functions that other children and adults experience. Some of these families contribute to their isolation because of a marked lack of relational skills in the parents. Not only do their neighbors find them hard to live next to but therapists also find them hard to have in their offices.

A second feature is the absence of something she labels as "*negentropy*." This is the opposite of entropy, a term that comes from physics, and reflects the fact that as an organism grows and develops, it becomes more and more disorganized and chaotic. Healthy families manage to reverse this tendency toward entropy and are hence negentropic. Incestuous families lack this ability, and it is reflected in such outcomes as decreased individual differentiation from the family and subsequent failure to develop a mature personal identity.

This absence of negentropy comes from impaired communication between family members and the absence of conflict resolution skills in the family. Communication is the vehicle for individuation and, when it is lacking, people do not develop. Conflict, when resolved, can be quite liberating and help the family move to another, more sophisticated level of functioning. When conflict is not resolved, and the family has to expend considerable energy to ignore its presence or avoid the emergence of conflict, individual growth and development along with family growth and development are curtailed.

Finally, Alexander described a third common feature that she labeled "*dynamic homeostasis*." Families do remain homeostatic, which is defined as maintaining stability and order over time. Healthy families are dynamically homeostatic in that they remain stable over time but continue to grow and develop as they move from one developmental period to another. Families develop in the manner described by Werner (1948), balancing differentiation (e.g., allowing increasing autonomy in family members) with integration (e.g., appropriate closeness between family members). Blocking the dynamic homeostasis in incestuous families is the presence of far too much enmeshment.

Enmeshment carries with it two features — one being the blurring of individual boundaries among family members, and the other being the dissolving of generational boundaries. This latter feature results in children becoming "parentified" or "spousified." Some clinicians have used the word role-reversal when describing mother-daughter relationships in incestuous families (Herman, 1981). Alexander subsumed this concept of role-reversal in her factor of dynamic homeostasis. However, she did not single out the victim, but wrote that every person in the family is affected by this overly close system. Gelinas (1988) echoed that in her description of incestuous families as relationally imbalanced.

A fourth feature, beyond the three described by Alexander, is also frequently present. This reflects my interest in the multigenerational dimension of sexual abuse, including incest, and also helps me to understand why it is so difficult for families to mobilize themselves and respond appropriately when the incest is discovered. This feature pertains to the *loss and desertion experiences* of the parents. The capacity for forming and maintaining secure attachments is impeded. This may have occurred as a result of their own parents being absent or due to their own history of physical or sexual abuse when younger. Loss and desertion become powerful organizing principles of their behavior, and parents follow Maturana's principle of structural coupling (Maturana & Varela, 1987), or repeating patterns over generations.

This helps to explain why two individuals of seemingly negative backgrounds can find each other and marry. They minimize the likelihood of loss in their own generation by marrying someone who is as equally fearful of intimacy as they are and by having children with whom they relate in a distant and nonempathic manner. The common finding of loss would be important to add as a basic feature to Alexander's three descriptors.

How do the characteristics of incestuous families compare to issues that seem to characterize families in general? Garbarino (1982) identified three broad issues that are common to all families: *family boundaries, internal organization,* and *family themes.*

Family boundaries define the relative separateness or connectedness of the subsystems in the family and regulate the flow of information and the flexibility of movement between subsystems. It is usually thought that there are individual boundaries, marital/parental boundaries, and sibling boundaries and that the family itself has an external boundary. As the family moves along its developmental course, boundaries change. However, the act of incest strongly indicates inappropriately weak or permeable boundaries between the parent and child, as in Alexander's (1985) description of enmeshment in the incestuous family. Father-daughter incest reflects a boundary violation between father and daughter, with its origins possibly in an overinvolved father-daughter relationship without overt sexuality. It also indicates a great deal of separateness between the partners in the marital dyad, which directly reflects Mrazek's (1981) findings of marital conflict in incestuous families.

With regard to internal organization or the pattern of family interaction, an incestuous family would have problems with communication (secretive), one dimension of internal organization (Gelinas, 1988). The expectations for interaction are also skewed. Rather than a pattern of intense father-mother interaction, there may be a pattern of intense father-daughter interaction and overt competition between mother-daughter. The interactions affect all family members and their expectations for family interaction in the future. This is evidenced by the familial transmission of incest, with incest in multiple generations.

Finally, family themes or goals are those commitments and values that the family has for its members and itself. They vary in terms of how explicit or implicit they are and also in terms of how general or specific they may be. Families that do not value or respect autonomy and individual rights include incestuous families. Garbarino (1982) wrote that family goals may be a key to the conflict in a family. For example, if there are mutually exclusive individual and family goals, the conflict may reach crisis proportions. An incestuous family has mutually exclusive goals, e.g., individual goals of the father for exploitation or indulgence and a goal of the child for autonomy and respect. The incestuous parent's goals are also not compatible with a goal for the longevity of the family as a healthy unit.

What is the evidence from other clinicians in support of Alexander's (1985) model? Fifteen additional clinical papers in this area were reviewed in order to determine their degree of agreement with the factors described above. The emphasis is clinical, in that none is empirically derived. One can see from Table 6-1 that the majority agree with these factors. The articles were reviewed and either a more general or a specific mention of one of these factors was determined. The greatest consensus was on enmeshment, followed by poor communication.

TABLE 6-1
Features of Incestuous Families

		Negentropy			
	Isolation	Poor communication	Poor conflict resolution	Homeostasis enmeshment	History of loss
Alexander, 1985	+	+	+	+	
Barrett et al., 1986	+	+	+	+	
Boniello, 1986	+	+	+	+	+
Eist & Mandel, 1968	+	+	+	+	+
Herman, 1983		+		+	
Justice & Justice, 1979	+	+		+	
Larson & Maddock, 1986	+	+	+	+	+
Lustig et al., 1966	+	+	+	+	+
Machotka, Pittman, & Flomenhaft, 1967		+	+	+	+
Meiselman, 1978	+	+	+	+	+
Mrazek & Bentovim, 1981		+	+	+	+
Pelletier & Handy, 1986		+	+	+	
Reposa & Zuelzer, 1983		+	+	+	
Roberts, 1984	+	+	+	+	
Sgroi, 1982b	+	+	+	+	+
Swanson & Biaggio, 1985	+			+	+

Additional Variables

Various features not included in this table were also mentioned by these and other authors. For example, Justice & Justice (1979) included the presence of a crisis that precipitates the onset of incest and supported this with findings from a life-events schedule completed by a group of parents. Further support for the finding that high levels of personal, social, and economic stress may be related to the onset of incestuous abuse comes from Gordon (1989), who examined stress levels in families in which a child was sexually abused by either a birth father or stepfather. His hypothesis was that for birth fathers to sexually abuse, stronger emotional links to their child would have to be overcome, and higher levels of stress would need to be present compared to families in which abuse by a stepfather occurred. He did find that families in which the birth father was the abuser showed significantly higher levels of drug or alcohol abuse, marital problems, and insufficient income than did families in which the stepfather was the abuser.

Herman (1983) was also correct in her theorizing that a significant subset of incestuous families are characterized by an exaggeration of patriarchal norms. Although this term may imply male dominance, the term "a dominant father" can be a misnomer in describing some incestuous fathers. In the same way that Wynne, Ryckoff, Day, and Hirsch (1958) coined the term "pseudomutual" to indicate families that appeared to be mutual but actually were not, the term "pseudodominant" would be more appropriate to those incestuous fathers who exhibit tyrannical styles within the family but are actually rather weak and inadequate in many other areas.

An additional feature identified by several authors (Erickson, 1986; Herman, 1983; Justice & Justice, 1979) pertains to the absence of the mother due to physical or emotional incapacitation or preoccupation with other child-rearing tasks. Herman (1983) described the mother in these families as being a victim "of her own reproductive cycle," in that these families frequently have a larger number and closer spacing of children. Erickson (1986), in a data-based study, described the children in her sample as being extremely unprotected because of chaotic rearing environments in which the mother literally is absent. The mother's absence appeared to allow these children to also experience numerous other types of abuse. In fact, she reported that the sexual abuse was not an isolated event in any of these children's lives, but that other instances of victimization were common.

Finally, substance abuse has also been mentioned by several clinicians as a contributing factor (Barnard, 1983; Gordon, 1989).

Thus, at least four additional features characterize some families, including greater levels of stress, an exaggeration of patriarchal norms, an absent or incapacitated mother, and an increased likelihood of substance abuse.

Some combination of this rather large constellation of possible characteristics of incestuous families is needed for incest to emerge. For example, substance abuse is not sufficient, but in combination with various other variables it may facilitate the emergence of incest. Research is needed to determine which of these features also characterize extrafamilial sexual abuse. A considerable overlap is probable.

The Role of Sexual Variables

Noticeably absent from Alexander's theorizing, and the theorizing of the majority of clinicians, is any mention of deviant sexual arousal patterns or criminality. Meiselman (1978) did mention that a history of sexual aberration exists for the mothers of incest victims, with the mothers being bimodally distributed: either viewing sex as aversive or being promiscuous. Larson and Maddock (1986) described a "sexualized dependency" in some families, and Roberts (1984) mentioned marital conflict, including sexual problems, as did Lustig et al. (1966). Boniello (1986) reported a lack of sex education in incestuous families, but the issue appears to go beyond the absence of sex education. In a paper that discussed factors related to the onset of sibling incest, Smith and Israel (1987) stated that sibling incest is more likely to occur in those families in which there is parental stimulation of a sexual climate in the home. They contend that this sexual atmosphere is engendered by a parent who is sexually avoidant and also by extramarital affairs by one of the parents.

Despite the fact that sexual variables of one type or another are routinely identified in sexually abusive families, there is still divergent opinion as to whether the child's sexual abuse or the disturbed family dynamics that accompany the abuse is the critical factor in predicting outcome for the child (Pelletier & Handy, 1986).

Empirical Research on Sexually Abusive Families

Little research has been done to document the existence of the elements that are supposedly common to incestuous families. What does exist is somewhat confirmatory of several variables mentioned earlier. Saunders and his colleagues, working primarily with Navy families (Murphy, Saunders, & McClure, 1986; Saunders, McClure, & Murphy,

1987), noted that incestuous families were characterized by an impoverished emotional environment. The family appeared to be focused around the victim and a special relationship seemed to exist between the perpetrator and the victim in contrast to relationships the perpetrator had with other children. Added to this was the fact that the relationship between the mother and the victim was frequently conflicted.

Erickson (1986) identified 11 sexually abused children from a prospective study of over 260 children and examined features common in these children's families. She identified a common history of sexual abuse in the mother's own childhood and noted that the families of these children were chaotic and could not provide appropriate protection to the children, leaving them vulnerable to exploitation. As a result, sexual abuse was just one of many traumatic events most of the children in her sample had experienced.

In a group of papers (Sroufe et al., 1985; Sroufe and Ward, 1980), which involved the same families as in Erickson's (1986) study, a subset of mothers at risk for physical child abuse or neglect was identified in a longitudinal prospective study as exhibiting "seductive" behavior toward their young children, usually male. Seductive behavior was rated as qualitatively different from affectionate behavior and was for the mother's own benefit. It was usually defined as sexual touching.

Mothers who exhibited this type of behavior, which Sroufe and colleagues equated with a dissolving of generational boundaries, (a) had a high incidence of incestuous relationships with their children, (b) were less able to set and keep limits in a playroom setting, (c) offered less support and guidance to their children, and (d) were more likely to use physical punishment than a matched comparison group of mothers. Mothers who were seductive with their sons were also derisive to their daughters, when a daughter was present in the family. Clearly the son was favored, but the relationship was ambivalent in that the mother was using the son to meet her "sexual" needs.

These two studies provide some empirical support for the features noted earlier, including enmeshment, poor conflict resolution, and loss or desertion as an organizing principle in these families.

More research is needed on how incest is transmitted multigenerationally and how a history of maternal incest might facilitate molestation of the children either in or outside of the family. In addition, more theorizing is needed that combines family features with features common to perpetrators and yields a more integrated theory. Such a theory would guide clinically appropriate treatment that would not allow the child to be abused further by the perpetrator or the more healthy family to dissolve.

What Is More Important — Family or Sexual Variables?

An issue that emerges frequently is the question of whether there is something about the family that "caused" the sexual abuse, particularly incest. This is an extremely contentious area of discussion. Several theories seeking to explain the origin of sexual abuse within the family have been proposed. Essentially two positions are represented: the family is seen as the etiologic agent or the incest is seen solely as a function of pathologic features of the perpetrator.

Regrettably, these positions do not appear to be easily reconciled. For example, a clinician may naively interpret the incestuous family system as typified by an autocratic, paranoid father and a mother who consciously or unconsciously supports the incest as a result of her own prior victimization or dependency. Support for this comes from the physical child-abuse literature, which characterizes abusive parents as having a history of being abused themselves and, as a group, being significantly more pathologic than comparison parents of similar education and SES level (Friedrich & Wheeler, 1982).

A family-systems' perspective on family functioning suggests that the emergence and continuation of sexual abuse in the family is a function of contributions by each member of the system. The parents' contribution may be an incestuous history in their own family of origin that has not been resolved; the child's contribution may be that he or she is the right age and sex. A victim-advocate stance, on the other hand, would find the concept of circular causality not only not useful but also morally bankrupt at this point and would place the full blame on the father. A related feminist stance would argue that sexual abuse is one more instance of female victimization and to accuse mothers as involved in this is further victimization (Caplan & Hall-McCorquodale, 1985).

There is truth in all of these perspectives. The initial emergence and subsequent maintenance of sexual abuse in the family appear to be a culmination of individual pathologic features of the perpetrator and a system that tolerates this behavior. Gelles (1974) argued this same point for conjugal violence. He developed a model of intrafamily violence that included a component pertaining to violence by parents toward their children. The family's microsystem — actual structure and interrelationships — is one element in the model. It is thought to be affected by (a) social position, (b) structural stress, (c) the offender's identity (derived from family of origin and the socialization of the offender), (d) social isolation, and (e) norms and values concerning violence. Family structure impacts situational factors which then lead to the violence. This is an obviously complex model that seems to do justice to a complex phenomenon.

If you refer back to Garbarino's (1982) three dimensions of healthy family functioning — boundaries, organization, and themes — incestuous families are not the only families that miss these goals. Poor boundaries, chaotic or overly skewed organization, and the absence of goals can describe various pathologic families. Evidence for the difficulty in making unilateral statements about the characteristics of incestuous families comes from Barnard's (1983) paper on the similarities in families who have problems with alcohol or incest.

Although it is true that alcohol is implicated as a contributing element in a minority of families who have an incest problem, the similarities are numerous and pervasive:

1. Generational boundaries are blurred.
2. The marital dyad is dysfunctional and operates as a fragmented or nonexistent parental dyad.
3. The marital sexual relationship has deteriorated.
4. Normal inhibitory anxieties are muted.
5. Affect is muffled and distorted.
6. Denial is rampant and "secrets" predominate.
7. Family roles are pathologically assigned and rigidified.
8. The family is isolated.
9. A profound state of homeostatic stuckness exists.
10. Sibling relationships are pathologically disturbed.
11. There is excessive separateness or connectedness within the family.
12. There are problems with trust/intimacy.
13. Problems with dependency are present.

Barnard's (1983) conclusion was that when clinicians are confronted by one of these two types, they should carefully investigate the potential presence of the other.

Finally, in a clinically relevant line of research, David Wolfe (Jaffe et al., 1986; Wolfe & Mosk, 1983) has generally failed to discriminate families in which violence was present from similar, low SES, disadvantaged families. Contrary to expectations that children exposed to violence would be more significantly disturbed, it appeared that family variables of disorganization and poverty were more important predictors of behavior.

Is the same true for sexual abuse? Elmer (1977), in a provocative study that has never been replicated, studied physically abused children who had been hospitalized and followed them over several years. She failed to find long-term differences between the physically abused children and other low SES children on several outcome measures, and she concluded that socioeconomic factors were primary and physical abuse was secondary in terms of impact. However, her follow-up sample was extremely small, accounting for only 20% of her original sample, and Cicchetti (1987), drawing from a much broader research base, concluded that physical abuse has an impact, over and above poverty, chaos, and family disorganization.

Comparable research is only now being completed with sexual abuse. For example, Briere (1989a) recently completed a series of studies with adults to indicate that there is something specific to sexual abuse, above and beyond family dysfunction, that predicted long-term outcome. Whatever the case, the therapist must be sensitive to what the clients perceive as primary — in some cases, they may perceive their issues to be something other than sexual abuse, and that may be the case.

In summary, with regard to family variables unique to sexual abuse, the literature suggests that it would be difficult for incest to emerge in families that have the four basic factors mentioned above without the presence of deviant sexual-arousal patterns, a history of sexual abuse in one or both of the parents, or criminal tendencies in the perpetrator. That is the point that Mowrer (1986; 1987) made in an effort to develop a bridge between family theorists and victim therapists. He wrote that family theory and theories on offender deviancy must be bridged in order to promote the most efficacious type of clinical practice. Without this deviant sexual-arousal pattern, families that have demonstrated the other features present in Alexander's model would more than likely be families in which depression and inadequate socialization would be common in children, along with increased acting-out behavior.

Nonincestuous Families

What can be assumed about the families of nonincest sexual-abuse victims? Do they somehow fail to protect the child so that the abuse is made more likely? Or is sexual abuse a totally unpredictable event? Some pertinent research that addressed this question dealt with risk factors (see Chapter 1). These factors implicate some family variables that also operate in extrafamilial abuse.

It was mentioned earlier that insights into this type of sexual abuse may also come from research on children's accidents. In this case, the sexual abuse of a child by a nonrelative or stranger is viewed as an accidental occurrence with minimal predictability. However, public health research has indicated that family dysfunctioning is frequently implicated in repeated accidents in children (Plionis, 1977), and a similar relationship has been identified between severity of parental punishment and childhood accidents (Langley, McGee, Silva, & Williams, 1983). A stressful, possibly aggressive, social or family environment also seems to be clearly implicated in childhood accidents (Jones, 1980; Westfelt, 1982). Finally, parental lack of knowledge of developmental milestones and injury prevention measures has been linked to risk of injury in the child (Matheny & Fisher, 1984).

What the literature on accidents in childhood suggests quite strongly is that various socioenvironmental factors contribute to the occurrence of accidents. Obviously, there will be abused children who come from healthy families, in which the event is random and a one-time or brief occurrence. To the extent that nonfamilial sexual abuse is similar to a "childhood accident," the same is true for this case; research into the social environment of these children is required in order to determine factors in the abuse process.

MULTIGENERATIONAL ISSUES

I would like to briefly review a case that places sexual victimization in a multigenerational context. A history of maternal incest appears to be related to subsequent victimization in a child. It is important to understand how that might develop. This incest can have an impact on the quality of life and psychological functioning of children and adults. In the case that we will review, the mother entered therapy after several losses, in particular, the loss of custody of her daughter to her ex-husband and the death of her mother. Loss is a common developmental trigger which serves to activate memories of abuse (Briere, 1989b; Gelinas, 1983).

Carla had been a patient at a large, group medical practice since she was 4 years old. Her medical record noted every visit she had had and every diagnosis at the time of the visit (Table 6-2). When I first met her, I was struck by the number of medical notations that I perceived to be incest-related. Her victimization by her stepfather began when he returned from World War II and continued for 14 years until she was 18 years old. When she was 4 years old, shortly after the abuse began, she was evaluated for suspected diabetes mellitus. Her presenting complaints were weakness, malaise, and frequent urination, including bed-wetting. The diagnosis was not confirmed. She presented at 5 and 7 years of age with vaginitis and with further bed-wetting at 8 years of

TABLE 6-2
Multigenerational Issues in Sexual Abuse

Mother		Son A		Son B	
Age, yr	Diagnosis	Age, yr	Diagnosis	Age, yr	Diagnosis
4	Suspected diabetes mellitus	3	Traumatic hemorrhage	4	Poison ingestion
5	Vaginitis	3	Puncture wound	6	School readiness
7	Recurrent vaginitis	5	Poison ingestion	9	Sexually transmitted disease
8	Bed-wetting	6	Femur fracture	14	Learning disability
18	Upper respiratory infection	7	Head contusion	15	Chemical dependency hospitalization
18	Glycosuria	8	Electrical burn	16	Chemical dependency hospitalization
19	Depressive reaction	10	Poison ingestion		
20	Psychologic testing	15	Psychiatric hospitalization		
21	Pregnancy	19	Chemical dependency hospitalization		
21	Post-partum depression				
24	Pregnancy				
24	Post-partum depression				
28	Pregnancy				
29	Scalp laceration				
30	Panic attacks				
34	Vaginitis				
35	Vaginitis				
36	Functional bowel disease				
37	Vulvitis				
40	Depressive reaction				
42	Vaginitis				
43	Group therapy				
46	Individual therapy				

age. At 18 years old, she was seen twice, once for an upper respiratory infection and again for possible diabetes. The latter was ruled out.

Her first involvement with mental health professionals came when she was 19 years old, had just gotten married, and was depressed. The depression persisted and she was briefly an inpatient in the hospital psychiatry unit; she had follow-up psychologic testing when she was 20 years old. She had her first child, son A, when she was 21 years old. Two months after the birth, she experienced a post-partum depression of several months' duration. The birth can be thought of as a developmental trigger. When she was 24 years old, she had son B, and this was also followed by five months of depression. At 28 years old, she gave birth to her third child, a girl. Shortly after the delivery, she was beaten by her husband, receiving scalp lacerations. Two years later, she experienced her first panic attack. Two subsequent bouts of vaginitis at 34 and 35 years of age were attributed by her to her husband's flagrant infidelity. She received treatment for a functional bowel disease also related to stress and for vulvitis at 37 years of age. She sought help for depression when 40 years old, and she divorced her husband at 42 years of age after another diagnosis of vaginitis. She began group therapy at 43 years of age, and she began to see me three years later. In retrospect, it becomes easy to identify signs of sexual abuse suggested by research that began to emerge when she was a child (Briere, 1989b). Carla had not discussed her sexual abuse until she began individual therapy.

Medical records for Carla's two sons clearly illustrate potential second-generation sequelae to incest, in the context of an abusive husband-wife relationship, and physical abuse by her husband of son A. When the boy was 3 years old, he had a hemorrhage to the head secondary to trauma inflicted by her ex-husband. He was accident prone and later that year was treated for a puncture wound. Poison ingestion occurred at 5 years of age. At 6 years of age, he was hospitalized for a femur fracture of suspicious origin. He reported falling down the stairs but the mother believed that he may have been thrown. A head contusion at 7 years of age was again secondary to being hit by his father. He needed medical treatment for two more accidents, an electrical burn and poison ingestion, this time in a veiled suicide attempt. Five years later, he was hospitalized in an adolescent unit, and then again at 19 years of age, in an alcoholism treatment program.

The second son had a somewhat different set of difficulties, although he also drank some insecticide at 4 years of age. Quite immature, he returned to the pediatrician at 6 years of age because his mother had concerns about his readiness for school. At 9 years of age, he was sexually abused by an adult neighbor and contracted a venereal disease. He received no treatment but was evaluated for a learning disability at 14 years of age. One year later, he was hospitalized for chemical dependency. He repeated treatment one year later.

Clearly, the long-term incest experience had a cumulative effect over several generations. Family-coping theorists would describe this as a "stressor pileup" (Patterson & McCubbin, 1983). The pileup of unresolved stressors and strains contributes to undesirable characteristics in the family environment. For example, Carla's sexual abuse dictated her choice of a mate. Always sure she never loved her husband, she said she married him because "he asked and I knew I couldn't get anyone better."

The extent to which her sons' subsequent difficulties were related to her abuse was difficult to determine. Borrowing from attachment literature (Bowlby, 1969), we might say that Carla's attachment to her own mother was insecure, leaving her with an internal working model of relationships that did not aid in developing secure and protective attachments to her sons. Her post-partum depressions also left her less available at critical early periods of relationship formation, leaving her children more prone to psychological problems. She admitted that she felt too overwhelmed to protect them or to leave her husband as a way of ending their physical abuse. She had little support from her extended family, whom she attempted to ignore once she left home. This absence of critical social support also kept her trapped.

An examination of these three people side by side illustrates the potential multigenerational ramifications of sexual abuse. You have, as Bowen (1978) wrote, a gradual erosion of individuation and personal autonomy from one generation to the next, leading to the multigenerational transmission of pathology.

Carla had never learned to protect herself, much less her children. When her son was molested at 9 years of age, it made sense to me that she did not seek treatment for him then as she had not sought treatment for her sexual-abuse experience. Her cognitive processes as a victim were probably projected onto her son — e.g., "I did something to cause my own abuse, I probably caused his, or maybe he did something to cause his abuse." These cognitions reflect the beliefs and rules of her family of origin.

TYPOLOGIES OF SEXUALLY ABUSIVE FAMILIES

Heterogeneity does exist in sexually abusive families, and understanding this diversity leads to better treatment. Initial attempts at understanding the diversity in these families were done on an individual, as opposed to a systemic, level. For example, characteristics of the father were emphasized. A classic example is Groth's (1979) bipartite grouping of fixated and regressed offenders. These are thought to characterize all those who commit sexual offenses against children, including incestuous fathers.

The two basic types reflect their primary sexual orientation and level of psychosexual development. The fixated offender has a primary sexual orientation to children. The regressed offender has a primary sexual orientation to age-mates. The offenses of the fixated offender reflect a chronic maladaptive resolution of life issues, whereas the offenses of the regressed offender reflect a maladaptive attempt to cope with specific life stresses. For example, it is this latter group that is thought to be most likely implicated in sexual abuse allegations that arise during divorce action.

MacFarlane et al. (1986) have written an excellent summary of the reasons why sexual abuse may occur during divorce proceedings. Too often, allegations at this time are accompanied by almost immediate disbelief. The reasons for the abuse include the potential of the father for being a regressed sexual offender, whose unmet emotional needs and concurrent reexperience of loss of a love object prime him for abuse, and also predisposing circumstances due to the change in living arrangements (e.g., shared sleeping quarters). It is these occurrences that remind us that sexual abuse is rarely a simply sexual act.

Groth (1982) outlined two prominent patterns of incest-prone families with respect to the role of relationship between husband and wife. These are the passive-dependent type of husband, with demands on the wife to be the competent partner, and the aggressive-dominant pattern, with the wife and family kept financially dependent on the father and socially isolated from extrafamilial relationships. Meiselman's (1978) experience with incestuous fathers led her to emphasize the "endogamic" nature of these men, whose features are predominantly those of Groth's fixated group. This chronically immature sexual orientation reflected either a personality disorder in the father or, less frequently, characterized a father who belonged to a rural or isolated subculture that had an increased tolerance of incest.

Groth's simplistic classification system, which has never been empirically validated, was expanded in a recent study designed to develop a system for the classification of child molesters (Knight, Carter, & Prentky, 1989). Incestuous offenders who had nonincestuous offenses were included in their sample of 177 men. (As an aside, they found the purely incestuous molester to be a rarity, underscoring the high likelihood for the father in the families we see to have a history of nonincestuous child molesting.)

Knight and his research team classified their molesters on two broad dimensions. The first included the independent dimensions of fixation and social competence, yielding four types of molesters—e.g., high fixation/low social competence and low fixation/high social competence. The second dimension pertained to the amount of contact the offender had with children. This led to further groupings including narcissistic, sadistic, and nonsadistic. The extent to which this classification system leads to different treatment outcomes has yet to be determined. It does speak to greater heterogeneity, however, of offenders and of families.

Other evidence for heterogeneity comes from family therapists in this field. Reposa and Zuelzer (1983) described two broad types, based on the families' patterns of separation-connection. One family type is centripetal, which binds children to the home and is characterized by an ingrown, overly close style. The other type, more chaotic and disrupted, is centrifugal, resulting in the premature expelling of children from the home (e.g., adolescent runaways).

Stern and Meyer (1980) suggested three types of interactional patterns of couples that appear to be linked to the occurrence of father-daughter incest: (a) possessive-passive, (b) dependent-domineering, and (c) incestrogenic. The possessive-passive couple is characterized by a patriarchal, dominant husband who controls a passive wife and children. Incest is usually reactive. The dependent-domineering couple pairs a weak husband with a more dominant, independent wife. Often a principal breadwinner, the wife may be unavailable to her children. The final pattern, incestrogenic, pairs two dependent, inadequate people who look to their children to meet their needs. Central to this dynamic is role reversal between mother and daughter.

Larson and Maddock (1986) developed probably the most elegant formulation to date, describing four different family types (Table 6-3). The central defining variable pertains to the "meaning" of the sexual abuse within the family.

For example, the rage-exchange subtype is highly pathologic; the abuse is a function of the pervasive anger in the family; and it is frequently characterized by force. Erotic-exchange families are pervasively sexual and many relationships are sexualized, leading eventually to sexual abuse. Clearly, the affection-exchange type is the most healthy of the four, and it appears to resemble the incestuous families described by McCarthy and Byrne (1988). They describe incest as "mistaken love," and it serves as a stabilizing process in an unstable family. As do Larson and Maddock, McCarthy and Byrne recommend that incest that fits this description be viewed in a less pejorative fashion in order for therapists to be most effective.

TABLE 6-3
Incestuous Family Types

Affection-exchange	Erotic-exchange	Aggression-exchange	Rage-exchange
		Characteristics	
+ Intent	+ Intent	− Intent	− Intent
Object connection	Object connection	No object connection	Object displacement
Nonviolent	Nonviolent	Often violent	Violent; life-threatening
Minimal power motive	Power motive present	Power motive present	Power motive primary
Individual psychopathology not critical	Individual psychopathology not critical	Individual psychopathology probably critical	Individual psychopathology critical
		Treatment Considerations	
Outpatient	Outpatient: group treatment	Outpatient/inpatient groups	Inpatients groups Individual
Involve entire family	Whole family	Whole family	Perhaps some of family
Perhaps stay home	Perhaps stay home	Separation usually very important	Separation critical

Note. Adapted from "Structural and Functional Variables in Incest Family Systems: Implications for Assessment and Treatment" by N. R. Larson and J. W. Maddock, in T. S. Trepper and M. J. Barrett (Eds.), Treating Incest: A Multiple Systems Perspective, 1986, New York: Haworth Press.

This model does hold some appeal, although it has never been empirically or clinically validated on an independent sample. First, it suggests that incestuous families are heterogeneous and treatment efforts need to be tailored differently for an affection-exchange family than for an aggression-exchange family. The variation of individual psychopathology in the parent figures is also borne out by the MMPI literature, which routinely reports normal-limits profiles in both fathers and mothers (Friedrich, 1988b). Affection-exchange families seem to be those families depicted in Giaretto's (1982) treatment program who are screened for appropriateness and who appear to have a motivation to keep all or part of the family intact.

Two of the categories from Larson and Maddock's (1986) model (aggression-exchange and rage-exchange) appear to characterize the families discussed by Anderson and Shafer (1979), who describe incestuous families as similar to individuals with character disorders. They believe effective intervention requires authoritative control and careful coordination among all professionals serving the family. The subset of families they describe appears to be only slightly more treatable than David Jones' (1987) subset of families that he labeled as "untreatable." The model in Table 6-3 has room for the appropriately pessimistic view that therapists may have about a significant percentage of the families that enter the treatment system.

A potential pitfall for the clinician, after reviewing this model and realizing that it is derived from the meaning the family attributes to the abuse, is that it may lead one to believe that for the affection-exchange families, or those least disturbed, the therapy task is straightforward and family therapy is either the exclusive treatment or is at least primary.

I would like to underscore the need not to give in to these families' intense needs to be reunited without also making sure that individual therapy for the child has occurred, the child's safety has been clearly established, and each parent has had a solid therapy experience over and above the family therapy. By comparison to many of the other families I see, when I meet a family that more closely fits the affection-exchange type, they seem healthier and I find myself sometimes not attending to the individual needs of the family members as closely as I do with members of other family types. Thus, I can get lulled into complacency when it is not appropriate.

A final typology to be considered comes from Faller (1988). She created a decision-making matrix to guide treatment decisions based on maternal and paternal factors. Two groupings of mothers — (a) independent and protective of victim and (b) dependent, unprotective, and poor relationship with victim — are crossed with two groupings of fathers — (a) well functioning in many areas, guilt about abuse, and nonextensive abuse, and (b) poorly functioning, no guilt, and more extensive abuse.

This creates four case types. Type I families have the best prognosis, combining a generally well-functioning mother and father. Type IV families have the worst prognosis, combining poorly functioning parents and extensive abuse. Faller stated, "When both parents are this seriously impaired. . . . Children should be removed from the home. . . . Parental rights should almost always be terminated."

Obviously, some families do not fit these neat categories because parental functioning represents a continuum. A common dilemma is a well-functioning father who has been very abusive. His extensive guilt and abuse may be a function of his obsessive-compulsive style, and altering his behavior could be difficult. Other dilemmas emerge for mothers who appear to function relatively well but are cool toward their children and not protective. Each of these cases must be carefully examined, and it may be that prognosis can be best determined by a course of individual therapy for the different family members after the safety of the child has been established.

In summary, this review of incestuous family characteristics and the literature on family typologies can only be interpreted to mean that sexually abusive families are relatively variable. A wide variety of intervention options is appropriate for families and their members. As a clinician, you must appreciate this variability and make decisions driven by careful assessment of the appropriate factors. It may require that you adopt a broader perspective of the families you treat.

An additional observation from the literature is that many of the variables identified are relevant to a large number of disturbed families. Although the sexual aspects of the abuse cannot be ignored, intervention on the other family issues can profit from the extensive literature on family treatment for various problem areas.

TREATMENT PROCESS

Development of a more integrated model of family treatment that combines both interest in the victim and interest in supporting the family is essential. Mrazek (1981) stated that therapists working in this area must achieve a balance of compassion and control. It is important to appreciate the relative intractability of many families and also to realize that an equally large number of families are motivated or can be directed to change. An overly punitive posture will work only with some families. We need to examine our own attitudes about the families we see. Are we generally controlling? Or at the other extreme, do we rarely have the capacity to be critical and directive when needed? Therapists at either extreme do not know how to balance compassion with control.

Solin (1986) described a phenomenon that has become more common.

The incestuously abused child is now perceived as a helpless victim . . . relieved of the onus of complicity and is extended concern, compassion, and unprecedented understanding . . . the offending father is increasingly held unequivocably accountable . . . culpable of an egregious act that is morally and legally beyond the pale.

This has resulted in a situation in which incest disclosure "catapults the family into crisis and shock." Solin reported that in the face of this overwhelming response by social service agencies, incestuous families respond defensively by displacing anger onto the therapist or social service agencies, or both.

This response pattern is particularly true for intact families. In a manner similar to the incest victim displacing anger at the father onto the mother for not protecting her, the entire family system now displaces anger onto the social worker and the therapist. This triangulation derails the treatment and thwarts the recuperative process. If the therapist is blaming the father, the family responds in a reflexive manner by supporting the father and blaming the therapist. The victim does not get a chance to "divest herself of imagined complicity."

Solin (1986) suggested that this displaced anger and resentment will subside if the therapist can understand the family loyalty to the father, endorse those feelings, and offer sincere empathy and concern to all family members. Those who have been highly critical of the offender, either to his face or to the family, may have lost all capabilities to be of therapeutic aid to the family. This finding by Solin suggests the need to have a more integrated model with which to approach families.

Gelinas (1988) described the therapy technique of multilaterality, a process in which the therapist takes into account every family member's needs and interests. It is important that the therapist not be an agent of one person exclusively, although it may be quite easy to do so with the victim. She stated that because of the family members' loyalty to each other, the therapist who does not deal fairly with everyone risks inciting their protectiveness of each other. The family could then exclude the therapist.

This assertion by Gelinas may be quite surprising to therapists who may believe that advocating on the victim's behalf sends a powerful, corrective message to the family. This rarely happens, at least not initially, because regardless of the level of pathology, family loyalty issues are paramount, and the therapist rapidly becomes the outsider if he or she fails to realize the complexities of family relationships. An outcome of this misguided advocacy can be that the ambivalent mother sides more fiercely with her husband and rejects the daughter, who is left with a caseworker whom she may blame for the loss of her family. The therapy is over before it starts. Interminable foster care is hardly the outcome of choice.

A more balanced approach, like that suggested by Gelinas (1988) and by Mrazek (1981), does not skirt issues of blame and responsibility for the incest. It is simply much more conducive to the development of the therapeutic relationship. In addition, other therapists in the picture (e.g., individual therapist for father, group therapist for child) can take a less-balanced approach than the family therapist.

Working Assumptions

Several assumptions underlie the various interventions and examples to be provided to incestuous families; some of these also apply to nonincestuous families.

1. The therapist must be active and willing to direct the therapy from the beginning.
2. The welfare and safety of victim and siblings are paramount.
3. Believe the victim and do not engage the offender in his denials.
4. Preferably, remove the offender, not the victim, from the home.
5. The appropriate authorities have been notified.
6. A therapist has assumed therapy case-management responsibilities and is coordinating treatment responses with social services.
7. Information can be exchanged with social services and the legal system.
8. It may be that reunification is not possible and that decision must be an option.
9. Within the above parameters, the therapist is willing to work with all persons involved.

If you fail to be active, set up appointments early, decide who will be seen and by whom, begin the coordination process, and track down the referral route so you know who else has dealt with this family and how, it is difficult to be successful. Again this activity is directive and conveys a willingness to be authoritative, yet it also communicates a willingness to be involved with the family as it begins to struggle with what is often the start of a major crisis. Some families are more jaded and have been either more resistant to treatment or treated inappropriately, and your activity is needed to help them refocus on the therapy process.

By making the children's welfare the paramount issue, you escape being typecast as a bad person, and you can cast yourself as sharing an interest in the children's welfare. Almost always, this requires that some members are removed from the home; it is hoped that the offender is the one removed. Again, if the offender can be removed, even in those cases that have a better prognosis, the family's structure begins to be altered in a manner that allows for greater individual autonomy in the family members. In addition, responsibility is clearly assigned to the father, and with the father out of the home, there is greater motivation for treatment. With the daughter out of the home, the same family could be relatively unmotivated.

The victim should be seen early and the proper authorities notified, if this has not been done. Use of the court to facilitate compliance can be quite helpful with many families. The father's protests and denials can be listened to briefly, but then they can be consistently blocked in a firm, clear manner that implies you will listen to him about other issues but not to his protests. If he is allowed to elaborate these denials over time and they are not blocked, his position becomes too entrenched to change later.

It is also critical that you are in a joint case-manager role with the social services caseworker. Herman (1983) stated, "No therapist can treat incest alone." We need the support of agencies, legal systems, and other treatment professionals. They may be inept, overworked, and all too eager to abdicate responsibility. That should not be allowed, and sometimes your level of commitment and professionalism are enough for them to take a greater interest and feel some hope for change. Your duties are to determine whether the father has been assessed adequately, who needs to be seen and by whom, to establish contacts with the other treating professionals, and, with many families, to do the vast majority of the therapy (e.g., individual, marital, and family). You are also then in a much better position to know whether or not progress is being made. As Gelinas (1988) stated, "There is no neutral gear in family therapy," and as primary therapist, you are in the best position to determine the source of stuckness.

Rather than wasting valuable time on untreatable families or on families that do not allow you to dictate treatment parameters, it is better to be clear about which families can and cannot be helped and to communicate that to the appropriate agencies. The county or state's attorneys who handled these cases should also hear your beliefs because they do not move to trial unless they hear convincingly that a case has a good chance of winning.

Issues

Rather than attempt to describe a relatively unitary approach to family treatment, this section will discuss nine processes/therapeutic issues that emerge across different family types and at different times. Some of the options suggested will, of necessity, be more applicable to some families than others. Family therapy is a framework through which to view the family and the areas of change that are needed, and it is also a therapeutic approach. Sometimes family therapy is done with individuals, combinations of family members, or the entire family. The interpersonal perspective is what guides the therapy with different family units.

The approaches that are used are derived from structural family therapy (Minuchin, 1974), strategic family therapy (Andolfi, Angelo, Menghi, & Nicolò-Corigliano, 1983), and functional family therapy (Alexander & Parsons, 1982). The structural approach is useful because of its emphasis on boundaries and the parental hierarchy, two areas that are skewed in these families. The strategic approach was developed with an appreciation of resistance and also of the importance of family members' perceptions of each other. It offers numerous avenues toward helping family members begin to see each other more positively, and it is particularly helpful in resolving estrangement between parents and children. A behavioral family approach, as described in the functional family therapy model, assists family members in learning how to communicate clearly, negotiate effectively, and set clear rules that specify the privileges and responsibilities of each family member. The therapist relies on modeling, prompting, and reinforcement to help the family achieve these ends.

Establishing a Therapeutic Relationship

The longer I work with intrafamilial and extrafamilial sexual-abuse families, the more I realize that despite the child's need and the power of the court, my presence is rarely desired. Therapy is not viewed as an opportunity for the family to have a positive growth experience. They do not come to my office eagerly. Rather, I have to anticipate that I will be allowed to have a therapeutic function only after some time has passed. Being controlling rarely helps me. Maybe it helps other therapists who come by that style more naturally. Rather, I try to join the part of the family I am seeing by openly discussing the various reasons why they would rather not be there with me.

For example, now that they are in my office, we have the option of spending our time productively or talking about why they do not belong there. I usually tell them that healthy families can admit problems, and if they want to show me they are healthy and not in need of therapy, then we need to choose some areas to focus on. I also repeatedly explain and clarify my role to them, and I let them know that I cannot expect them to like me on any level. None of the families I have seen over the past years have ever been involved in counseling before, despite persisting problems in one area or another. This speaks to their degree of isolation. Thus, I have to educate them about the therapy process and gradually work to develop a relationship. Some of my more needy families are actually harder to work with than those that are initially resistant.

Always be prepared for the fact that even when you can tell that the family is working, your relationship is not necessarily secure. Rather, expect their ambivalent relational style to occur several times. For example, Ben had been molested by his uncle, and Ben and both parents were seen early on. He seemed to be doing significantly better after two months and I felt good about my relationship with all the family members. Then, at the beginning of a session, the mother stated, "We've been coming here and working hard and you haven't given us anything in return. We still don't know his diagnosis. We're wondering whether we shouldn't just quit." After I internally processed my initial reactions of hurt, anger, and defensiveness, I replied that she was right, provided a diagnosis, and then helped them set several additional goals. At the end of that session she informed me that I had "earned my keep" that week, and they continued to see me for another several months, much of the time as a couple.

With some families I need to be more controlling and I let them know I will be; I try to use their language, even if it might seem offensive (e.g., "kick a little ass" was a mother's phrase for getting strict), and positively connote their resistant behavior (e.g., "You make me work hard," "You're keeping me on my toes").

None of these solutions are magical; the key rests in your appreciation of the need to join in many different ways and to develop some way to appreciate the various family members. For example, hostile, rejecting mothers are difficult for me to "appreciate," but I try to remind myself of their own abuse, praise their honesty, realize the dilemma we put mothers in, and be clear about my goals with them (e.g., "I won't beat around the bush like some counselors might. I will try every session to find that part of you that loves your daughter and recognizes her hurt. Because you and I both know it's in there").

The following is an excerpt from a session with a young mother, Maureen, whose elementary school-age daughter, Shannon, her only child, had been molested by the mother's boyfriend. Because Maureen was often openly critical of Shannon, this session, our fourth, was with Maureen and myself. Family therapy does not simply mean the number of people present in the session. Prior to this segment, I had encouraged Maureen to talk about her continuing affection for Ryan, her boyfriend.

Therapist: So, you're telling me Ryan is no longer in your life. You're upset, you're pissed off. Finding a man is hard enough with a kid. This sounds like a big sacrifice on your part. Something a mother would do.

Maureen: Mary (the caseworker) would never say that. God, I hate that woman. She said I had to get him out of the house or she'd have to place Shannon in foster care.

Therapist: And you did that.

Maureen: Yeah. I'm not happy about it.

Therapist: I seem to remember you were in foster care. A few times.

Maureen: Yeah.

Therapist: And you didn't want Shannon to have to go through that too.

Maureen: I did it because of what Mary said.

Therapist: We do things for lots of reasons. One reason is Mary. Another reason is you're a mom. Shannon's mom.

Maureen: I know that! What's that got to do with it?

Therapist: Moms try to think of what their kid needs.

Maureen: Tell that to Mary.

Therapist: I'm trying to convince you first. That's what we're doing here. I'm helping you figure out how you can show people you're really Shannon's mom.

Maureen: Yeah, sure.

Therapist: Right. It's hard to believe. Now we have two things to convince you of. The first is that I can help you. The second is you're Shannon's mom.

Maureen: You've said that enough times.

Therapist: I can be a stuck record about it.

If you routinely find yourself able to relate to only one or two members in the families you see, then reexamine your views and attitudes carefully, with a supervisor, to help you adopt a more multilateral approach. Try to attend to which type of family member you are most likely to establish a relationship with, e.g., child victim or depressed mother. This can help you to get a handle on your own issues.

Involvement of Various Family Members

It is usually strongly contraindicated to see the family members as a group at the beginning of the treatment process. Rather, in a more typical case, individual sessions are held with the victim, mother, each sibling, and the father. These are scheduled as soon in the therapy process as possible and the emphasis is on the assessment of the individual family members, the degree to which the sexual abuse has organized the family, and the meaning the family makes of the sexual abuse.

It is important also to facilitate early conjoint meetings with the mother and the victim, particularly in those cases in which the mother is at least neutral in her attitude toward the child. It is also in these early conjoint sessions that you can determine the degree of conflict and role reversal that is present.

Expanding the focus to include the mother and remaining children is a logical next step. It allows you to see her capabilities as a parent more clearly. You can determine at this time the degree to which she is effective, the presence of other behavioral problems that may also need treatment, and if her attitude toward the victim is significantly different from the attitude she has toward the other children.

During this time, individual sessions with the victim continue and individual or group sessions for the mother are also initiated. Therapy for the father must also be ongoing and coordinated if offered by a different therapist or agency.

Seeing both spouses together is a matter of judgment, again depending on the relative health of each member. If you have been able to have the father removed from the home, and the mother has not yet been able to see herself as separate from her husband, the conjoint marital sessions may need to be limited. However, it is also important to make a determination of the viability of the marriage; a significant percentage of the families I see end in divorce even though their initial intent was to remain intact. The ability of the non-offending spouse to consider the option of divorce may exist only when she has reached a level of individuation within the spousal subsystem that she had never previously attained. As the individual members appear to be increasingly committed to the therapy and reunification process, marital sessions are held regularly.

When family therapy sessions begin varies from family to family. Larson and Maddock (1986) wrote that for a small subset of affection-exchange families, family therapy can begin early. I have not been convinced clinically that that is wise. More cautious therapists, including myself, prefer that the family sessions not begin until the offending parent has assumed complete responsibility for his actions, has been carefully assessed psychologically, and is involved in individual or group therapy. The mother and children need to be clear about their goals, the mother needs to be able to demonstrate appropriate parental authority, and some therapy movement needs to be occurring before the father is reintroduced to the whole family.

Individual and joint family goals need to be clearly articulated, using the goal-setting techniques discussed in Chapter 4. The model described by Barrett, Sykes, and Byrnes (1986) uses an apology session as a potential vehicle to bring the father into the family sessions on a more regular basis. However, they caution that this session must not occur until the therapist is confident that this intervention will not have a detrimental impact on the child. This usually requires some amount of progress.

Empowering the Mother

In many sexually abusive families, the mother is relegated to a significantly lower position in the parental power hierarchy. There are some mothers who function in a more autonomous manner, but in these families there often is a recent stressor, a period of estrangement between the parents, or parent-child estrangement that has contributed to the emergence of the sexual abuse. Thus, she may appear to be somewhat more autonomous, but in her functioning with her children she may be quite conflicted.

My efforts at empowering the mother occur within the context of individual and group therapy and also in the family sessions that include her with her children. Enhancing her parenting competence is a critical step toward more normal family functioning. It is here that I target symptoms in the children that lend themselves to a behavioral-management approach, and I provide ample support to enhance the likelihood that she will be increasingly successful. Within the family sessions, too, I frequently find that one of the victims is more competent parentally, and we formally negotiate how to elevate the mother in the parental hierarchy.

A family consisting of Twyla, 33, Tina, 11, and Trey, 6, is useful to consider here. Tina had been molested by an adult male in their apartment complex. All three were present at this session, which was focused on Tina's behavioral problems. Initially, we were discussing Tina staying out too late.

Tina: I don't have to listen to you. I can come home when I want.

Twyla: See Doctor? I try and try, but she just doesn't listen to me. She never has and she never will.

Therapist: Well, you wouldn't be here if you were giving up. Let's see. Now, Tina, your mom and I are going to put our heads together so we can come up with some ideas to let her be mom and you be Tina. And you be Trey.

Twyla: He doesn't bother me none.

Tina: I don't want to come home after school right away.

Therapist: What would your mom have to do to get you to come home?

Tina: She couldn't.

Therapist: Mrs. Brown, we'll win on this one yet. But maybe we have to start smaller. Like something you want Tina to do at home. Something you can win at. What's a problem that happens in the home?

Twyla: She picks on Trey. She doesn't do her homework. She only wants to watch her shows on TV.

Therapist: What about homework? You say she doesn't get that done?

Tina: I do too.

Twyla: Well, at the last minute. You're always watching TV.

Therapist: You've probably wanted to keep the TV off until she's done with homework.

Twyla: Yeah. But she'd turn it back on.

Therapist: Not if you really meant it. And not if you got through to her that you like her. You know. Like she minds you and you do something nice in return.

Twyla: I don't have any money if that's what you mean.

Therapist: No, you have lots of things an 11-year-old would want. I mean, what if you say, "No TV until homework is done. Then we play a game together."

Twyla: But Trey needs some time too. She'd want to play cribbage and he can't play.

Tina: He always gets the attention.

Therapist: I think, I think she's saying she needs you, Twyla. I know moms get dragged in a hundred directions, but what could you do with Tina?

Tina: Make popcorn.

Therapist: See, an idea. I think Tina wants you to succeed at getting her to do her homework.

For several sessions after this one, our focus was on expanding Twyla's positive and parental interactions with her children, particularly Tina. As mentioned before, the success of behavioral programs rests on the quality of the parent-child relationship.

A previous history of sexual abuse must be addressed also, and this can actually precipitate further underfunctioning in the mother. At those times, psychiatric intervention with antidepressant or antianxiety medication might be necessary, and because the mother can be stabilized rapidly, this return to more adequate functioning is empowering to her as well.

Routinely, the mother's social network is sparse, and she may be estranged from family members as well. For example, in Chapter 4 we described the family consisting of Claire and Tara. With Claire, the mother, we specifically established goals and contracted with her for making changes that would increase her contact with other people, including her AA sponsor, attending AA meetings, and socializing more with co-workers. It is here that support groups can be invaluable, and previously isolated mothers can be literally turned on to the greater possibility of social relationships.

The use of positive connotation and reframing, two techniques derived from strategic therapy, are useful here as well. The mother has heard many times that she is weak and inadequate, and she has rarely received praise for any of her efforts. For example, when Claire originally refused to socialize more, I did not become more controlling — at least not immediately. Rather, my tack was to praise her for her honesty with me and tell her that other mothers I saw would promise while knowing full well that they would not comply.

Because Claire had been a schoolteacher and Tara needed assistance with her reading, I countered her protests that she could not "do anything right with her" by contracting with both Tara and Claire to allow Claire to listen to reading and check homework, and I described Claire as fulfilling the "part of being a mother that is teaching." She routinely described herself as a failure as a parent, and I worked to counter this negative self-perception by stating that parenting involved numerous tasks, including teaching. Because she had been a teacher before, it was my assumption that she could also be a successful teaching parent.

None of the empowering can be done in a coercive manner. Here is clearly a situation in which a blend of compassion and pushiness is needed. However, without correcting the long-standing isolation and returning the maternal role to normal, the family will simply continue to exist as previously.

The typical pattern with families in which there are multiple generations of maltreatment and insensitivity to children's needs is to make
some corrections in their functioning with the help of therapy, but to
fail to realize that they need equal amounts of help at other transition
points in the family life cycle. For example, at a recent conference I
attended, a case was presented in which parent training, over a several-
month period, was able to correct a mother-infant relationship marked
by failure to thrive. Yet at 6 years of age, the child returned, prior to
foster placement, because of neglect and physical and sexual abuse
(Wolfe, 1989). The correction in the relationship when the child was
several months old did not persist. One shot, brief interventions rarely
do. Episodes of sustained intervention are needed. Behavioral programs
may bring quick initial results, but unless the ambivalent parent-child
attachment is also altered, we have simply taught parents a few more
coercive techniques.

Conflicted Parent-Child Relationships

This is an extremely common family issue. When present, evidence
for impaired parent-child relationships usually involves several children.
The male children may be idealized inappropriately and consequently
undercontrolled, and female children may be devalued and overly
punished. There are numerous combinations of various maltreatments
that are possible. From the beginning, the therapist needs to return this
situation to normal by stating that it is expected that mother-daughter
relationships will be impaired and then help the parties articulate the
specific issues that are operative.

It is also useful here to create the expectation in the mother that her
goal has always been to be a more effective parent than her own mother.
Now that she has the opportunity, she can actually achieve this goal. I
also help her at this time to identify the ways in which she has been
different from her parents. These differences may be subtle, but they
need to be connoted in a positive manner.

Some case material is again useful here. Let's return to Tara and
Claire, described earlier. Claire was an avid reader of stories of horror
and of the occult. Both Claire and Tara were present in this session,
which was the sixth one we had.

Therapist: You know, Claire, you've said some things about how you
and your mom never got along, that she never was very supportive
of you.

Claire: I could tell you stories that would make a Steven King novel seem tame.

Therapist: Terror, huh?

Claire: Pure, unadulterated terror.

Therapist: Sort of a reign of terror.

Claire: Let's just say it was *The Shining*, *Christine*, and *The Pet Semetery* all playing simultaneously.

Therapist: And in 3-D. So you grew up during the reign of the queen of terror. What was her name again?

Claire: Susan.

Therapist: Queen Susan. Somehow it doesn't sound sinister enough. Not an evil enough name.

Claire: Yeah. I could think of a few.

Therapist: I'm sure you could. (Turning to Tara.) Did you know about this? Your grandmother Susan and all the things she did to your mom?

Tara: I don't know, do I? (To Claire.)

Claire: You don't need to know all those things. Besides . . .

Therapist: You're still pretty loyal to her. Not gossiping about her to Tara. That's a nice feature about you. Loyalty, I mean.

Claire: What's so hot about that? She doesn't give a shit.

Therapist: You're right. But you know, you are trying not to be a terrorist to Tara. You're practicing antiterrorism.

Claire: I wish she'd act like she appreciated it sometimes.

Therapist: Well, if she did, the world would be fair and you'd never have lived with the Queen of Terror.

Claire: Yeah.

Therapist: The world isn't fair. But by hanging in here with Tara, by showing her yourself, by not being a terrorist to her, you're trying to make it fair.

Claire: Well, I do try. It's hard.

Therapist: That's my point. You are trying to make it a better, fairer world for your daughter. And you have every excuse in the world not to. But you are.

Claire: I lost you on that one.

Therapist: Well, it was a compliment. And sometimes when people don't get many, it's hard for them to hear it. To soak it in. Let me say it again.

Claire: No, I think I got it.

Therapist: Well, just in case, you're doing a better job with your daughter than your mother did with you. Did you hear that?

Claire: I guess.

Therapist: (To Tara.) Do you think she did?
Tara: I guess.

Frequently, the difficulty is the fact that the mother's own relationship with her mother is impaired, and her relationships with most females are difficult. The victimized child represents failure to her and
reactivates her own physical-abuse or sexual-abuse memories. The
mother's perception of having to attend therapy may be that it is tragic.
Rather than allowing this perception to persist, I help the mother come
to the realization that (a) her mother had never done that for her, (b)
her daughter has now provided her an opportunity to work on her own
sexual-abuse issues, and (c) I repeatedly point out the similarities between the two and help them see those in a positive manner.

In the case of Claire and Tara, Claire's world view was that all people
needed to learn how to be tough and aggressive. What I did as a therapist, to counter Claire's neglect of Tara, was to repeatedly point out that
she and Tara shared a similar history of disappointments and that it was
important that she be there as a tough parent for Tara so that Tara could
bounce against her strength and be toughened herself. After Claire's
first successful attempt at setting clear and nonpunitive limits with
Tara, we discussed that incident in terms of Tara learning that rules
were rules and that tough people had to face the consequences. Tara and
Claire's relationship never became a model of nurturing, but it did
become far more positive and significantly less conflictual.

Finally, the parental estrangement with the child may begin to be
corrected if you can help the parent realize that the child's behavior
reflects the child's need for the parent. This is sometimes useful with
male victims. The mother of an acting-out, 7-year-old boy who was
overwhelming to his detached mother began to be more involved with
her son in a positive way after hearing repeatedly from me that "he is
going to continue to get more and more extreme in his behavior until he
finds where you have your limits. We need to help him learn that you
can show him some appropriate limits, because being so out of control is
actually very scary for him."

For example, we had dozens of interchanges very similar to the following, sometimes twice in the same session. The goal was simply to
alter how the mother saw her son.

Therapist: So it looks like you needed to put him in time-out several
        times each day this past week (looking at a daily behavior log the
        mother brought in). Is it getting easier? Tim, are you, is your mom
        getting better at this?

Tim: Maybe.

Mother: How much longer will this take? I think it was worse this week.

Therapist: So what do you think made him so scared this week? So scared he had to show you by being out of control.

Mother: I don't know what you mean. Every time he does something bad, you tell me he's scared. I don't think he's scared. He does it to piss me off.

Therapist: Well, there may be something in that. But what might have made him scared? Let's just stick to the scared thing for now.

Mom: Well, he saw his dad on Thursday.

Therapist: There. You said it. You put your finger on it. You know exactly what I'm talking about. Being scared when he sees his dad. Flying out of control. Needing you to put him back in control. You see that, don't you?

Mom: Yeah.

She began to alter her original view of her son as unmanageable to that of a child who was in need of her protective attention.

This segment from a therapy session underscores a point made earlier in the book, that sexual abuse leads to a disorder in the child's ability to regulate affect or emotion. A child learns how to modulate activity level and emotional level in a healthy way, via dyadic interactions with a parent who is neither overly intrusive nor overly excitatory. Tim's father was both, to an extreme. No wonder Tim had a difficult time being "in control" after seeing his dad, no wonder he was thought to have an atypical attention deficit disorder, and no wonder his friends all thought he was "too pushy."

Assumption of Responsibility

The assumption of responsibility must always be a precondition for family reunification and continued family therapy sessions. Whether this is done in the formal apology session described clearly by Trepper (1986) or is something that evolves over the course of several sessions, it is essential that the offending parent assume responsibility for his actions and the consequences of them and contract explicitly that this will not happen again.

The sincerity of the father's apology will frequently be tested, for a number of reasons. As the individual members of the family gain greater personal autonomy, various feelings that the victim has toward her father and mother may emerge over time. These will include anger, and it is important that these feelings be allowed full expression rather than be squashed simply because "he has already said he was sorry." In fact, it is this capacity by the various children to be more autonomous than previously that helps to create a different family structure and decrease the likelihood of further victimization.

The words of the apology session(s) are rarely the most important aspect. Actions, repeated many times, are critical. Sometimes we, as therapists, want closure on these tough cases, are too willing to settle for anything that seems apologetic, and therefore often introduce it too early in the therapy process, effectively stopping the momentum for continued change and work.

Creating Personal Safety

A focus in therapy that must begin early on is the creation of personal safety. Gelinas (1988) indicated how having family members describe a typical day and draw a map of the house can reveal things that are pertinent to the issue of safety. For example, in a drawing of a house, she became aware that a long-term incest victim had to pass through the parental bedroom to get from her bedroom to the nearest hallway. Clearly, the father had significant control and was successful at gaining it with the family. In order to negate further victimization, this type of living arrangement needed to be corrected.

A marker that indicates a more successful resolution of safety issues is in those families in which the victim can express anger at the non-offending parent for lack of protection. Here is an example where multi-laterality is important. One of your therapeutic tasks is to support the developing competence of the mother, and this can be done by allowing the victim to ventilate appropriate anger. The mother's ability to hear the anger can be framed as "You are now giving your daughter a clear message that you are strong enough to hear what she has to say, and letting her know that she no longer has to worry about protecting your feelings."

Marital Therapy

An essential goal of family therapy with incestuous families is the establishment of a strong adult coalition (Reposa & Zuelzer, 1983). In those families in which the adult relationship is viable and the adults choose to continue it, marital therapy is a necessary component of treatment. Long-standing patterns of relating need to be corrected and the power imbalance between the parents needs to be altered. These patterns are not changed simply by discussion in therapy. Extra-therapy activities, contracted by the couple, that include each member altering roles and behaviors, are critical.

The mother must operate from a far more egalitarian posture than ever before, and the father's control in the relationship must be curtailed. Their sexual relationship is also distorted and usually not satisfying. This is clearly an area in which the changes made by the mother can be seen. Her developing autonomy must be demonstrated in a clearer manner of getting her needs met in the relationship. The issue of separation and divorce may emerge, sometimes for the first time ever. The father may have the greatest difficulty in accepting these changes.

Some therapists recommend severely curtailing the father's range of responsibilities and duties within the family, thus creating a marital-parental relationship that is also quite unbalanced. With some couples, this is probably all that can be attained, given their personal limitations. However, this frequently sets up an equally untenable relationship that continues the father in a role of less mature person, and in some cases this appears to invite further victimization. In fact, the several couples that I have seen who fit relatively easily into the pattern of dominant wife and submissive husband had behaved in that manner prior to the abuse, and to continue in the same format was to maintain an inappropriate status quo.

A reading of Bograd (1986) would be very helpful here. She described the loss of objectivity the therapist risks in working with severely dysfunctional spousal systems. What do you do when a contract for no violence, for example, is violated? Our need to feel successful, our need to be empathic to these issues, and the push from internal and external sources for a resolution, whether premature or not, can get in the way of good therapy.

Determining Successful Outcome

Gelinas (1988) suggested four criteria that can be used to measure successful treatment outcome:

1. the definite termination of incestuous abuse
2. a healthier family structure, with greater individual autonomy in all members

3. enhanced communication
4. improved conflict-resolution skills.

Additional suggested criteria are:

1. significant improvement in the marital relationship with all
   parties acting more adequately
2. a decrease in the daughter's level of parentification and an increase in her self-esteem and assertiveness.

These criteria, with few exceptions, are applicable to intra- and extrafamilial abuse.

Herman (1983) suggested slightly different criteria, stating that safety for the child victim is not established simply by improving the sexual
or marital relationship of the parents. Her criteria involve a correction
of the mother-daughter relationship to include the mother feeling able
to protect herself and her children, and the daughter believing that she
can use her mother for protection. She stated, "Probably the best gauge
of successful treatment is the child victim's subjective feeling of safety
and well-being, the disappearance of her distress symptoms, and the
resumption of her interrupted normal development."

Increasingly, my belief is that these families often leave treatment too
early. We are tired of them and they are tired of us. Additionally, goals
were never clearly articulated at the beginning of therapy and a true
measure of success is not available. For example, in the marital realm, if
a legitimate goal was for the wife to have equal say in the family
finances, this could then be ascertained as termination was approaching. The family would also have a much clearer idea about what needed
to be accomplished prior to the end of therapy, and they would not be so
prone to view the therapist as the person who is keeping them in therapy, rather than assuming responsibility for their own progress.

Because I routinely obtain objective personality assessment of parents
as they enter therapy, a repeat administration of the MMPI is also
helpful to me in making a determination about the increased resilience
and decreased depression in the mother, the reduced defensiveness and
enhanced self-control in the father, and a decrease in overall distress in
the adolescent victim or indicators of appropriate school performance
and peer relationships from the victim's teacher.

It is important that we have objective criteria to determine treatment
outcome because of the high level of intensity and the long time that we
have spent with these families, and because our subjectivity is too great.

We all hope for therapeutic success and are frequently much more will-ing to give the family the benefit of the doubt than is appropriate.

For example, in one family, the 16-year-old girl was a classic brittle-overcontroller (Earls et al., 1987). Her MMPI at intake revealed an enormous level of personal alienation and depression, but soon into therapy she and her mother appeared to become healthy. I was more naive at the time and was pleased with their progress; reunification became our focus in therapy and the father was included in the sessions. As the family began to clamor for termination, the daughter became more overtly distressed, and the MMPI showed greater distress at that time than at the beginning of therapy. It was at that point, after 11 months of therapy, that she haltingly stated that, although the overt incest had ceased, she continued to be bothered by her father's use of pornographic materials in the home and was fearful for her younger sister's safety.

Needless to say, this necessitated a reassessment of our therapy goals, and I encountered marked resistance from the father as I negotiated with the court to force him to return to individual therapy sessions and deal with his personal issues. Needless to say, everyone in the family was extremely upset. It is these types of experiences that make a therapist much more cautious about reunification and much more thorough in the evaluation of the family and its individual members.

Regarding sibling incest, the criteria for returning the offending ado-lescent sibling to the home are several, and the family needs to hear them early on in the therapy. After the sibling is working in his own therapy and is now ready to join family sessions, the family's move toward their goals can be assessed more accurately. For example, a depressed 12-year-old victim became animated and talkative when her 16-year-old brother was in the sessions. This concerned me because at no time had I seen a real change in her relationship with her adoptive mother, who was actually her aunt, although the girl exhibited few overt behavioral problems.

Briefly, suggested goals prior to returning home are:

1. an admission of guilt by the offender
2. appropriate parental authority
3. improved behavior in the victim and in her relationship with the protective parent
4. completion of individual/group therapy for the adolescent per-petrator
5. an expanded social network for the victim.

Monitoring

Because of the long-term pattern of behavior that is frequently present in these families, the end of regularly scheduled therapy does not coincide with the end of all therapy contacts. Rather, the family needs to be moved to a less frequent therapy schedule with regular follow-up sessions over the next several years. Gelinas (1988) recommended that the family come in every three months for the next one or two years, and then every six months, until either all the children are grown or the therapeutic changes are well ingrained. These guidelines are not unreasonable given the intractability of some of the offenders.

Even for those better-functioning families, the follow-up sessions are useful because these families are more than likely to have other problems emerge as the families continue to develop. The rigidity present in the untreated family may soften significantly, but that does not rule out the likelihood that, as children grow and mature, problems with discipline and parent-child estrangement reemerge.

I hope it is clear that family therapy allows an appropriate arena for confronting sexual abuse and an arena for positive change in family functioning, leading to a better long-term prognosis for the victims. In extrafamilial sexual abuse, the family issues that are operative are often quite similar, including mother-child estrangement, role reversal in the victim, and the persistent lack of safety for the child. In fact, there are incestuous families about which I feel greater optimism for future success than some extrafamilial abuse families that I have seen, in which the mother continues to keep potentially unsafe men in her life. These individuals are never involved in the therapy, because of their transient nature, and thus the safety issue is much more difficult to confront. Given that the family context of the child is central for appropriate personal development, altering that context so that it is more facilitative of autonomy and safety is essential to therapeutic success.

7

Group Therapy With Child and Adolescent Victims

> Intimacy is that type of situation involving two people
> which permits validation of all components of personal
> worth.
>
> *H.S. Sullivan*

Probably because he was isolated as a child, Sullivan had particular sensitivity to the importance of close peer relationships. He contended that beginning sometime between the ages of 8½ and 10 years, the child finds a same age peer. This relationship is the arena where the child "begins to develop a real sensitivity to what matters to another person" (Sullivan, 1953).

Given that peer relationships are frequently impaired in sexually abused children and social support is essential to coping with stressful events, group therapy approaches can be quite useful in the overall treatment plan. In fact, the group therapy experience can provide opportunities for therapeutic movement not available within the context of either individual or family therapy (Hazzard, King, & Webb, 1986):

1. The intense isolation and sense of deviancy can be diminished in the victim.
2. Social skills can be enhanced.
3. The intensity of individual therapy can be avoided.
4. The ability to talk about another person's problem rather than one's own problem avoids the threat of immediate self-disclosure.
5. Dependency on peers may actually be more reliable than depending on the adults in the child's or adolescent's life.

The disclosure of a powerful and nagging secret in an empathic setting can provide enormous relief to the victim. In addition, the opportunity to discuss one's victimization and the accompanying emotional reaction counteracts the incestuous family's secrecy and denial of the problem. Group therapy also allows the therapist to move beyond the somewhat limited view of children obtained in a one-to-one relationship and to see them in a social setting. For example, I did not realize the full extent of a child's hyperresponsibility and parentification until I saw her in group, helping everyone except herself. Because I had not yet seen her with her mother, this was helpful to know, and I could anticipate the role she assumed in her family and what it might take to change that.

Berliner and Ernst (1984) stated, "Group treatment may be the best therapeutic approach to address the victimization issues." Other clinicians have written that not only might group therapy be the treatment of choice for addressing the interpersonal problems of the incest victim, but also that group therapy can recreate the incest family experience, thus providing more momentum for change (Alexander, Neimeyer, Follette, Moore, Harter, 1989). These authors were discussing treatment for preadolescent victims and Gagliano (1987) concurred for adolescent victims. The therapeutic elements of interpersonal learning, the instillation of hope, universality, group cohesiveness, and catharsis are thought to be operative in groups of victims (Yalom, 1975), even child victims.

As is too often the case in therapy with sexually abused children, little is known about the efficacy of various treatment modalities. Group treatment of victims is the most widely used therapy form for victims of all ages. Two recent papers, one with adult victims (Alexander et al., 1989), and the other with child victims (Nelki & Watters, 1989), have suggested that group therapy is effective.

Alexander et al. (1989) found that two different, 10-week group approaches were more effective at post-treatment and 6-month follow-up than a waiting list control group. Fifty-eight women completed the study. Outcome measures included depression, general distress, and social adjustment.

Nelki and Watters (1989) studied the outcomes of six girls, 4 to 8 years of age, after a nine-session structured group experience. Significant improvement was noted on a brief problem checklist when pretreatment scores were contrasted with scores assessed two months after the group ended. No other outcome measures were used.

Although group therapy was not the only modality used with the 45 boys in the study reported earlier (Friedrich et al., submitted), it was the primary treatment for many of the boys. The group format was open-ended and sessions were semi-structured, but significant improve-

ment was noted in various areas of functioning at the end of treatment — e.g., general behavioral problems, sexual behavior problems,
and school performance.

Documenting the efficacy of our treatment is an important component of treatment. Not only do we learn if our efforts are successful but
assessing children before and after therapy can also serve to guide our
treatment. Table 7-1 lists measures suggested to assess several dimensions
of child and family functioning. These readily available measures can
be implemented in treatment programs and used to guide treatment
and demonstrate efficacy. With a little effort, many agencies could
publish studies with larger sample sizes than that by Nelki and Watters
(1989) and evaluate children across a greater variety of dimensions than
simply the 33-item behavioral problem list they used.

GENERAL CONSIDERATIONS

One of the emphases of this book has been on the heterogeneity of
sexually abused children and their diverse treatment needs. Another
emphasis has been on the importance of context — i.e., family and social
networks. Let us return to some of these basic assumptions. Are there
some children for whom group approaches are more appropriate? What
are the ways to design a group so that it maximizes the child's therapeutic needs?

A large number of models exist, usually dependent on age. Fowler,
Burns, and Roehl (1983) described the content of a preschool group (2 to
6 years old) that appeared to be primarily activity group therapy (Schiffer, 1984). Their 7- to 12-year-old group was more cognitive and in-
terpretatively focused and the teen group (13 to 18 years old) was more
crisis-oriented and usually included sex education. Some groups are
short-term and primarily educative (Berliner & Ernst, 1984; Friedrich,
Berliner, Urquiza, & Beilke, 1988b) and range from four to six sessions
that are highly structured and focused primarily on the victimization
experience, courtroom preparation, and prevention. Another common
model is somewhat longer and assumes a broader therapeutic focus. For
example, Nelki and Watters' (1989) nine-session format has a specific
aim each week — e.g., allow expression and understanding of difficult
feelings in week 5. The comprehensive format described in Mandell and
Damon (1989) takes the child and caregiver, in parallel groups, through
10 modules, each taking from three to eight sessions.

As indicated in most of the programs described, there will be a subset
of sexually abused children who will not be able to tolerate the intensity

TABLE 7-1
Recommended Assessment Battery to Measure Treatment Effectiveness

Parent Report
1. Parental Depression and Pathology (SCL-90-R; Derogatis, 1983)
2. Parental Social Support (Moos, Cronkite, Billings, & Finney, 1983)
3. Life Events Checklist (Moos et al., 1983)
4. Child Behavior Checklist (Achenbach & Edelbrock, 1983)
5. Child Sexual Behavior Inventory (Friedrich et al., 1989)
6. Dissociative Events Schedule—Children (Putnam, 1987)
7. Self-Administered Alcoholism Screening Test (SAAST, Swenson & Morse, 1975)
8. Sibling Behavior Problems (Moos et al., 1983)
9. Family Environment Scale (Moos et al., 1983)

Teacher Report
1. Child Behavior Checklist (Achenbach & Edelbrock, 1983)
2. School Situations Questionnaire

Child Report
1. Intelligence (WISC-R Short Form)
2. School Achievement (WRAT-R)
3. Self-Esteem (Harter, 1982)
4. Depression (Child Depression Inventory; Kovacs & Beck, 1977)
5. Child Assessment Schedule (CAS, Hodges et al., 1982)
6. Safety Interview

Therapist Report
1. Child Involvement in Therapy
2. Parental Involvement in Therapy
3. Global Rating of Quality of Parent-Child Relationship

of group treatment and may need prior individual therapy or may benefit more from an open-ended group.

Cole and Barney (1987), writing about adult groups, discuss the "need for caution in promoting disclosure of a powerful, guilt-ridden trauma." Group therapy may not pace the disclosure of abuse as precisely as individual therapy may, for example. A child who is resistant to disclosure may be overwhelmed as the participants recount their victimization. "There is the potential for group treatment to elicit anxiety well beyond the tolerance of individual members" (Cole & Barney).

Sometimes children in sexual-abuse treatment groups become overwhelmed even without disclosure, seemingly contracted by the other members' thinly veiled distress and sexual talk (Friedrich et al., 1988b). Cole and Barney (1987) used post-traumatic stress reaction theory to explain why this phenomenon exists. The traumatized individual experiences phases of denial that alternate with intrusive phases. Because the natural regulation of affect is a process that is disrupted as a result of victimization, the trauma victim may oscillate between these extreme phases and spend little time in a more neutral or moderate band of distress that allows for resolution.

The group process is intense. Yet, when managed appropriately, with therapists who work hard to modulate the group members' distress, it can be less intense and anxiety-provoking than the individual therapy experience. For example, the child may feel less exposed in a larger group and may have fewer concerns about safety. Because the modulation of affect is something many of these children have not learned, working with them in a group context where anxiety can become manageable suggests group treatment approaches for a wide range of sexually abused children.

Different issues present themselves depending on the sex makeup of the group. Although Berliner and Ernst (1984) talked about the utility of a coeducational group, particularly with younger ages, most groups are same sex. The majority of the clinical literature is clearly on female groups, given the preponderance of female victims. Sex differences in male groups seem to show up in greater activity, more overt sexualization, and less ability to inhibit their impulses (Friedrich et al., 1988b).

However, a careful reading of the Nelki and Watters (1989) paper, reporting a nine-week group approach with six young female victims, identifies such behaviors as inappropriate closeness and cuddling, loud and boisterous discharges of affect, attempts at undressing other group members, and destruction of papers and pencils during group art projects. Depending on the content and membership of the group, sex differences may not be readily noticeable.

The experiences described by Friedrich et al. (1988b) and Nelki and Watters (1989), both with latency-age or younger children, do not preclude utilizing groups for intervening with young male or female victims. What clinical experience increasingly says is that screening for appropriate participants is important; very brief and intensely focused groups are not recommended for younger males; and more effort needs to be made to titrate the emotional intensity of the groups.

Rather than introducing new topics in rapid succession, time must be allocated for the introduction and processing of such emotionally laden topics as "fault" and "owning one's body." Validation of the reality of the victimization on the one hand and the victim on the other is another by-product of group treatment. The adult therapist's influence pales in contrast to the influence of same-age peers.

Another opportunity that groups provide that other therapeutic approaches do not is the ability for different groups of individuals, currently in therapy, to meet with each other. For example, a female adolescent group has profited from meeting on several occasions with an adolescent offender group. Mothers can meet with daughter groups, a process built into several models (Giaretto, 1982; Mandell & Damon, 1989). Steward, Farquhar, Dicharry, Glick, and Martin (1986) wrote that children from various abusive backgrounds can be effectively treated in the same therapy group, and they have included physically and sexually abused preschoolers in the same groups.

As is always the case in clinical work, differences of opinion exist. Some clinicians do not feel comfortable advocating group therapy for abused or traumatized children, particularly younger children. Abused children with poor boundaries have been reported to assume the problems and difficulties of other group members. The initial regression seen in some children, particularly in intensive and short-term groups, may rock the already shaky family stability. Other clinicians argue that a traumatized child needs first to have the undivided attention of an adult therapist. However, if little is truly known about the efficacy of individual child psychotherapy, even less is known about the efficacy of group approaches for children (Weisz et al., 1987).

It is disappointing that the numerous groups that are run throughout the country are not done in such a way that pretreatment, post-treatment, and follow-up measures can be administered through the various agencies so that we can know if what we are doing is helpful. For example, although clinically rich, the structured format suggested in Mandell and Damon (1989) has never been empirically validated. Until this occurs, we need to use our clinical experiences to design the various types of therapeutic contexts that can be helpful.

FORMAT ISSUES

A basic format issue is the duration of the group. This is dictated not only by our clinical wisdom but also by expediency, the group of children that is available to be served, and the focus of the agency that is involved. I am not opposed to short-term groups if we do not delude ourselves into thinking that they are to be used for anything more than diagnostic purposes and maybe for imparting some information and the beginnings of a sense that the child is not alone in the victimization. Brief educative formats are increasingly used because of the number of children needing intervention and the difficulties that disorganized families have in managing anything more than a few sessions in a row.

If we are going to use a structured approach that is primarily focused on resolving the victimization experience, preventing further abuse, and empowering the child for future life experiences, I believe that a minimum of 16 to 20 sessions is needed. This allows for greater group cohesiveness, the experience of peer support, and the emergence of some central issues in a supportive context. Group process can also emerge in this longer period. Some time during each session can be allocated to focus on each member's interactions with the group as a means of developing new ways of relating to the group specifically and other people generally. In addition, the structured, time-limited format helps to keep the focus on the task at hand. Clear time boundaries also provide a welcome contrast to the lack of structure present in the child's frequently chaotic and overly intrusive family.

If the circumstances support a longer-term or even open-ended group, I see this as the most optimal for adolescents in particular. This format is more demanding of the clinician, however, and threatens to be less structured. Highly unstructured group approaches simply do not work with extremely disturbed children (Curry, 1989). Yet the longer-term format can be more respectful of the heterogeneity of children who can be seen in groups; it also enables the group to continue to work for long stretches at a time without the initial start-up and get-acquainted period that is typical in the first few weeks of any new group. New members give older members repeated opportunities to work through their abuse experience in a more gradual manner, as they share with the new member(s). In addition, the older members' self-perceptions can alter positively as they view the changes they have made in contrast to a newer member.

SCREENING CRITERIA

From the outset of this section, I need to state that regardless of the number and the needs of the children available, all sexually abused children do not belong in group treatment, particularly not as their first and only exposure to therapy. Screening criteria used for the adult women in a study reported by Alexander et al. (1989) included serious suicidal ideation, psychosis, and severe substance abuse. Children available for group treatment must also be screened as to their suitability. To not do so runs the risk of making the group experience less than useful and even damaging.

Screening is not a luxury that can be ignored. If four children are available, and only two seem suitable, it is preferable to have a group with the two children deemed suitable, even if the critical mass is not reached. Because screening guidelines and techniques are less than perfect, a trial group involvement may need to be arranged. Problems are created when removing the child from the group. If an individual therapist is available, that is usually sufficient. However, the same behaviors that precluded group treatment make this child more than the usual challenge in individual therapy.

What are appropriate screening criteria? Obviously, psychotic and mentally retarded children would be difficult to incorporate into a group, and they should be excluded. Mandell and Damon (1989) suggested several other basic criteria, including:

1. the potential to talk about the molestation in group
2. the ability to control impulses and tolerate limit-setting
3. "sufficient ego strength."

The authors go on to state that children who deny or greatly minimize their victimization present management difficulties, but they also stated that the group can effectively and therapeutically erode the child's denial. In the case of parallel group treatment, in which parents and children are seen in separate groups with parallel agendas, separate screening criteria for caregivers are also appropriate.

The assessment process outlined in Chapter 3 can be useful in the screening process. What Mandell and Damon (1989) called "sufficient ego strength," I operationalize from projective assessment, particularly the Rorschach. I have reviewed the Exner-scored Rorschach tests of the last dozen children for whom group treatment was not used because of their behavior or who were removed from group after the first several sessions.

Their total behavioral problem score from the Child Behavior Checklist was not the uniformly discriminating variable. Rather, it was the differential between available emotional resources (EA = human movement and chromatic color) and level of emotional distress (es = animal and inanimate movement added to achromatic color and shading responses). This ratio, es, represents the various unsettling feelings and needs of the child. In all but two cases, es was two to three times, at the least, greater than the child's EA, or available emotional resources. The ratio, EA, is presumably equivalent to ego strength. The overt behavior ranged from quiet and withdrawn; to anxious, depressed, and suicidal; to anxious and sexualized; to sexualized and aggressive. Thus, by behavior alone, these 10 children were quite diverse. The remaining two who were also screened out had severe conduct disorders. Most of these 12 also had difficulties discussing their molestation in a screening interview.

COMPOSITION

Once a group of children has been screened as suitable, concerns regarding actual group composition must be addressed. A core of somewhat better-socialized children in each group who are able to talk and connect with various members is critical. It is also important to have a similar developmental age represented. For example, preschoolers usually do not belong in school-age groups, and latency-age children do not belong with early adolescents.

It is important to not have the six- to eight-member group dominated by primarily conduct-disordered or oppositional children. One or two at the most is recommended. In smaller groups of fewer than six members, the presence of even one severely disturbed child will disrupt the group for weeks and even months on end. Children who are markedly impulsive and have poor boundaries and who have absolutely no sense of the timing of interpersonal relationships are also difficult to manage in a group setting. You will end up spending a great deal of time supporting the parents or caregivers of the other children in the group because the children are overly activated by the presence of these one or two children.

The group usually requires some minimal number to be successful. With younger children, three to six children are recommended (Steward et al., 1986) and reportedly as many as 13 can be accommodated in an adolescent group (Blick and Porter, 1982), although I have not seen groups this large be effective in the short term. If the group is small, I believe the composition should be more homogeneous, both with regard to sex and to type of victimization experience. I have also worked successfully with groups of two children, usually boys. If a co-therapist is not available or the children would be too activated in a larger group, this may be an appropriate option.

Some groups can take on a rather unusual constellation. It may be that with younger, more infantile children, separation issues are so predominant that the mother also attends the group. An excellent description of the initial dilemma that presented to the therapist and how this worked out positively is presented in Pescosolido and Petrella (1986); the ambivalent mother-daughter relationship resulted in such separation anxiety in a young girl that her mother attended the group. Apparently, the mother also had separation difficulties, and she actually expressed pain when her daughter grew to the point that she was able to have her mother leave.

CO-THERAPISTS

Working as a therapist with a group of three or more children can be an arduous task. That is not the only reason why co-therapists are strongly advocated. More important reasons are that the therapeutic tasks can be more readily divided, modeling of appropriate interaction between adults can be educative and healing, and in some ways it can allow for a more natural working through of the black-white thinking that these children frequently do. Co-therapists need to anticipate that they will alternate in good guy-bad guy roles. This is more likely in longer-term groups.

However, there are some precautions. The co-therapy relationship, particularly in longer-term groups, can be intense. In one of the more enlightening and personal papers I read in preparation for this chapter (Gottlieb & Dean, 1981), the authors discussed their personal experiences working as male-female co-therapists for an adolescent group of sexually abused girls. The two groups that they ran were seven months long. Working out male-female issues, including sexual attraction between the two of them, being sensitive to their own sexual issues and how that impacted their relationship with the girls, and even discussing some of these issues openly with the members of the group are discussed in this paper.

The co-therapy relationship is something that also depends on the nature of the group. Because of the brief educative format of their groups, Berliner and Ernst (1984) report that on occasion they have used county attorneys and other individuals from the community as co-therapists. This is something that can be done given the fact that the relational issues are not as important or intense in briefer groups. In addition, these experiences can sensitize nonmental-health professionals in a powerful manner to the issues these children face.

The co-therapy relationship does evolve over time. It is not a relationship that springs to life full-grown when the group begins. Mutual regard and respect are essential, as is a similar philosophy of what is important. Whether or not the co-therapists should be the same or opposite sex has not been decided in the clinical literature. Some therapists believe that a male-female combination is too threatening and invites seductive behavior or projection that interferes with group process. Others believe that whatever issues develop are potentially useful for therapy. Nelki and Watters (1989) utilized a male-female co-therapy team and recommend this approach. My group work with latency and adolescent-age male victims has strongly reinforced the power of a male-female co-therapy team over a male-male team.

In any case, a co-therapy team can be invaluable at generating discussion, helping children move into new and threatening areas, and modeling a more cognitive, problem-solving approach for the children. The co-therapists may find that one of them is better than the other at introducing difficult topics in a way that does not overwhelm the children. Or some children will clearly relate better to one co-therapist than the other, allowing an important relationship to develop. The importance of discussion between the co-therapists should be appreciated. Important teaching can occur in a nonthreatening way when children hear co-therapists discuss issues such as shame, which may be too difficult for the children to directly examine.

PHYSICAL ENVIRONMENT

A number of issues are important in the determination of the group's environment; the foremost is a sense of safety and, for younger children, the ability to play. Where the group therapy takes place can be quite important to context-sensitive children and adolescents. A mistake I made in a group I led was that the room was too large and had more than one exit, which seemed to activate the rather chaotic and impulsive nature of the boys in the group. Keeping on task and managing their behavior was made even more difficult because of this room choice. It was also much harder for process discussions to take place, because there were too many opportunities to flee. Sound-proof rooms are also important, or you run the risk of disturbing your colleagues.

The environment also consists of the children who are present; marked fluctuations in attendance from one session to the next are not conducive to therapy. Thus, contracting with parents about attendance and making provisions for attendance to be as regular as possible by providing transportation or babysitting are important. Scheduling parent and child groups at the same time can enhance overall attendance.

In addition to providing safety in the environment, the therapist also needs to build in nurturing. Provision of juice or snacks should not be used as a "behavioral modification strategy to elicit compliant behavior, but rather as a tangible sign of nurturance by the therapist" (Steward et al., 1986). The provision of food is mentioned almost universally among the group therapy papers reviewed as an important element of the treatment process.

TREATMENT ISSUES

Treatment issues vary from one group to the next depending on the nature of the group, the therapists, and the participants. Blick and Porter (1982) identified four issues:

1. ventilation of anger
2. socialization
3. preparation for court
4. sex education.

Gagliano (1987) focused on:

1. sex education
2. discussion of the incest
3. alleviation of guilt
4. discussion of parental roles and types.

Gagliano also particularly focused on fathers and their styles of manipulation. These goals are quite ambitious for the short-term group that she discussed.

Another, probably overambitious, set of goals to be covered in nine weeks was presented in Nelki and Watters (1989):

1. meeting strangers safely
2. yes and no feelings
3. secrets
4. touching with people you know very well
5. telling someone
6. anger and punishment
7. fault and responsibility
8. your own body.

Only one session was allowed for integration at the end, in the context of parent-child group meeting.

Mrazek (1981), in 1½-hour sessions over a course of six months and modeled on activity group therapy, focused on:

1. providing a safe setting to facilitate the discussion of feelings regarding individual and family problems, including their sexual experiences
2. providing male and female adult role models
3. allowing the girls to relate to peers who had similar sexual experiences
4. enhancing the girls' overall social skills.

Steward et al. (1986), in their group with preschoolers, articulated seven goals to be accomplished in an open-ended group extending from eight months to two years:

1. helping the children articulate thoughts and feelings
2. encouraging their developing abilities to ask for help
3. providing an experience with a caring and comforting adult to deal with issues of abandonment and loss
4. enhancing social skills
5. helping develop a realistic sense of competence
6. supporting mastery of normal milestones
7. confronting the egocentric assumption that abuse is their fault.

In addition, their format allowed for regular home visits that also enhanced the likelihood of a positive therapy outcome.

Although the existing literature on group work with younger, primarily female victims is expanding, significantly less material is available regarding the treatment issues of latency age and adolescent boys who are victims. Some of these boys may also have victimized other children, and if their sexual aggression is primary, that needs to be addressed prior to their involvement in a victims' group. The topics that I have found central, and which are covered typically in 22 to 28 weeks, depending on the group, are:

1. who I am (positives, negatives)
2. the family I am from
3. my victimization
4. guilt and shame
5. my sexuality
6. my feelings about my perpetrator
7. my perpetrator potential
8. preventing further victimization
9. setting goals for now and the future.

Sessions typically last 70 to 85 minutes; ground rules prohibiting aggression and sexual touching are introduced at the first session and as needed throughout. In our effort to modulate the intensity of the group, portions of videotapes of previous sessions are regularly played for discussion and to offer opportunities for integration. Each boy schedules a time to discuss his victimization during the time we are focusing on that issue, and this is videotaped, notes are taken by the therapists, and the group provides feedback about how thoroughly and appropriately this was done.

Guidelines from Smets and Cebula (1987) have been useful in structuring how we have the boys talk about guilt and shame. Their concept of levels in group progress related to the boys' ownership of their sexual victimization of others has also been useful. From the beginning of the group, usually in the screening sessions, goals are set for in the group and outside of the group, and these guide the sessions and are used to motivate the boys and assess their progress. The outcomes we have witnessed argue for the utility of the group format.

The longer-term groups appear to have more opportunity to address the other diverse difficulties with which these children present, rather than focusing primarily on the abuse. Many of the shorter-term groups reported in the literature, with their heavy didactic component, are overly cognitive. If a cognitive focus, exclusive of an interpersonal focus, was the only emphasis, groups would have little value (Curry, 1989). Are we serving our security needs or the child's needs by being brief and overly structured in the groups we run?

The goals of adult groups can provide some guidance here. An open-ended men's group discussed by Singer (1989) focused on:

1. interpersonal relationships
2. powerlessness and control
3. validation of the victim and victimization.

Topics in the more structured group of Alexander et al. (1989) included:

1. feelings of being different
2. positive and negative perceptions of self
3. feelings of helplessness
4. issues of trust
5. family secrets
6. ambivalence toward mother.

Therapists with adults usually do not have to be as directive and structuring as I find myself being in group settings with children and adolescents. The types of guided exercises described in Mandell and Damon (1989) are ideal for many younger groups and generate therapeutic movement. I find myself using group exercises, pictures from magazines and the Projective Storytelling Test (Caruso, 1987), and art activities in many of the group meetings to generate discussion of emotionally laden topics.

Prevention is an important treatment issue and the group can serve to empower children to react appropriately to further threat of abuse. The most important empowering agent, however, is the parent figure. Although Giaretto's (1982) groups appeared to be carefully screened for success, his ideas and those of others (MacFarlane, Waterman, Conerly, Damon, Durfee, & Long, 1986; Mandell & Damon, 1989) about parallel group therapy, involving mothers and children at different segments in the therapy, are important to the success of prevention. In fact, that approach is probably the only way to work with preschool and early school-age children regarding this topic. With the acquisition of greater assertiveness, to prevent further abuse, or any new skill identified above, the liberal use of role-playing and coordinating with other caregivers to develop and maintain out-of-group behavior is critical.

Another commonly identified treatment issue is to enable the children to discuss thoughts and feelings about problems, including their abuse experiences. Structured sharing exercises, art projects, discussions between the co-therapists, and the modeling of openness by a more verbal or more seasoned group member can all be extremely useful. Videotaped segments from other groups can be a good starting point. The art project may help to express a personal dilemma. I have noticed that group members may be more open to discussion while working on their project than if they were sitting in the group circle. The same is true for snack time. While eating, some extremely important discussion can emerge. These examples reflect a child's need for being indirect, at least initially, in the sharing process.

Because of the importance of bringing the child's abuse experience to the therapy setting for discussion and resolution, some additional comments on how to do that in the group setting are warranted. Discussion of the abuse indirectly, via art projects or listening to the therapists discuss a prototypical child's emotional reactions, are two ways to modulate the intensity of affect that may emerge at this time. There are ways, so to speak, of keeping the child within the "therapeutic window," or that moderate distress area between denial and intrusion (Cole & Barney, 1987).

Various less direct techniques are possible. The child may write about the abuse on a worksheet to be shared at a later date. An art exercise that has the child draw the perpetrator is a nice precursor to a later discussion about what actually happened. Using some of the video material available for purchase can prime the child for a more manageable disclosure, as can a group discussion of "hypothetical" abuse situations, some of which approximate the child's actual experience. I have also had success with a video technique in which the child talks about the abuse while being recorded in front of the group. The child is then in charge of the actual playback of the disclosure, stopping the tape to add something. Something about speaking to a camera enables some children to feel less threatened than if they spoke directly to a group.

When a child begins to be overwhelmed in the group, this can be indicated in different ways—e.g., hyperventilation, vomiting, an urge to leave the room, increased activity, "unconscious" sexual behavior (touching the male therapist). Calling a stop to the disclosure, putting it on hold, using deep breathing or other relaxation techniques, and reminding the child where she is so as to reorient her to the setting are possible options. Sometimes at this stage in the group, it is necessary to divide the group into portions, some devoted to work, others to play or less structured activities. Victims often think "magically" about their victimization—i.e., if they talk about it, it will happen again. Thus, for children to begin hesitantly to talk about the abuse, and then find themselves revictimized by unmanageable affect, is something that must be guarded against.

Because of the brevity and narrow focus of many groups, numerous other, equally important issues such as loss may not emerge unless we remind ourselves that the sexual victimization may not be the central issue for the child at this time. Structured exercises that promote a meaningful discussion of family issues are also recommended as equally important.

The simple provision of an hour or more per week of supportive attention cannot be underestimated, although its impact may be difficult to measure. The quickly developed and intense bond I see some children form speaks both to their neediness and to the potential positive impact of the therapy, even if brief. I interviewed an adult incest victim who had adapted quite well but wanted one or two sessions to discuss how to handle an upcoming family reunion. During the interview, I asked, as is customary for me, what adults she remembered "were there for her" when she was growing up. Without hesitation, she mentioned a maternal aunt and a 9th-grade gym teacher. I was curious about the teacher, and the woman said that she just seemed interested in her, would sometimes ask how things were going, and did not ridicule her about not wanting to dress for gym class. The teacher left after one semester. If this woman could have experienced that type of positive effect in such a brief time, some children in our groups will also. That woman helped confirm for me that what I do, even in relatively brief interactions, can be helpful.

In conclusion, group therapy can be an important, even primary therapy experience for sexually abused children. Attention needs to be paid to appropriate group composition and to creating a sense of safety in the group so that the children's energies can be focused on the opportunities the group provides.

Group formats provide not only an opportunity to impart valuable information and initiate resolution of a child's victimization but can also be an essential arena for the child to try out new changes in a supportive atmosphere in which positive corrective feedback is possible.

8

Hypnotherapy With Sexually Abused Children

Rape is a crime against sleep and memory.
Pat Conroy, The Prince of Tides

Although individual, family, and group therapies are routinely discussed as standard and acceptable treatment modalities for sexually abused children, the same is not true for hypnotherapy. Primarily, this is because hypnotherapy is much more widely practiced with adults, as evidenced by only one standard text in the area of hypnosis with children (Gardner & Olness, 1981). A second reason is that hypnotherapy continues to be misperceived by professionals and the public. Hypnosis is also often associated with a loss of control, which is clearly a third reason for its lack of wider acceptance. Few of us could imagine a situation contributing to potentially more out-of-control feelings than sexual abuse. A parallel exists between the reticence a large percentage of therapists exhibit in failing to help the child talk about the abuse and the lack of endorsement for hypnosis by these therapists; hypnosis is erroneously thought to be tantamount to being out of control. Most of us are aware of stage hypnotists and their posthypnotic suggestions designed to make people look foolish. Whether these are true examples of the craft of hypnotherapy or not is not the question. We are left with a powerful impression of someone being out of control.

Nothing could be further from the truth. Hypnosis is often defined as a state of relaxation coupled with a narrowing of focus and heightened suggestibility. Hypnotherapy is the use of hypnotic techniques in the practice of psychotherapy. Individuals do not lose control when hypnotized, and they cannot be made to do things they choose not to do. Hypnosis does not require complex and arcane induction (e.g., swinging watches or prisms). Although direct techniques are widely used (e.g., eye fixation or eyeroll), a large percentage of therapists use indirect induction (e.g., suggestions or imagery); indirect techniques are quite suitable for children.

Some may think that hypnotherapy strips away defenses and renders the person vulnerable to primary process intrusion. Others have the misconception that hypnotherapy should not be practiced with anyone who is not completely intact. Both of these beliefs are erroneous. Solid contemporary literature counters these assumptions (Baker, 1981). In addition, children are usually perceived, as a group, to be better hypnotic subjects than adults (Gardner & Olness, 1981).

HOW TO CONCEPTUALIZE HYPNOSIS

The practice of hypnotherapy can be viewed in at least two ways. The first is that hypnotherapy is a specific collection of techniques that assists in the practice of therapy and behavior change. For example, the profound relaxation that accompanies hypnosis is counter to the anxiety that many sexually abused children experience, some chronically and others prior to specific events (e.g., school, tests, visits with offender, court testimony). Additionally, children can be taught self-hypnosis quite readily (Gardner & Olness, 1981), and the use of this new skill can engender a sense of competence and feelings of greater mastery over the environment. No one could argue against the importance of these positive experiences.

Rather than creating greater vulnerability in the child, hypnosis can be used to shore up a child's defenses, again contributing to a decrease in anxiety and an increase in mastery. For example, intrusive thoughts can often be countered with suggestions, while in a trance, of the child's ability to put those specific thoughts aside until the appropriate time arises, presumably in therapy, to discuss them. In addition, a child can be taught to control the degree to which thoughts and memories occur, and how to choose them to come forward at the child's own pace. The decrease in the child's motivation to do schoolwork on the one hand and a heightened distractibility on the other can also be handled hypnotherapeutically.

An important concomitant of hypnosis is that it rapidly enhances the therapeutic relationship. Greater mutuality and trust are frequent additional benefits that are as important as any of the others mentioned earlier.

In addition to these more specific uses of hypnotic techniques, designed to decrease anxiety and intrusive thoughts and to enhance mastery, concentration, and motivation, there is a broader definition: Hypnotherapy can be viewed as a general framework that guides the entire therapy process. For example, refer to the earlier definition of hypnosis, that is, relaxation coupled with a narrowing of focus and heightened suggestibility. In therapy, one does not need an overly tense and rejecting client or one who is too easily distracted and unable to focus on the salient issues. Because change is the goal, it is important to have a more compliant individual in the therapy office. Finally, given that therapist-patient rapport is central, the enhancement of this relationship, a by-product of the hypnotic process, is also critical to the success of therapy.

I see hypnosis as helping in the development of each of these important therapeutic elements, both as a result of direct trance work and also more indirectly. In fact, much of good therapy can be conceptualized from a hypnotherapy perspective. For example, in order to facilitate a relationship, there must be a meshing of the therapist and the client. This fitting-together process comes about via pacing and mirroring. Pacing refers to the simultaneity of process, with the client not feeling either overly pushed or directionless. Mirroring refers to the fact that there is congruence between the therapist and the client. An affectively sad state is mirrored by the therapist via slowing down, matching some of the pain with posture or tone of voice, and showing acceptance of the individual's current state. For the therapist to reject his or her own discomfort and try to move the client past that sadness would be the antithesis of mirroring, and it would not be good therapy.

In addition, the language of hypnosis is quite interesting and fits with the definition of a general framework of therapy. The positives are emphasized along with the innate ability of the person to find his or her way. For example, when I make either direct or indirect suggestions, I may say something like, "You'll find that you will increasingly feel more capable of. . . . " It is important not to use words like "try" or "maybe." These imply the possibility of failure to the person who is thinking in a much more concrete manner in a trance (e.g., trance logic).

The divorce that exists between the different fragmented elements of the person or between thoughts and affect is also better resolved with the ability of hypnosis to create deep relaxation; hypnosis facilitates a working through or a reconnecting of these disparate parts. Clients in a waking state may be very confused and not able to comply when the therapist asks them to drop their usual veneer and comfort the small, hurt child that lives within themselves. Yet in a trance, this is a natural request that is usually met with compliance and subsequent integration of the client.

Further support for hypnosis as a general framework comes from the belief held by many family therapists that families are powerful trance agents (Ritterman, 1983). Children pick up on subtle cues and may behave quite differently within the family than individually in a separate and different context. It is useful to think of the hypnotic messages seen in incestuous families—e.g., do not disclose, do not be aware of what is going on, my needs are less than the offender's needs, the family is everything and the individual is nothing.

I have seen several children, and particularly adolescents and adults, who described a type of sleepwalking state or a drugged feeling as they became aware that incest was about to recur. One adult client reported, "I knew by then of course it was wrong, but I felt frozen and like there was nothing I could do." The duty of the therapist is to substitute a new "trance," so to speak, and to disrupt the harmful cueing that operates. I see the multigenerational perpetration of incest as a reflection of the fact that incestuous families use very similar cues, and without therapy or personal change the adolescent or young adult becomes entranced and enters a relationship that is toxic and recreates abuse in another generation. Thus, hypnosis is both a general framework to guide therapy and a specific set of techniques.

SPECIFIC USES OF HYPNOTHERAPY

It is relatively easy for me to see the applicability of hypnosis to a diverse set of problems exhibited by sexually abused children. These range from the mundane to the arcane. Later in this chapter I will discuss the use of hypnosis with two of the more arcane, hysterical seizures and conversion reactions. Here I will review several specific uses and present case material.

Treating Toileting Difficulty

We cannot lose sight of the fact that sexually abused children may exhibit difficulties in many areas of their lives. A common presenting problem is difficulty, frequently of secondary onset, with toileting. A child who has had no problems with daytime or nighttime enuresis suddenly exhibits problems in this area, possibly as part of a larger constellation of regressed behavior. Or a child, frequently male, may develop problems with encopresis secondary to abuse, sometimes sodomy, either due to pain at elimination or reflecting the literal thinking of the child.

The typical parent is quite torn, wanting the child to show no problems, despite the abuse, and feeling unsure of how lenient or firm to be. In addition, peer relationships may be disrupted. As a result of toileting difficulties the child may feel compelled to turn down offers of sleepovers, or he or she may be ridiculed in school by classmates.

Hypnotic techniques are mild, nonintrusive, and frequently effective with these conditions, although more so for enuresis than encopresis in my experience. By the time I see encopresis cases secondary to sexual abuse, usually an intensely negative parent-child system has developed or been further elaborated from a preexisting set of dynamics.

Enuresis

Enuresis can be treated quite easily. The procedure I use is to have a conjoint discussion, including the parent(s); explain, via sample drawings and discussion, the biology of voiding; and talk about the bladder "talking" to the child and the child "talking" to the bladder as naturally occurring processes during the course of the day. This leads to the conclusion that we need to keep each "talking" to the other during the night or other times when the child has difficulty.

Relaxation, usually with imagery or a psychomotor technique, e.g., rag doll or coin drop, is induced and "conversations" are held with the bladder, usually with some suggestions of mastery and competence included by me at this time. The child is then asked to repeat the relaxation process on his or her own, prior to the end of the session.

It is also possible during this interview to assess motivation to change and possible pitfalls and to discuss what can be done about these. The family is sent home and the child is instructed to void before bed and then spend several minutes, prior to lying down, sitting on the edge of the bed, relaxing, and "talking" to his or her bladder. Usually the drawings are sent home with the child and the child is asked to look at them on a regular basis, so as to focus his or her conversation. When this is done as prescribed, 90% of the children I have seen for this type of problem are helped significantly within the first two to three weeks. There are usually more obstacles to successful treatment when daytime enuresis is the primary presenting problem, due probably to different contributing dynamics.

An example is helpful here. In an early session with a mother and her 8-year-old boy, Clark, who had secondary nighttime enuresis subsequent to fondling by a male adolescent, we began to talk about his wetting.

Therapist: Do you know what I mean when I say that your bladder, this round thing here in the drawing we made, talks to you? Sends you messages?

Clark: Sort of. No.

Therapist: Okay. Let's go through it. You know when you have to pee during the day? Huh?

Clark: Yeah. I feel it. I feel full.

Therapist: Right. You feel full and you know you're full because your bladder sent a message to your brain that you need to pee. It talks to you with these messages.

Clark: Oh, okay. How does it send the message?

Therapist: It uses your nerves. They are like telephone wires in your body.

Clark: Oh.

Therapist: What happens at night, when you pee in bed, is that you aren't listening to the messages. You used to. You didn't wet the bed before Robert. But now, for some reason you've decided not to listen.

Clark: I want to hear them.

Therapist: Exactly. You want to hear the messages from your bladder. You want to hear it say to you, while you are sleeping, "Clark, I got to go pee. Get me to the bathroom." And that's what we'll do now. Get you to hear the messages again at night. Okay?

Clark: Okay.

A light trance was then induced and I held a conversation with Clark's bladder. He talked to it again in my office, and once before bed that night; he had only one accident during the next four weeks. This was in direct contrast to almost nightly wetting. Also aiding the rapid turnaround was a supportive parent-child relationship and a boy with no history of previous problems.

Encopresis

Encopresis is more difficult to treat, either behaviorally or with hypnosis. Frequently, the symptom is related to a larger pattern of oppositionality and parental inefficiency and inconsistency. Behavioral treatments can be intrusive and coercive (Wright, 1975) with regular enemas and suppositories. These approaches may be more difficult to implement when there is a prior history of sexual abuse. I try in these cases to establish a strong relationship with the child (facilitated by hypnosis), remove the child from the parental umbrella by making the encopresis an issue between the child and myself, use drawings of digestion and elimination, hold conversations with the bowel, and provide images of easy, slippery passage followed by relief and a sense of control. Some contracting also occurs between the child and me.

An example of a successful outcome was a 5-year-old boy who experienced rectal tearing when sodomized by a family acquaintance. The resulting pain prompted constipation, and elimination was accompanied by pain and some bleeding. This created a prolonged period of staining and bowel leakage, and he was in the pediatrician's office regularly. The boy still would not defecate regularly despite the use of large quantities of mineral oil. His mother was a positive source of support in his life, and the three of us had several discussions about defecation and pain. I used some hypnosis to demonstrate its power against pain (he had a severe sore throat that disappeared with some suggestions of warmth and comfort). His mother was recruited as a hypnotist and she would keep up a running commentary of appropriate images while he sat on the toilet several scheduled times each day. After several successful eliminations that produced no pain, he resumed a more normal bowel pattern.

Addressing School-Related Symptoms

Another set of symptoms are school-related and include distractibility, poor concentration, and apathy. Children may also exhibit disturbed peer relationships, particularly related to overintrusiveness or poor personal boundaries. Children can be taught self-hypnotic techniques to increase their ability to focus on their schoolwork, and self-hypnosis can augment the cognitive-behavioral training that is currently in vogue with children (Kendall & Braswell, 1985). In fact, I have augmented some of Kendall's self-statements with a prior hypnosis-induced relaxation, and I believe this enhances the utility of cognitive-behavioral methods. These self-statements help to orient a child to the task (e.g., "I will keep my eyes focused on the work in front of me") and persist in the task (e.g., "I will be able to ignore events around the room that used to distract me").

Motivation

However, motivation is probably a larger issue, reflecting the child's damaged sense of self. Motivation is directly related to the child's self-esteem or self-efficacy. Supportive parental attitudes toward the child are central to the child's development (Harter, 1981). Not only has the abuse interfered with development, but the frequently concomitant negative parental relationship has also made the child more vulnerable to derailing. Thus, schoolwork can be overwhelming.

If you have not spent time recently watching children learn how to read or perform simple mathematical problems, the basic building blocks of education, you may have forgotten how much effort and focus this process requires. The overachievement in school by some sexually abused children never ceases to amaze me, but it reflects the compartmentalization of their life that the abuse forced them into. It is as if they are saying, "This part of me can do well in school," or "This part of me is drawn to self-destructive relationships."

This compartmentalization is captured extremely well in several subtypes of bulimic women (Root et al., 1986), who perform in an overadequate manner in school and employment areas, but whose interpersonal relationships are fraught with problems. The high rate of sexual victimization in bulimic samples is not surprising (Root & Fallon, 1988).

How is motivation addressed hypnotically? Several approaches seem to work gradually:

1. the liberal and frequent use of mastery imagery
2. exploring the child's ambivalence about performance directly while in trance
3. helping to bring about incremental improvement in performance.

Mastery imagery is one of my favorite uses of hypnosis. Initially, I learned to use it with pediatric cancer patients as a way to improve their hopefulness, decrease their use of narcotic medication, and maximize their immune systems' response to their illness. It is a powerful technique that allows you to build up a child and it creates minimal resistance.

Several years ago, a young boy was referred to me for treatment. Sexually abused by his paternal uncle and stepfather, he was in foster care after parental rights had been terminated. Phillip had adopted a rigid defensiveness, the extent of which I had rarely seen before. My efforts to compliment this 10-year-old boy or to express pleasure at seeing him were met with comments such as, "You're just saying that," "Why do you say those things when you don't really mean them?" and, "Now what do you want me to do?"

However, Phillip loved skateboarding and was relatively adept. We began to spend part of each session entranced in skateboarding imagery, with Phillip performing fantastic feats of derring-do. Essentially, I would make some suggestions about relaxing, suggest a pleasant place or two, and then instruct Phillip to imagine doing his favorite skateboarding tricks. This would bring an even greater level of relaxation, made noticeable by his increased limpness and a big smile on his face. I would make approving sounds or comments when it seemed appropriate. This enabled us to have a period in which he allowed himself to be viewed in an unconditionally positive manner by both of us. It did not surprise me that our relationship was enhanced, he began to be more competent at school, and he was much more receptive to the verbal nurturance his foster parents and I were providing.

The second approach to facilitate motivation hypnotically is to explore the child's ambivalence about performance. It is appropriate that the child be ambivalent about success — wanting to be successful but fearful of its consequences. A successful performance may create an internal dilemma in the child about the good-bad feelings with which he or she is struggling. While the child is in trance, the two of us can talk about this ambivalence, and suggestions can be made about the child's feeling positive about himself or herself.

Finally, although hypnosis can quickly remove some symptoms, when it comes to mastery and motivation the improvements are usually incremental. Hypnosis enhances the relationship and allows the child to be more open to your positive input. This by itself can enhance self-esteem. Children can also be taught to observe themselves in a new way, seeing evidence of successful performance where they may not have seen it before due to their negative self-images.

Redefining Personal Boundaries

I have also seen some positive results regarding personal boundaries, although measuring whether they are transferring to peers is often difficult. In a boys' group I co-led, during the first two months I was struck repeatedly by a general deficit in these latency-age boys regarding interpersonal distance (e.g., too much touching, coming too close to each other, lack of respect for each other's property or personal rights when speaking). This prompted me to spend 8 to 10 minutes of each session over the next two months in group hypnosis, each boy sitting physically separated, with eyes open, and initially becoming relaxed. Some mastery imagery followed this and then we focused on body boundaries, with them listening to my suggestions of knowing where "they stopped and other people started" and "listening to the part of them that knew how close to stand to each other."

I borrowed these suggestions in part from some of the seminal work done by Elgan Baker (1981) on hypnosis with borderline and psychotic individuals, two groups with definite problems in the area of interpersonal boundaries. In an article with Michael Nash (Nash & Baker, 1984), he reported on research that found greater hypnotizability in children who have been physically abused; they related it to the children's overly developed skills at dissociation or distancing themselves from pain.

The boys in my group were also instructed during the trance to give themselves reminders about touching, standing too close, and allowing other people their turn. A return to the mastery imagery rounded out the group trance work and the group continued with its usual process. Due in part to the passage of time and also to the boundary work done in trance, the remaining three to four months of the group were characterized by significantly improved boundary behavior.

Aiding in Recall of the Abuse

A further dilemma exists with children who are unable to benefit from a discussion of the abuse because they have blocked it out of awareness in some fashion. The same is true for adult victims, who as a result of some precipitating event, usually a loss, become vaguely aware of earlier sexual abuse, but are unclear of its nature, extent, and event perpetrator. My greatest experience is with hypnotically aided recall with adults. Children are usually closer to the event, and the use of drawings and storytelling, and a great deal of patience are usually all that is needed. However, with adolescents and adults, hypnotically assisted recall may be quite useful.

This probably arouses anxiety in those readers who still are uncertain about the importance of uncovering traumatic events to the recovery process (review Chapter 4). However, the affect associated with a prior, unresolved history of sexual abuse does not have to be overwhelming to the client, particularly when a gradual, hypnotically assisted recall is utilized. Guidelines for this type of approach are spelled out clearly in a recent volume by Brown and Fromm (1986). Let's now discuss a case in greater detail that combines some of the elements discussed in this initial portion of the chapter.

Jennifer was 9 years old at the time she was referred to me by her local county social services center. Her mother had become aware just recently that Jennifer was behaving in a sexually aggressive manner with the two younger sons of her mother's best friend. Only three months earlier, Jennifer had told her mother that her stepfather, from whom Jennifer's mother was divorced, had molested her approximately a year and a half earlier, beginning when Jennifer's mother was pregnant with her second child and continuing for approximately six months. This sexual abuse had involved oral-genital contact on several occasions and some threats to maintain silence. Jennifer had visited with the social worker briefly after the initial disclosure but no follow-up therapy had been arranged. Now, with the threat of losing her best friend, Jennifer's mother did arrange for a consultation and followed through with a prolonged course of treatment; the initial portion had a substantial hypnotherapy component.

At our first consultation, Jennifer, her mother, and I met and discussed Jennifer's behavior in general and the behavior with the two young boys in particular. Later in the interview, I saw Jennifer alone and I asked her to speak generally about how she was feeling. Jennifer was unusually poignant when she stated, "A lot of times I think about dying." She went on to talk about her feelings of embarrassment and her mother's anger toward her. She was only able to speak in general terms about her previous abuse and admitted that it made her "feel bad," and seemed surprised to hear me say, "I think your being sexual with these boys is connected to what your stepfather did." This freed Jennifer to talk a little bit more deeply, and she was able to describe the feelings that she had at the time she molested these two young boys. Essentially, she felt "sort of like killing myself but then I wouldn't and I would go do that with them." She drew a picture of those feelings for me and they were a formless blob of black and red.

When asked if she would like to make those feelings more manageable, she said very eagerly, "Yeah, for sure." I then introduced the concept of hypnosis to her and told her about finding a favorite place in her mind, which to Jennifer was the previous summer's camping experience through the local YMCA. A deep trance was induced using imagery for induction, and when I made some general suggestions about putting the feelings into safe places so that they would not bother her unless she felt she was in a safe place and could talk about them, Jennifer got up from her chair, moved around the room while still in a trance, and placed what she later described as her "boxes" in different locations in my office. The following excerpt from the trance work is derived from my notes and is not exactly verbatim. It came toward the end of the initial trance.

Therapist: . . . and it feels so nice and safe to be at camp. Remembering all the things you did so well. Away from all the worries that bother you. Far away from them all. Remember how well you swam, how fast you went. In the same way you went far away to camp, you want to put these red and black feelings far away from you. You want to send them off somewhere. Maybe we can imagine boxes, little boxes that we can put these feelings and memories in. Leave them here in the office. You don't need to have them bugging you during the week. Just imagine you're now putting these yucky feelings in little boxes here in my office. You and your mom can drive home tonight and you will feel safe and relaxed, remembering how strong and good you felt at camp. (At this point, Jennifer began to get up from her chair, eyes still closed, and moved around the room.)

A result of this initial intervention was the cessation of further molestation of the two boys. On several occasions, I initiated opening up one of the boxes and Jennifer reluctantly spoke about the contents, which essentially were a collection of vague and negative feelings. The rest of the 13 months of therapy consisted of conjoint sessions with Jennifer, her mother, and younger sister, focusing on the mother-daughter relationship, and facilitating more consistent and positive parenting.

A breakthrough in the therapy occurred when Jennifer's mother was able to see for the first time how similar she and her daughter actually were. The individual therapy during this time used Harter's (1977) technique of allowing Jennifer to see herself in terms other than "all bad," or just "red and black." This process involves both differentiation and integration of new, positive self-percepts, much of which was initiated with hypnosis.

In summary, hypnotherapy was used at the beginning of the therapy as a way of helping Jennifer gain mastery over her impulses and establishing more clearly the link between her abuse and the sexually inappropriate activities in which she was involving these two small boys. Once these feelings were "put away," Jennifer was much more able to focus on the therapy process. When therapy was terminated, progress both at home and at school was reported and symptoms were minimal. However, I did not sense a complete resolution to the abuse experience, and it may be that therapy will resume at a later date. This is certainly possible because she will soon enter adolescence and Jennifer's mother and I parted on good terms.

CONVERSION REACTIONS AND DISSOCIATION

Hypnosis has utility for working through more unusual reactions to chronic victimization. In conversion disorders (previously, hysterical neurosis, conversion type), physical functioning is altered or lost as an expression of psychological conflict (American Psychiatric Association, 1987).

The symptoms, many of which suggest a neurologic disease, usually develop under extreme psychological stress and appear suddenly. The usual age at onset is adolescence or early adulthood, but they also occur in childhood (Rae, 1977). This phenomenon is much less common today than previously, and when it does occur, it appears that there is some relation to lower intelligence and greater social isolation. Goodyer (1981) reported that they are more common in girls and do not appear before the age of 5 years. Because the individual is believed to attain both "primary gain" (the unpleasant event is kept out of awareness) and "secondary gain" (support or protection that is not usually forthcoming), behavioral and family interventions (Dollinger, 1983) have been attempted with reported success.

Pseudoseizures, or hysterical seizures, also have been described as a consequence of sexual abuse (Goodwin, Simms, & Bergman, 1979). Gross (1979) suggested that "for all girls presented to the clinician with symptoms of hysterical seizures, a detailed history should be taken to explore for the possibility of incest." Gross used a combination of psychotherapy and hypnotherapy to treat three of the four cases described. None of the adolescent girls were aware of the connection between their seizures and the incest; all displayed indifference to their symptoms; and all benefitted from secondary gain, which allowed them to be away from the threatening father and also to gain some sympathy from the mother.

Both Gross (1979) and Goodwin et al. (1979) viewed the seizures as protection from further victimization. The belief was that a "sick" girl was now safe from molestation. This type of "literal" defense is true both with the several pseudoseizure sexual-abuse patients I have seen and with another adolescent female who developed a leg-foot paralysis, seemingly to be less available/attractive to her father. Incidentally, when he was confronted with her accusations, he acknowledged partial guilt and also expressed concern about having contributed to her paralysis, whose onset apparently ended the abuse.

In this section, I will briefly describe my work with the four girls I have treated who had pseudoseizures, each of whom developed these as part of a reaction to sexual victimization. Hypnotherapy followed a relatively standard course for these girls, all of whom were easily hypnotizable. The connection between the incest and the seizures was explored during several sessions by using open-ended questions. Two of the four girls had previously made accusations, but these had been ignored. These two were the most readily forthcoming about the abuse (one and two sessions versus three and five sessions, respectively). A 14 year old, whose most overt symptoms decreased but who continued to feel "woozy and faint," was taught self-hypnosis and used this as a way to decrease the frequency of these feelings.

A rather large task remained after the removal of the symptoms, because family relations were severely disrupted by the confirmation of sexual abuse for each girl. In one case, the mother angrily told me, "Can't you see she'll do anything for attention?"

In addition, each of these girls seemed more personally fragmented and less mature than other similar-age victims whom I have seen, making individual therapy more difficult. Hypnotherapy was used during this time as a way to provide a safe "holding environment" in the therapy room (Sands, 1986). Michelle, a 13 year old, would sometimes ask me to "talk like you do," meaning use my slower, more modulated trance voice.

Pseudoseizures are in the domain of dissociative responses. Dissociation is defined in the DSM III-R as

> a disturbance or alteration in the normally integrative functions of identity, memory, or consciousness. The disturbance or alteration may be sudden or gradual, and transient or chronic. If it occurs primarily in identity, the person's customary identity is temporarily forgotten, and a new identity may be assumed or imposed . . . , or the customary feelings of one's own reality is lost and is replaced by a feeling of unreality. . . . If the disturbance occurs primarily in memory, important personal events cannot be recalled.

The most extreme manifestations of dissociation are individuals with multiple personality disorder (Kluft, 1984). Greeted with skepticism by many clinicians, several recent reports have presented small case samples of children with multiple personality (Bowman, Blix, & Coons, 1985; Malenbaum & Russell, 1987; Weiss, Sutton, & Utecht, 1985) or with incipient multiple personality disorder (Fagan & McMahon, 1984). Each of the children described in these case reports was multiply sexually abused or traumatized in some other fashion.

Although I have seen numerous instances of dissociation during projective assessment and when the child and I are discussing the abuse, I have had direct or consultative involvement with only three children who claimed a dual identity and who also had significant periods of dissociation. One presented with a torn rectum and bruised labia at the emergency room with her aunt one evening and she remained in the hospital for several days. Only 6 years old, Gwendolyn eventually disclosed, over a 12-month period, persistent sexual abuse. Other instances of oral sexual assault, witnessing a murder, witnessing battering between her mother and other men, and also being left alone for several days at a time were uncovered. On three occasions, she identified herself to me as a different child, complete with new name, and would act differently for a brief period, never lasting more than one minute. Her self-mutilative behavior was distressing to her several sets of foster parents, did not decrease with behavioral programs, and seemed to occur after some reminder of previous traumatic events.

Only after I used hypnosis, with suggestions of not harming her body, along with additional suggestions of safety, did her self-mutilative behavior stop. Although she is still in therapy in another setting, additional progress is slow. I saw hypnotherapy as being useful with her, particularly to the extent that it allowed her to feel internally safe and less fragmented and reached her on the level that "someone did hurtful things to you and you do not need to do hurtful things to yourself."

Diagnosis of dissociative disorders invites muddy thinking. At times, when I have raised a skeptical voice about the frequency with which I hear some clinicians diagnosing them, I have felt unheard by and somehow disloyal to the field of victim therapy. Yet I am aware of the marked suggestibility of people with dissociative disorders and question whether our interventions, on occasion, can be iatrogenic. I would rather that these individuals come to see themselves not as oddities, but rather as individuals who, despite being profoundly traumatized, have been rather creative in their self-protection, preserving a portion of intactness somewhere inside that can now be allowed to emerge and grow.

Along these lines, some recent research has added support to the belief that the kinds of clinical interview procedures used in the diagnosis of multiple personality may encourage and legitimize enactments of this syndrome (Spanos, Weekes, Menary, & Bertrand, 1986).

The use of hypnotherapy in these more arcane cases should not detract from its overall utility for enhancing the relationship, providing a sense of safety, increasing a sense of mastery and integrity, and decreasing specific abuse- and nonabuse-related symptoms. It provides both useful tools and a framework for your therapy with this difficult population.

9

Management of Sexually Reactive and Aggressive Behaviors

Every persecutor was once a victim . . . someone who was allowed to feel free and strong from childhood does not have the need to humiliate another person.

Alice Miller

Any book dealing with the psychotherapy of sexually abused children and their families should have a chapter on the treatment of sexual behaviors in sexually abused children. However, that is often not the case. I believe there are several reasons for this. The first reflects our own unease at acknowledging children as sexual beings, particularly subsequent to sexual abuse. In a recent survey of 110 inpatient psychiatric institutions, sexual behavior exhibited by sexually abused children in the treatment setting was identified as one of the more difficult behaviors for staff members to manage (Kohan et al., 1987). Inappropriate staff responses found in the study included avoidance, disgust, restriction, and punishment. The authors stated that the staff's lack of knowledge regarding the handling of overt sexual behavior contributed to greater anxiety and ineffectiveness in their response. This seemed to lead to more feelings of incompetence and inappropriate actions. Our personal frame of reference usually does not include children "grabbing" adults in a sexual way.

A second reason probably has to do with the sex of therapists working with sexually abused children. From my discussions with female therapists around the country, I believe that my male colleagues and I see more sexual behavior than they do because of our differential stimulus value to children. Males may cue sexual behaviors in children who have been sexually abused by males. Some children are much more pansexual and may interact sexually with any adult or child, but the majority of children are more cue-specific and males can and do trigger this behavior. Given the fact that more females than males are therapists for sexually abused children, they may not see the sexual behavior that I see in the therapy session, nor may the child's mother.

A third reason has to do with parents' defensive mechanisms. If the parents know that their child has been sexually abused, and they feel guilty about it and blame themselves for it occurring, they are going to be much more prone to denying the existence of sexual behavior even though it is present. Parents of many sexually abused children have blinders for deviant behavior. (That explains the type of spouses they choose and the inconsistent parenting they exhibit.) Sometimes they notice it, and sometimes they do not.

A clear example of this is in a family I am currently working with, which consists of a mother and two boys, 8 and 4 years of age. A large part of the first several months of therapy focused on helping her to recognize how aggressive her boys were toward her and to identify that some other behaviors with each other and with her were sexual in nature. For example, they were destructive of property in the room, pulled her hair, pinched her breasts, and punched her bottom as she walked down the hall.

An essential part of my therapy was training her to observe her children's behavior appropriately. If I had simply allowed her to report to me what behaviors were going on each week, I would not have known whether or not she had truly targeted the appropriate behaviors, and we would never have made the gains that we have. I was somewhat relentless, talking first in the session about what we would do in response to the children's aggression toward her or each other, deciding on a consequence (e.g., in-room time-out, no candy rewards), and then asking her what needed to happen after each display of behavior. She could get so caught up in her own legitimate woes that she would completely miss many behaviors. I am convinced that her basic dependent stance has kept her in the therapy and reasonably cooperative. Another patient might have not hung in as long as she has.

A final reason is related to the fact that our treatment field is divided into two generally nonoverlapping camps — victim therapists and offender therapists. Seeing a child as both a victim and a perpetrator requires mental gymnastics and flexibility. Much of victim therapy appropriately is supportive and depends on the development of the relationship. Offender therapists typically eschew the relationship as irrelevant, something that gets in the way, and rely heavily on confrontation. Thus a dilemma exists.

How do you treat a young, sexually aggressive child? — as a victim? an offender? both? If both, in what order? Support and compassion for older offenders, prior to their owning up to their responsibility for their sexual behavior, are clinically seen as inappropriate. Do these guidelines also apply to children who molest other children?

I believe that both schools of therapy can contribute to the development of appropriate therapies for young sexually aggressive children. However, it will require a great deal of effort and an appreciation that there is heterogeneity among child and adolescent offenders, some requiring treatment weighted more heavily on the offender side, others requiring a more victim-focused treatment.

Given that sexual behavior is one of the more reliable indicators of sexual abuse and is one of the more frequent sequelae of sexual abuse, this is an important treatment area. In addition, we know that a certain percentage of sex offenders were sexually abused as children. The field is still unclear about those mechanisms that transform sexual-abuse victims into victimizers, but I think it is safe to say that children who are sexually abused who then become victimizers are making a powerful statement that their earlier victimization was not resolved. Thus, we should be sensitive to both the short- and long-term implications of sexual behavior.

Lucy Berliner and her colleagues at the Harborview Sexual Assault Center in Seattle, Washington developed a set of diagnostic criteria for child sexual behavior disturbances (Berliner, Manaois, & Monastersky, 1986). In their model, they see these disturbances as having three levels that are ranked on severity. The most severe is coercive sexual behavior. This includes aggressive sexual contact and socially coercive sexual contact. The first would involve physical force, including injury. The second would imply the use of threat and social coercion. Berliner et al. stated, "This behavior always warrants assessment and intervention. It should be considered serious, unacceptable, and may be associated/ found with other antisocial behavior."

The second level is labeled developmentally precocious sexual behavior. This includes attempted or completed intercourse but, although the behavior is both explicit and intentional, no coercion is present. The authors felt that these behaviors are not always evidence of psychological disturbance but, because they are developmentally out of the ordinary, require evaluation. The evaluation should address such variables as:

1. the child's age
2. the family contacts

3. how and where this behavior was learned
4. the frequency and persistence of the behavior
5. whether or not the child has continued access to sexually explicit materials or the opportunities to watch sexually explicit activity.

The third and final level is labeled inappropriate sexual behavior. Various behaviors are included in this category:

1. persistent masturbation
2. masturbation in public
3. masturbation causing pain/irritation
4. touching the breasts/genitals of others
5. asking others to touch the child's genitals
6. excessive interest in sexual matters
7. sexualization of nonsexual situations
8. sexually stylized behavior imitative of adult sexual relationships
9. sexualized content in play, art, or conversation
10. repeatedly or publicly showing genitals.

Again, these behaviors are not necessarily evidence of psychological disturbance unless:

1. they occur in inappropriate situations or contexts
2. the child's development is interfered with
3. the behavior persists despite intervention
4. there are multiple sexual behaviors reported
5. the sexual behavior is accompanied by other disturbed behavior.

What can be gleaned from the writings of Berliner and her colleagues is that sexual behavior in children exists along a continuum, with some of the behavior being quite extreme, indicative of psychological disturbance, and warranting coordinated intervention. What I would like to focus on in this chapter are sexual behaviors that are coercive and inappropriate, and also sexual behaviors that I label as reactive. These reactive sexual behaviors seem to emerge as a function of the sexual abuse, but they do not appear to be coercive in nature — at least not initially.

In the next section we will review the modest amount of literature on sexually aggressive children and adolescents and try to extrapolate information from the literature on adult offenders that might be useful to understanding and treating sexually aggressive children. A further subset of behavior is sexually reactive behavior, that is, behavior that is immediately reactive to the abuse and creates management difficulties.

Sexually reactive behavior may not have an aggressive component to it but may simply be a heightened sexuality in sexually abused children, either transient or more prolonged in nature.

LITERATURE ON SEXUALLY AGGRESSIVE CHILDREN AND ADOLESCENTS

Three recent papers focus on the issue of sexually aggressive behavior in sexually abused young children. All three of these papers go beyond the limited body of case report literature (Arroyo, Eth, & Pynoos, 1984; Yates, 1982), and each discusses a larger number of children.

The first paper evaluated 22 children, 4 to 11 years of age, who had been referred for sexually aggressive behavior (Friedrich & Luecke, 1988). These were then contrasted with 22 boys, 5 to 13 years of age, who had completed a sexual-abuse treatment program. Sixteen of the 22 children who were referred for evaluation were identified as sexually aggressive, meaning that they had behaved in a coercive manner, their behavior was persistent, and it involved genital contact with a child who was at least two years younger than the perpetrator.

A relatively standard assessment procedure was used with each child. Twelve of the 16 sexually aggressive children were male. They received primary DSM-III diagnoses of conduct disorder (8), oppositional disorder (4), adjustment disorder (2), dysthymia (1), and schizophrenia (1). The majority lacked appropriate social skills and were seen as sexually preoccupied, evidenced not only by their overt behavior but also by their responses on projective assessment. Accompanying school problems were a universal finding for those children who were in school. Their types of offenses against children mimicked the abuse that they had received. The quality of their parent-child relations was characterized by a history of maternal absence and neglect, projective identification of the child, and a general absence of emotional support provided to the child. When support was provided, it was rarely adequate. Fifty percent of the mothers had a previous history of chemical dependency.

Powell (1987) presented data on 15 children who were drawn from a consecutive sample of children referred to a program at UCLA for sexually abused children. She followed this larger sample over the years and identified the 15 children who had later committed a sexual offense. Usually these offenses occurred when the children were between 14 and 15 years of age. The majority of the children who were later seen as sexually aggressive were male (11 of 15); this sample had been abused for an average of 2.7 years. What seemed to discriminate the sexually aggressive children from sexually abused children who were not sex- ually aggressive was reflected in the poor quality of parent-child rela- tionships, and the greater extent and severity of the abuse that they had experienced.

Finally, in the largest study done to date, Johnson (1988) identified 47 boys between 4 and 13 years of age who were described as having molested children younger than themselves. Coercion was involved in all cases, and each of these children was treated in a child perpetrator program in southern California. Approximately 50% of the boys had been sexually abused prior to their own sexually abusive behaviors, and 19% reported a history of physical abuse. There was a history of sexual and physical abuse in the majority of the families of these children as well as a history of substance abuse. Almost half of the children who were sexually abused by these boys were siblings. The average number of victims was two; the age range of the victims was 1 to 7 years and they were an average of 2 years younger than the offender.

Burgess and her colleagues (Burgess, Hartman, & McCormack, 1987) did not study sexually aggressive young children per se, but they did follow up on 34 young people who had been sexually abused as children six or eight years after the abuse had occurred and contrasted them with 34 subjects who had not been abused. The authors were particularly interested in understanding what "may operate in conjunction with sexual abuse that leads to the externalizing behaviors of drug use, juve- nile delinquency, and criminal behavior." So their study is pertinent to the concerns in this chapter.

The authors found that boys who were in adult and peer sex and pornography rings for an extended time, who were not supported upon disclosure, and who were socially excluded and dropped out of school were much more likely to become involved in delinquent and criminal behavior. Children who were molested for a briefer time and whose families were more stable and nonblaming did not display delinquent or criminal behaviors significantly more than their non-sexually abused siblings. The boys who had more negative outcomes also were far more likely to have a history of physical abuse prior to the sexual molestation. Thus, the intervening variables that made for a better prognosis were clearly family- and abuse-related.

Burgess and her colleagues felt that the boys who had a poor outcome "managed their flashbacks through the extension of drug abuse, and the ring-specific behaviors of compulsive masturbation, prostitution, and aggressive acts continued and escalated." The pattern of results provides support for the "victim to patient" process decribed by Rieker and Car-

men (1986), which is an interaction among abuse events, family relationships, and other social contexts.

The conclusions from the three papers reviewed, in addition to
Burgess, seem to state clearly that sexually coercive children represent a
significantly more challenging treatment group than the typical sexually
abused child. Not only was their abuse more severe but also supportive
family contexts were unlikely. Somewhat more literature is available on
adolescent sex offenders and we will examine that in the next section.

LITERATURE ON ADOLESCENT SEX OFFENDERS

Several fairly recent studies provide typologies of adolescent sex offenders and offer the realization that this is actually a rather heterogeneous group of individuals. A typology is useful to the extent that it can
provide concrete descriptions of behaviors, personality and family correlates, and motivations for each type of offender. This provides a
framework for suggesting appropriate treatment modalities and strategies for each type of adolescent perpetrator.

O'Brien and Bera (1986) reported on 350 adolescent offenders treated
through the PHASE program in Minnesota. These adolescents were
divided into seven distinct groups based on their behaviors and associated personal and family variables. The types included:

1. the naive experimenter
2. the undersocialized child exploiter
3. the pseudosocialized child exploiter
4. the sexually aggressive
5. the sexually compulsive
6. the disturbed impulsive
7. the group-influenced.

The labels are actually relatively explanatory. This seven-category typology initially was a two-type classification. The prognosis is seen as
most bleak for types 2, 3, 4, 5, and 6. This typology was derived infor-
mally from clinical experiences.

The MMPI was used as the vehicle to empirically develop a typology
for 262 adolescent males who had committed sexual offenses (Smith,
Monastersky, & Deisher, 1987). The authors derived four clusters. The
first two clusters had normal range profiles on the MMPI, with Group I
seen as shy, overcontrolled, and quite anxious. Moral rigidity was also
noted. Group II also had a normal range profile and was seen as socially

outgoing, not having impaired judgment, but exhibiting problems in the area of emotional overcontrol. Group III was seen as the most disturbed and was demanding, narcissistic, argumentative, insecure, and overly reliant on personal fantasy. Group IV was undersocialized and isolated and exhibited distrust, alienation, impulsivity, and poor judgment.

It appears that far greater heterogeneity is seen among older adolescent offenders than among young children who are sexually aggressive. For example, the younger the child, the more likely the child has also been sexually abused. In addition, sexually aggressive behavior is usually a function of an ongoing oppositional or conduct disorder. With older children and adolescents, however, other contributing variables result in different personality manifestations.

Becker (1988) provided some useful information on what variables seem to be operative in adolescents who later offend sexually (see Table 9-1). Three groups of variables (individual, family, and societal) are thought to contribute to initial offending. For example, an adolescent with a history of physical or sexual abuse, in a covertly sexually coercive family, and who is involved in an antisocial peer group would be at risk for initial offending. Reoffending is viewed as probable depending on one or more of four variables:

TABLE 9-1
Characteristics Leading to Initial and Repeat Sexual Offenses in Adolescents

Initial offending*	Later offending

Individual characteristics
  Impulse control
  Conduct disorder
  Impaired cognitive abilities
  History of physical or sexual abuse
	Reoffending
	  Initial offending pleasurable
	  Minimal consequences
	  Deviant behavior reinforced via
	    masturbation or fantasy
	  Socially deficient

Family characteristics
  Sexually or physically coercive—
    overt
  Sexually coercive—covert
  Interpersonally isolated
	No further offending
	  Negative consequences

Social factors
  Societal condoning
  Antisocial peer group	

*Adapted from "The Effects of Child Sexual Abuse on Adolescent Sexual Offenders" by J.V. Becker, in G.E. Wyatt and G.J. Powell (Eds.), *Lasting Effects of Child Sexual Abuse*, 1988, Beverly Hills: Sage.

1. the nature of the consequences for the first offense
2. whether the offending was pleasurable
3. whether or not the adolescent reinforces this emerging pattern of deviant behavior with fantasy or masturbation
4. the adolescent's level of social skills.

It is also useful to examine some relevant literature on adult offenders at this time. Although Groth (1979) developed a typology categorizing adult offenders into two groups — fixated as opposed to regressed — little empirical support for this dichotomy has surfaced. Adult offenders are quite heterogeneous and the percentage reporting a prior history of sexual abuse varies from one study to the next, depending on whether incarcerated or treatment samples are being used. In a review of the MMPI literature on sex offenders, I noted that not only was there not a typical sex offender profile but also that the MMPI revealed an enormous amount of heterogeneity (Friedrich, 1988b). This supports the idea that there is no such thing as the "profile of a sex offender," nor is there an MMPI profile or personality test profile for incestuous fathers.

The increasing variability noted among adolescents, contrasted with their preadolescent sexually aggressive counterparts, is seen also in adults. Clinical experience with adult pedophilic sex offenders has implicated four identifying characteristics of this population (Lanning, 1986):

1. a long-term pattern of behavior
2. children as preferred sexual objects
3. evidence for well-developed techniques in obtaining victims
4. sexual fantasies that focus primarily on children.

The degree to which these four characteristics identify adolescent and younger child offenders has not yet been determined, and I am not advocating relying solely on adult-derived criteria for understanding sexually aggressive children.

Some of the sexually aggressive children, particularly those who have larger numbers of victims, are characterized by these features. The first child I saw who clearly was sexually aggressive reported preoccupation with sexual activity with children, had a specific age group that he preferred, used candy and other enticements to get access to these children, and had been sexually acting out with children for at least a third of his life. He was only 9 years of age and already had multiple victims. As you would expect, he had been molested for several years.

HOW IS SEXUAL TRAUMA LINKED TO
SEXUALLY AGGRESSIVE BEHAVIOR?

Various theoretical perspectives provide some explanation regarding how sexual trauma and sexual acting out are related. The first perspective that should be reviewed is a behavioral perspective, given the fact that considerable work has been done by behavioral researchers in the area of aggression and delinquency. Beginning with Bandura (1977), who proposed that modeling was critical in learning new behavior, the concept of modeling has explained how it is that children see aggressive behavior and then act on it. Predisposing variables, making it even more likely for children to interact aggressively after witnessing aggression, were being male, being less socialized, and coming from more punitive families.

Another behavioral concept is paired-associate learning, which posits that there is a link between a behavior and an affective response (Wolpe, 1973). A behavior is more likely to be repeated if it is paired with an affective response that is pleasurable. Aggression is accompanied by the release of neurotransmitters that reinforce the aggression; this increases the likelihood of further aggression. In addition, sexual aggression carries with it satisfaction from aggression and sexual activities, making the likelihood of recurrence even greater.

Social learning perspectives would also be useful in understanding the development of aggression and conduct problems over time, because sexually aggressive young children are usually oppositional or conduct-disordered concurrently with their sexual acting out. Patterson (1986) developed a model from his extensive research indicating quite clearly that disrupted family-management skills lead to the development of antisocial child behavior. The noncompliant and coercive features of the child's behavior put the child at maximal risk for rejection by normal peers and for academic failure. This results in further parental rejection and solidifies the child's developing loss of self-esteem.

Children's levels of aggression are quite stable over time; by the time peer relationships are problematic, the child is well on the way to an antisocial pattern of interaction. This is sad given that, after the family, normal peer group exchanges are critical contributors to the child's learning about empathy, reciprocity, and cooperation. Omitting peer relationships from normal development could mean that the child will have an inadequate basis for later developing intimate or enduring relationships.

Substance abuse in the parent is another contributor to family management problems and thus to antisocial behavior. Recently, Patterson (1986) reported that maternal heavy drinking correlated with inept monitoring and decreased parental involvement. Finally, males are more prone than females to being socialized in a manner that allows for acting out rather than acting in.

Several psychodynamic perspectives are of importance here in understanding sexual aggression in children who have been sexually abused. Object relations theorists report that children internalize representations of experiences with different people and will then act according to these internalizations (Guntrip, 1969). A child who receives consistently positive nurturing that is unconditional and satisfying will internalize these dimensions of the caregiver and will interact in future caregiving roles in a manner that is quite similar. A child who is sexually abused is going to be more likely to internalize that into his or her behavioral repertoire.

This concept is similar to the developmental psychology concept of a "functional map of relationships" discussed in Chapter 2. When a similar situation presents itself, that is the model that is called forward and possibly acted on. Objects are essentially people who interact with the child and the sum total of their interactions is incorporated into the child's emerging being. The degree to which these interactions are not overly exciting makes them more likely to be incorporated into some type of coherent sense of self. If they are overstimulating or overly exciting, it is likely that they will be split off and not incorporated into a coherent sense of self, but they will still exist in the child's potential behavioral repertoire.

This is where more traditional psychodynamic formulations of dissociation and primitive defenses come into play. These split-off experiences, or object relations, in one way or another are dissociated or kept out of awareness. This is why it is traditionally thought that people who act in a dissociative state are unaware of what they are doing and will deny the existence of their actions. Their understanding of themselves precludes the existence of this behavior.

More specific to traditional views of ego defense mechanisms are the processes of undoing and identification with the aggressor (Freud, 1966). Although the latter concept can also be seen, from social learning terms, as directly related to modeling, e.g., the child is abused and thus abuses, Schafer (1968) wrote that identification with the aggressor is more likely to occur only with children temperamentally prone to be more active and less inhibited.

New research in developmental psychology, particularly cognitive development and social development, also provides ways to understand sexual aggression as seen in the sexually abused child. For example, it can be stated that a child who is sexually aggressive is nonempathic in that instance. Empathy, which has both cognitive and affective components, is one of five core moral emotions according to Damon (1988). It means "reacting to another's feelings with an emotional response that is similar to the other's feelings." In order to react to another child's feelings, the child must first recognize accurately the other's feelings.

The cognitive ability to discern another's inner psychological state is called perspective-taking. Initial skills in perspective-taking are usually quite limited. Thus, children's empathic responses will increase in frequency and scope only as they become more cognitively sophisticated. By the end of the second year, children have a firmer grasp of others' needs and feelings as distinct from their own. Over the next few years they become more aware that every person's perspective is unique and that someone else may have a different reaction to a situation. This enables them to respond more appropriately to another's distress. Children learn to make a more objective assessment of another's needs while putting themselves in the other's place in order to locate the true source of distress.

> Empathic dysfunctions can create the conditions for serious antisocial behavior. Young people convicted of violent crimes often express their lack of feeling for their victim's distress. This can take several forms, all of which serve to promote or justify the violent act. (Damon, 1988)

This lack of empathy was documented in a study I conducted with Luecke (1988). A 6-year-old boy, sodomized by his stepfather and sexually assaultive of his younger sister, delighted in slamming a drawer on my hands, laughing gleefully at the pain he caused. This lack of empathy also underscores the need for empathy training in therapy that is focused on sexually aggressive children and adolescents. A lack of empathy may be evident in sexually abused children, but the full effect of this may not be seen until they are parents or caregivers and then fail to be sensitive to the needs of their own children.

The second developmental strand involves socialization and peer relationships. Lack of socialization and failure to accept rules of normal behavior are common in sexually aggressive children. The socialization process begins in a child's first significant relationship, that is, with the parents, most typically the mother. Failures in the attachment of the parent to the child contribute to the child's failing in relationships with peers. Instead of learning how to negotiate or compromise, the child learns an inconsistent and sometimes explosive pattern of relating. Because the child is frequently demeaned, he or she learns how to demean others. It is difficult to see how the demeaning that is so central to the confrontational style of most offenders' therapists can be truly helpful unless it is balanced by careful attention to also developing the relationship.

The extent to which these perspectives explain sexually reactive behavior depends on the child. Sexually reactive children may simply be reflecting recent and profound disorganization that is then resolved and sexual behavior problems are not seen later. However, sexually aggressive children appear to have this behavior more firmly entrenched.

MANAGING SEXUALLY REACTIVE BEHAVIOR

We will first discuss managing sexually reactive behavior in sexually abused children and then turn to the more difficult task of managing sexually aggressive behavior in children. To reiterate, by sexually reactive we mean sexualized behavior that appears to be in direct response to recent sexual abuse. This would include masturbation, increased sexual exploration, exhibitionism, and a temporary breakdown in the children's interpersonal boundaries.

What is needed first is a careful assessment of the child in the family context so that a seemingly unmanageable case can be made more manageable. Many clinicians lose their usual clear-thinking abilities when it comes to sexual behavior; starting off by objectively collecting data can be one way of orienting oneself to this task.

The first assessment step would be to identify whether or not the child's behavior is normative for children of that age or for children with a similar history of abuse. There is an increase in sexual behavior generally between 4 to 6 years of age in many children. This will be true for children with a history of sexual abuse and the discovery of the abuse may overlap with this age. Thus, a parent's reaction to the child's "newly discovered" sexuality may be in part a reaction to normative behavior. Using the Child Sexual Behavior Inventory (Friedrich et al., 1989) as a way of assessing the full range of behaviors is helpful. Any coercive sexual behavior identified should raise a red flag, but even those children with 8 to 10 items checked, reflecting a heightened interest in sexual behavior, may simply be more aptly described as sexually reactive.

I am reminded at this instance of a family I saw in which the young girl had a carcinoma of the vulva. This had been diagnosed when she was quite young and by the time I saw her, when she was 4½ years of age, she had become quite focused on her perineum; her compulsive masturbation was becoming a real problem both medically and personally to the parents. Her repeated physical examinations in the context of a teaching hospital had had a powerful focusing effect on her toward her perineum. After the consultation, we changed the manner in which she was being managed medically, removing all other observers from the room and using only one pediatrician. In addition, her parents were instructed how to extinguish this behavior, e.g., restricting it to a specific room and time, responding matter-of-factly, and praising her when she did not masturbate.

I followed the child for several years and by the time she was 6 years old, she had lost the genital focus that she had earlier exhibited. It appeared that her earlier preoccupation with her genitals, plus the normal increase in sexual interest at that age, had combined to make the increase in sexual interest even greater. But the fact that she had not been abused and that the family responded appropriately allowed her to have a normal developmental transition through the 4- to 6-year range, with a subsequent decrease in sexual behavior.

My mention of the normal parental response is important because how the family reacts to the child's sexual behavior determines, in part, whether or not the sexually reactive behavior becomes of greater concern. Recall that the victim becomes a patient due in part to how the family reacts to the abuse (Rieker & Carmen, 1986). Families that are used to dealing with their children's behavior in a consistent manner may continue to do so and may extinguish the sexually reactive behavior quite naturally over a short time. However, parents who have a history of responding consistently with regard to other behaviors may become quite disoriented when it comes to sexual behavior; their previous excellent parenting may now fall apart and they may react variably and inconsistently.

Another family dimension that may be useful to think about involves the dichotomy of parents into erotophobic and erotophilic. This dichotomy came about as a way of explaining an individual's erotic orientation. Parents who are on the phobic end may respond overly punitively or with greater anxiety to a child's sexually reactive behavior. Parents at the erotophilic extreme may actually perpetuate the child's sexually reactive behavior due to their own higher level of sexualization and their inability to perceive that the child's behavior is out of the range of normal and reflects a cry for help.

One mother who could be categorized as erotophilic put significant restrictions on her somewhat flamboyant heterosexual behavior after she realized that her daughter's sexual behavior was being exaggerated by the home environment. As we were finishing up a successful course of treatment, she told me, "I needed to get my life in order so that I could help my little girl not be so screwed up in her head about sex."

Related to family reaction is the meaning that the family attaches to the behavior. Burgess et al. (1987), in their paper on antecedents of socially deviant behavior, detailed quite clearly the range of appropriate and inappropriate parental responses to the disclosure of the abuse. If the parents view the sexually reactive behavior as now meaning that their child has been hopelessly contaminated, they are not going to be able to manage it adequately.

One of the boys discussed by Friedrich and Luecke (1988) had a mother whose primary concern was whether or not her son's predilection for young female victims as opposed to male victims could leave her assured that he would not be homosexual. When I refused to give her a clear answer but expressed my deep concern for her son's behavior, she basically lost interest in the therapy process.

The meaning the family attaches to the child's behavior may reflect an underlying strain in the parent-child relationship. The child's being abused is going to have a depressive impact on many parents and this may cause them to underfunction as parents for a while. When this is combined with a parent's being unable to see what the child needs, this further increases the likelihood of persistent sexually reactive behavior.

Here is another instance in which an MMPI from the parents can be useful. Does their profile reflect a normal increase in depression and anxiety subsequent to their child's abuse, or does it actually suggest their usual interpersonal style is passive-aggressive and thus inconsistent? This allows you to plan your treatment approach.

Finally, it is important to assess who is clearly in charge in the family and whether or not the child's sexually reactive behavior is of such degree that some other children in the family are no longer safe. Becker (1988) discussed how initial offending in adolescents becomes more entrenched in some to the point that they become persistent sexual offenders. One of the behaviors that contributes to reoffending is the adolescent's finding that the initial offending was pleasurable; deviant sexual behavior is then reinforced.

The same may be true for younger children. Johnson (1988) found that much of the sexual aggression in her sample was directed at siblings — the most available targets. If the family cannot create safety for other children in the family, due to a parent's inability to assert a parental role consistently, then the child's likelihood of persisting in this behavior is much higher and intervention should be planned accordingly.

Let us take as a modal example of sexually reactive behavior the compulsive masturbation frequently seen in the sexually abused child after abuse. Over the years, I have evolved a five-part plan for working with families in this area.

1. Assess parental attitudes and behavior related to the masturbation.
2. Shape positively the child's nonmasturbatory time.
3. Create a time and place for the child to masturbate.
4. Normalize the masturbation.
5. Deal with the child's abuse experience because this, in part, is driving the masturbation.

Regarding the first component of the intervention, assessing parental attitudes and behavior related to the specific instances of masturbation, it is important to be specific about what sexual behavior the parents have observed and where. It is important to find out how the parents reacted to the child's behavior, either punitively, appropriately, or by ignoring the behavior. Do the parents have an idea about the origins of the masturbation and its relationship to the child's sexual abuse? Some parents I have worked with have not seen the connection so that simply establishing the masturbation as a consequence of the abuse has helped them to have some empathy for the child and to adopt more appropriate management.

Here is also the opportunity to determine the nature of the parent-child relationship and whether it is positive or strained. Sometimes we are working with foster parents who have not had much interaction with the child, but who do have some fairly rigidly held beliefs about the negative aspects of sexual behavior, including masturbation. Here also you have the opportunity to teach the parents a little bit about behavioral observation and to obtain baseline data that includes time and place and the parents' usual reaction to the masturbation.

After a determination of the frequency of the child's behavior, intervention can be established. It is important for the parent to positively reinforce the child at times that the child is not masturbating when he or she might have in the past. This can be in the form of positive verbal statements, e.g., "Sometimes when you're sitting on the couch you touch yourself but I'm glad to see that you're sitting on the couch now and you're not doing that." The parent can also work to keep the child busier during the usual times the child has masturbated in the past.

The third component may be difficult for parents who are punitive or whose sexual beliefs are quite restrictive. In many ways this part of the intervention is paradoxical — you are asking a child who is exhibiting some impulse-control problems to now display the behavior. Negotiating this with the family requires your having a working alliance with the child's caregivers. I have had some difficulty with families with rigid fundamental religious beliefs. However, the important component is that the family and the child work out a preassigned time and place for the child to masturbate. If the child is observed masturbating at a time and place other than the preassigned time and place, the parent is instructed simply to gently remind the child about the agreement. The child then is requested to go to his or her room for a few minutes. As the child becomes more compliant, the program can be phased out.

It is also important to normalize the child's masturbatory behavior. The most usual way would be to link it directly to the sexual-abuse experience. When families require a more direct type of intervention, I attempt to tie it directly to the family. I may make a statement such as, "He is going to need to do that as long as he thinks people have a hard time understanding what happened to him." This is reserved for families who are usually more unsupportive and inconsistent with the child and who are making the child a scapegoat. My intervention with them, and this usually needs to be repeated several times, attempts to make the child's behavior interactive. The child is not going to stop until the message is clearly received by the rest of the family.

For example, I worked with a young mother and her young school-age daughter who was distracting her classmates and teacher with her sexual behavior, particularly vigorous masturbation. The father's visitation was suspended, but the mother was lax about allowing contact. We were making no progress, and I confronted the mother about my suspicions that the daughter was still seeing her father and reacting to his presence, even if no overt abuse was occurring. At about that time, the father was jailed on several outstanding warrants and was out of circulation for almost six months. The daughter's rapid cessation of masturbation in the first four weeks of his being jailed finally convinced the mother of the direct relationship between her daughter's behavior and exposure to the father. This then gave the mother the resolve to discontinue contact once the father was released.

Finally, I believe that compulsive masturbation that continues to persist after these benign types of interventions is related to a lack of resolution around the abuse experience. In these cases, use of the traumatic events interview in several supportive sessions may be helpful to the child. I have seen a marked decrease in masturbation frequency after a few gentle uncovering sessions that focused on the abuse experience.

This approach can be utilized with various sexually reactive behaviors. In a supportive environment, the passage of time after the abuse may result in a reduction in sexual behavior (Friedrich et al., 1986), but this approach can greatly speed the process.

MANAGING SEXUALLY AGGRESSIVE BEHAVIOR

Rather than considering the full age range of children who are sexually aggressive, I focus here on sexually aggressive children 12 years of age and younger. (For guidance with adolescent sex offenders, you might turn to Bolton et al., 1989; O'Brien and Bera, 1986; and Becker, 1988.) There is greater heterogeneity among adolescent sex offenders. This is thought to be related to the fact that there are multiple pathways leading to sexual offending in this age group, including some having a history of sexual abuse and others not. On the other hand, younger children are far more likely to react to an actual instance or instances of abuse, particularly abuse that has been persistent and aggressive.

It is useful to have as a mind-set, when one is attempting to manage sexually aggressive behavior in young children, that it is a disorder of conduct. Social learning-based approaches that are useful with conduct-disordered children are also useful here. For example, it is a type of behavior that is closely related to a behavior like stealing. Stealing as well as sexually aggressive behavior provides the child with potent and immediate reinforcement. In addition, it is secretively done and frequently the child escapes consequences. I would like to refer you to a slim volume by Patterson, Redi, Jones, and Conger (1975) that can be extremely useful in guiding your intervention with the larger aggressive component common to these children.

Despite the fact that these children usually carry with them a diagnosis of conduct disorder, intervening only with the oppositional or conduct disorder is probably not going to be sufficient to also turn around their sexually coercive behavior. More often than not these are boys from the two most negative family types described by Larson and Maddock (1986): aggression exchange and expression of rage. For the sexual abuse to have persisted for as long as it did, usually with accompanying physical force, and then for the family's response to the abuse to be as inappropriate as it usually is with these children, indicates that this is not going to be the type of family that is easy to engage and work with. On the contrary, these are probably some of the most difficult and frustrating families that I have seen.

The fact that they frequently drop out of treatment is a mixed blessing, because on one hand you may be personally relieved that this onerous family has now disappeared, but on the other hand, you know that the behavior is only going to get worse and other children may be victimized. Thus, it is important at the very beginning to make sure that you have the backing of the appropriate agencies and systems to work with this family and that the family members understand that they must be involved in treatment.

Let's return to assessment. It is a way to make unmanageable cases more manageable. First, sexually coercive behavior is not normative. The family needs to hear that. Getting that message across so that it can be acted on positively is very difficult. The family is willing to listen to new negative things about the child because frequently he or she is viewed negatively already. Your comments would simply join a chorus of negative statements about this child.

What must be done is to motivate the family early on by pointing out that the child's behavior is not normative, that something needs to be done before it gets significantly worse. The child is stating loudly and clearly that he or she is in need of help and part of the child is worried that the situation could get worse. Usually you will find markedly ambivalent mother-child relationships in a family in which parents have not assumed authority the way they need to. In addition, there may be numerous unprotected siblings and other smaller children in the immediate vicinity who are vulnerable to sexual coercion. Their presence may dictate some changes in the treatment approach, e.g., does the child need temporary out-of-the-home placement?

TREATMENT PROCESS

Borrowing largely from social learning theory and the work done by Patterson et al. (1975) and Alexander and Parsons (1982), the treatment process with sexually aggressive children in the family context begins with the identification of small goals, often not related to the sexually abusive behavior per se, and the implementation of a family-wide behavior-management program. It is important that these initial goals are small and comparatively easy to accomplish so that the parent can feel empowered. Usually one is treating a single mother who needs to carve out increasingly larger areas of competence as a parent. Since she is the key to your continued successful therapy, the formation of a therapeutic relationship with her is critical.

These families activate a controlling and blaming style in therapists and it is important that you do not fall into that trap. It may be necessary to complement the social learning approach with some strategic or paradoxical elements, e.g., anticipating failure or prescribing some symptoms.

As Patterson et al. (1975) articulated, these families are characterized by a coercive interaction cycle. The parent and child are used to interacting with each other in a coercive and controlling manner. This existed prior to their coming to your office and usually prior to the abuse. The mother is multiply entrapped (Wahler, 1980), meaning that few of her relationships are working for her. She needs far more support and guidance than is available through an hour a week of family therapy. Getting her involved in group support will help her to work with you so that a clear, firm, but less coercive parenting posture can be established with the child. However, she may put off other people or be so distrustful that group involvement is not a likely option.

In the event that the child is being scapegoated and focused on as the source of all problems in the family to the exclusion of the other children in the family, the therapist might decrease the coercive process by "spreading the symptom around in the family." This family therapy technique is used to create a more systemic focus and to point out to the family that other problems also exist. This is not to remove from the offending child responsibility for his or her actions.

Another way to help the family see the offending child more positively would be to frequently reframe the child's behavior. The child's sexual aggression and his continued acting out "remind us all of what happened to him. He won't let us forget how badly he feels." With one boy, who was locked in an intensely negative relationship with his mother, the mother did grudgingly admit after six or seven sessions that he was becoming easier to manage. Part of her difficulty was that she had left her boyfriend after finding out that he was the perpetrator and still felt quite ambivalent about that. Additionally, she had lost a source of support.

Over and over again I stated to her something along the line of "I think from the fact that he is improving he is trying to tell you that you made the right decision to leave Bob." Another mother, who had a long history of sexual abuse that was not resolved in her own life, began to see her child a bit more positively with my ready use of the reframed statement, "You know your bringing her in to work on her problems is allowing you the opportunity to begin to work on your own abuse. In some ways she's done you a favor."

It is also important to maintain close contact with other people in the child's life, particularly from the school. Obtaining behavior ratings from the teachers will help you determine whether or not the same symptoms that you see are also being reflected there. Working with the school to change educational programming or to enhance the child's competence in school is also critical. You need to have many people in the child's life telling you if the child is changing or not. If the mother is not very competent about informing about inappropriate behavior, other sources are needed.

This is also the opportunity to address the parental history of chemical dependency and unresolved abuse. Assessing for problems in these areas is critical and arranging and facilitating follow-up that can help the parents begin to focus on chemical problems and previous abuse are important. Jesse (1989) points out that it does little good to treat sexual abuse without addressing substance abuse.

Finally, this is rarely brief treatment. Kazdin (1987), in his review of treatment outcome with conduct-disordered children, indicated that childhood antisocial behavior is stable over time, the prognosis is likely to be poor, and antisocial behavior in childhood predicts similar behaviors in one's offspring. He stated that four techniques appear to be especially promising in the treatment of antisocial behavior:

1. management training for parents
2. functional family therapy
3. problem-solving skills training
4. community-based treatment.

With regard to management training for parents, more dramatic and durable effects are evident with protracted or time-unlimited programs extending up to 50 or 60 hours of treatment. Thus, this is a lengthy process.

I would like to describe a relatively typical "successful" case with a sexually aggressive boy and his family. Numerous features in the individuals were unchanged, but from a perspective of behavior change, the boy stopped abusing and the family was functioning in a healthier manner.

The therapy took place during a 21-month period, and there have been several follow-up sessions since the end of this first period of therapy. The Hanson family was an easy family to dislike. Physically unattractive, sometimes unwashed, and always poorly groomed, they would show up early for appointments and "spill out" over the waiting area. Other people there would move away, leaving them isolated in a corner of the waiting room. This seemed to fit their rejected, isolated status in all other areas of their life. They were referred to me after their 10-year-old son, Darrin, was reported to have molested several boys while in a summer camp for children from disadvantaged families.

During the course of therapy, we also found out that he was sexually coercive with his younger brother, Doug, who was 5 years of age. It was not until much later in treatment that we learned that Darrin had been molested by his maternal uncle, approximately one year earlier, during the course of a 3-week cross-country truck ride. Darrin was sodomized numerous times in the back of his uncle's semi-trailer truck.

Mrs. Hanson, who was 20 years younger than her husband, was the oldest of three siblings. Because her mother was a chronic schizophrenic and in and out of the state hospital, she raised her two younger siblings. Although devoted to her father at the time treatment began, she also revealed, during the course of treatment, a long history of sexual abuse by him.

The Hansons lived in a home on the edge of Mr. Hanson's father's farm. Mr. Hanson worked for his father, who also had a history of paranoid schizophrenia and a long history of physical abuse of Mr. Hanson even into adulthood. Mr. Hanson was the oldest of three siblings, and he farmed with his younger brother who was also physically abusive toward Mr. Hanson. Mr. Hanson denied a history of sexual abuse. The parents met while visiting their respective parents at the state hospital where both had been court-ordered for short-term stays.

As is often the case, Darrin's school and peer difficulties were viewed by Mrs. Hanson, the spokesperson of the family, as a greater concern to her than Darrin's sexual behavior. Data obtained from school indicated that Darrin was learning disabled, achieving primarily at the second-grade level, and was also quite inattentive. He had no friends, due in part to the fact that the family lived several miles from their small town. Mrs. Hanson was extremely ambivalent toward Darrin, alternately stating, "He is a great kid," and then indicating in the next breath, "I could strangle him half the time."

Because Darrin was not forthcoming about who had abused him, nor was Doug forthcoming about his own abuse, each parent was interviewed extensively and completed an MMPI. Mr. Hanson's MMPI was suggestive of a rather isolated and dependent individual who was moderately depressed. Mrs. Hanson's MMPI suggested that she was depressed, angry, and inconsistent in her parenting. My sense after several sessions with them was that they had not sexually abused Darrin, and family and individual therapy sessions were scheduled on a weekly basis.

In keeping with my belief that initial goals should be small and easily accomplished, we set a goal for Darrin to complete his daily homework and get it turned in on time. We developed a behavioral program that Mrs. Hanson began to implement and results were quickly forthcoming. This gradually extended to Mrs. Hanson having greater control over TV watching, eating habits, and physical conflict between the two brothers.

After approximately eight family sessions, two new issues emerged. The first was Mrs. Hanson's dilemma about what to do with her mother, who was living in a nearby nursing home and continually harassing her over the phone; when Mrs. Hanson would visit her, her mother would be physically abusive to her. Mrs. Hanson also began to voice displeasure about her relationship with her husband. Apparently, he was completely subservient to his father, who would call at all hours of the day and night to complain about one thing or the other. Mr. Hanson would dutifully field all requests and put up with much verbal abuse over the phone. Each spouse wanted the other to make changes with their respective parent and each contracted with the other to take steps to circumscribe their contact with the abusive parent. Mrs. Hanson was far more successful than her husband, but over the course of the 21 months of therapy, he did get himself named in his father's will, decreased his father's phone calls to five or six times a week, and told his father that he was not going to be pushed around anymore. Mrs. Hanson, on the other hand, cut off all contact with her mother and felt that that was the best she could do.

By this time Darrin informed us who had molested him, and it did not take Doug long to tell about Darrin having molested him. Because of our concern about Darrin and Doug's relationship, we had already gotten the family to put them in separate bedrooms and Mrs. Hanson was somewhat more careful about the boys spending unsupervised time together. Creating greater safety for Doug became a focus of the family sessions. At about this time Mrs. Hanson began a part-time job which added immensely to her self-esteem. This was approximately 12 months into the therapy.

School consultation continued and Darrin was placed on therapy with methylphenidate. During the first 12 months of therapy, he had made approximately 15 months of progress in school, and although still relatively friendless, he was not as disruptive on the bus and reported having more friendly contacts with peers.

After several months of seemingly smooth sailing, with continued progress noted in both boys and the parents, Mrs. Hanson separated from her husband for approximately six weeks. Although their relationship had never appeared to be satisfying to either of them, it appeared to be relatively stable and I was quite surprised. Mr. Hanson brought his sons in twice during the separation and looked devastated. The boys' behavior deteriorated markedly. Two months later, Mrs. Hanson called back to resume therapy and announced that she had returned home a month earlier. After several weekly sessions, the family sessions became more marital in focus and less frequent.

At the end of treatment, Mr. and Mrs. Hanson were more satisfied with their marriage, had defined clearer parental roles with their two boys, created more appropriate boundaries between themselves and their disturbed parents, Doug was at grade level in school and had a close friend, and Darrin was approximately one year behind in all subjects. Although without a best friend, Darrin was seen by his parents and teachers as more appropriately sociable.

This family was different from many of the families I have worked with in that both parents were present and in a relatively stable relationship. Both seemed to view the therapy appointments as their only regular opportunity for socialization and thus became committed to them quite rapidly. Although Mrs. Hanson at times would praise my efforts with them, she would usually strike back the next session by being much more critical of me and demanding results. I nurtured my relationship with her, the true parent in the family, by attending very closely to any physical changes that I saw her make as she became less depressed, e.g., haircut, new glasses, or washed hair.

The success of the initial interventions that we chose was aided by the fact that Darrin and his mother did not have a truly coercive relationship. Rather, it was more of a sister-brother relationship, with Darrin presenting as somewhat immature, socially awkward, and anxious rather than as oppositional or conduct-disordered. He genuinely seemed to welcome her taking greater authority in the family. Once the family context became relatively stable, he could talk about his abuse more readily. Further evidence for the family's growth is the fact that Mrs. Hanson has a female friend from work; she also takes her sons to church each week, where they socialize with other people.

An excerpt from therapy can illustrate more clearly the nature of the therapy and our relationship. This portion is from session 9, when Mrs. Hanson was struggling with what to do with her mother. My goals were to support her decisions and tie her difficulties setting limits with her mother to her developing abilities in setting limits with Darrin.

Mrs. Hanson: Well, what are we coming here for if you're not going to tell me what to do?

Therapist: Okay, what I want you to do is work out something so that you don't have to feel abused by her.

Mrs. Hanson: But she's my mother. She just has to call me and I feel I have to go get her for a visit.

Therapist: Well, what if you just didn't go pick her up?

Mrs. Hanson: I can tell you never loved your mother.

Therapist: Well, uh. You're a tough lady. Maybe you got me there.

Mrs. Hanson: See, I told you.

Therapist: Can I start over again? Back to what to do with your mom, I mean.

Mrs. Hanson: You can do whatever you want to.

Therapist: Okay. You know, Mr. Hanson, you've got a tough wife over here.

Mr. Hanson: Yeah.

Darrin: Yeah.

Therapist: Okay. What do I keep bugging you to do about Darrin not doing the things you want him to do? Taking money from your purse and things.

Mrs. Hanson: You want me to punish him. Get him to mind.

Therapist: Exactly. Show him who's the boss. All I want you to do is take the ability you have gotten with Darrin and use it to show your mom who's the boss.

Mrs. Hanson: But you don't do that to your mother.

Therapist: I'm not asking you to. . . . You know, I'm not going to get anywhere by arguing with you, Mom.

Mrs. Hanson: Good.

Therapist: Yeah, you got me. But I will ask you this. What should . . . what would you tell a friend of yours to do if every time her mom came over to visit her, she got beat up and her kids got scared?

Mrs. Hanson: You're trying to trick me, aren't you?

Therapist: Yeah. Probably.

Mrs. Hanson: Well, I'd tell her to protect herself, to not go get her.

Therapist: Right. You're the mother to your kids. You don't have to be the mother of your mother. When you try to be her mother, it's harder to be Darrin and Dougie's mom. Do it for them. Not for me.

Mrs. Hanson: I don't know.

Therapist: Mr. Hanson, I want you to help your wife. I want you to help her by telling her not to go get her mom the next time she calls from the nursing home. Can you do that?

Mr. Hanson: I don't know. She sort of does what she wants.

Therapist: Well, what if I wrote a prescription? Doctor's orders. You can't see your mom for three months because she's hazardous to your health. She gets in the way of you being the mom you want to be.

Darrin: Yeah.

Therapist: You want her to do that, huh? See, Darrin wants you to do that. He's quite the helper.

Mrs. Hanson: I'll think about it.

The session continued pretty much this way, but several weeks later, Mrs. Hanson did refuse to pick up her mother from the nursing home after she called demanding her to get her. Mrs. Hanson informed her mother that I had ordered her to have no contact. This was the first step in her eventually stopping all contact.

In summary, sexual abuse does activate some behavioral problems relatively unique to the abuse. These sexual behavior problems range along a continuum of severity, related to the severity of the abuse and the dysfunction of the system. When intervention occurs at this early stage, the child is more likely to relate better to peers, and hopefully, the likelihood of revictimization is decreased on a short- and long-term basis.

10

The Person of the Therapist

Sometimes what is called therapy is only a continuation
of early unintended cruelty.

Alice Miller

Writing this book has been a process of personal exploration. One of my goals was to explore some of our internal processing as we work with these children and their families. I believe the book would be incomplete if the important topic of the therapist as a person was not raised. Books that focus on therapy have the opportunity to go beyond techniques and address the therapist. This is particularly the case with sexual abuse, a clinical phenomenon that defies the usual "functional map of relationships" that therapists bring to their clinical work.

Many therapists receive early and intensive training in their family-of-origin to become therapists. We learn early how to comfort, soothe, listen, and direct. However, many of us have not had to deal with such phenomena as exploitation, abuse of power, parental alienation, violence, and a precocious introduction to sexuality. It is true that a percentage of mental health professionals in this field have a previous history of victimization. This is even more the case with alcoholism counselors. A person's effectiveness is not predicated on their previous personal experience with a similar issue. It is based on personal maturity and integrity, among other variables. However, we cannot expect to resolve our victimization via the therapy of victims.

Society has gradually been made aware of alcoholism, physical abuse, suicide, and sexual abuse. This has not been without considerable difficulty, and when we move out of our collegial relationships we find that much ignorance and disbelief remain, along with a persisting view that children are second-class citizens. The response of outrage by the Vienna Medical Society at Freud's initial postulation of the seemingly ubiquitous nature of father-daughter incest persists, although maybe less overtly. If we are completely honest, we will admit that we do sometimes find ourselves not wanting to believe that something abusive has happened. There are days, even weeks, when we are convinced that if we have to see one more family or one more child involved in sexual abuse, we will not make it. As Summit (1988) articulated so well, we share in the negative hallucination of not wanting to believe what is before our very eyes.

None of us wants to believe that the personal tragedies we see daily have actually occurred. This is one reason why sexual abuse has only relatively recently emerged fully as an issue. For example, I sat in on a case conference in 1974 in which incest was raised but dismissed as an explanation for a child's behavior. In retrospect, incest was the most likely explanation for the young boy's sexual acting out. I did not begin to see sexual abuse as a common clinical phenomenon until 1978. That was in my role with my wife as group home houseparents for eight adolescent females, with all but one reporting persistent and severe sexual misuse. Yet the sexual maltreatment of children has been with us from the beginning. The relative stability of the incidence levels for the past 15 years clearly indicates that it is not a new phenomenon.

COUNTERTRANSFERENCE

The first topic discussed in this chapter is countertransference or, simply stated, our reactions to our clients that are based, in part, on who we are and what we bring to the therapy process. My use of the term is broader than it is usually used in psychodynamic circles. Given our early "training" to be therapists in our own families, we can expect that some of what we bring to therapy are overdeveloped skills at listening, facilitating, controlling, and supporting. Each of these, in some portion, can be useful as long as it is applied flexibly and we do not take the family's refusal to cooperate as a personal affront. Where we run into problems are in our rigidity, our personal unresolved victimization, and our defining ourselves as successful only through our therapy. It is essential to be able to (a) identify what our personal issues are, (b) know how they interfere with doing good therapy, and (c) take steps via personal therapy to ameliorate the impact of these personal issues.

In a paper pertinent to this section, several therapists wrote about countertransference issues and concerns regarding a small number of boys and girls they were treating who had been involved in long-term sexual relationships with a parent or parent surrogate (Krieger, Rosenfeld, Gordon, & Bennett, 1980). Sexual behavior in these children was a common initial presentation, and the authors believed that their "seductive behavior reflected, in part, a test of the safety of the therapeutic situation . . . a safe nonimpulse-ridden environment was provided and the seductive behaviors disappeared."

The therapists reported that the children's behavior was sexually arousing, they found themselves irritated and annoyed, and were troubled by their reactions, fearing that their discomfort would result in covert expressions of anger and distancing. The authors of this paper are to be commended for their honesty in daring to speak directly about how these children and their behavior affect us. Thus, we should not feel alone in our reactions to these children, and follow this example by openly and honestly processing our reactions to our clients with our colleagues, supervisors, and therapists.

Many of the clients we see are not easy to like. In fact, many reflect their poor attachment history in forming ambivalent and avoidant relationships, complete with poor social skills. I have further evidence I am in for a tough time with a family when secretaries and appointment clerks recount the difficulties they have with the family after limited contacts.

For example, I saw a family in which the older son had been molested by an uncle. Family members rarely showered and had many personal habits that were irritating, including regularly reminding me that I was not helpful. Yet they kept the majority of their appointments and made some progress. When they attempted to express their gratitude by bringing a gift box of cookies, nuts, and sliced fruit, all jumbled together, and wanted me to taste a piece of brownish-looking divinity that had an apple slice stuck to the side, I bit the bullet, so to speak, and had a bite. The mother's obvious pleasure at my gesture was striking, and it reminded me again that acceptance, wherever it begins, is a basic human need and must be conveyed, despite the obstacles.

There are various reasons why sexual abuse is a difficult issue to manage personally. First, although we know that children get misused, and despite our generally espoused belief that we value and prize children, we frequently fail to confront our tendencies to see children as second-class citizens. This happens despite our best efforts to be child-sensitive. Adults want children to assume responsibility for their own safety, and when they do not, our initial tendency is to blame them for what happened.

Second, sexual abuse combines sexuality and the misuse of dominance, two issues that few of us deal with maturely until after many years of experience or therapy or both. I hope that each of us knows with what families we work best, and which types are more personally difficult. For example, if we experienced role-reversal and conflicted but enmeshed relationships in our family of origin, we may not read as accurately these common features in sexually abusive families. This may lead us to intervene less effectively, becoming more a part of the system and less an agent of change. The opposite may also occur. We may be hypersensitive to these issues and rigidly react by unnecessary distancing or negativism. It is important that we know and act accordingly. Think about the fact that each of these families allows us another opportunity to monitor our own health and progress toward maturity.

A third area of difficulty is that the role of the therapist gets blurred and advocacy issues and casework management concerns can become primary. After spending so much time training to become a therapist, why is it that we spend so much time on the phone to caseworkers, attorneys, and police? Rather than having clients validate our image as a good person by coming regularly and canceling rarely, we see people who come because of a court order, who do not appreciate our efforts, and who need far more than we can offer. We have to redefine our job, sometimes reluctantly and usually without much training in these new areas foisted on us.

Who has the opportunity to take a low-intensity graduate course in interviewing sexually abused children? No one. Do any of us really like being viewed as an extension of law enforcement or the social services? What about the binds we find ourselves in with attorneys? This is particularly true with those difficult-to-read situations, involving very young children in contested custody cases, that are not served well by the adversary system.

I found I had to put aside my accepting, therapist self and become very dictatorial about seeing all parties instead of just one, being retained by the court rather than by an attorney, and performing the evaluation I thought was necessary. However, the personal price one pays by then "playing Solomon" in the court setting is also difficult to bear, particularly because in this arena the child's needs are again secondary, and the personal needs of the parents are primary.

The simple question of how best to serve the child in the multiplicity of roles we find ourselves in can present baffling options. For example, because I want to be thorough but yet sensitive to the child, do I try to get the important extra information that might be forthcoming by watching the alleged offender with his child, or do I choose not to put the child through the extra anxiety and go with my other information, even if it is skimpy? The approach of observing the interaction may result in a better long-term solution. Not making the mother and child anxious may be a better short-term solution. If you are tired, beleaguered, and upset with either or both of the parties, what do you do?

Fourth, the issues for many children will hit therapists where they may have difficulty, e.g., boundary permeability, sexuality, and empathy defects. For example, with the overly intrusive styles of some children and families, therapists have to learn how to be clear about their own boundaries. This can be very difficult for someone who early on was elected in his or her own family to a caretaking role, in which another person's needs are more important than one's own.

Sometimes I have seen a therapist respond to these dilemmas by being overly rigid about any physical touch or aggression, setting limits in ways that are rejecting rather than helpful. The process of establishing rigid rules may make us less anxious, but it may not truly serve everyone we see. However, to ask that decisions be made on a case-by-case basis may be too much for someone who is struggling with how to create that necessary balance between acceptance and clarity of boundaries.

Sexuality is always a difficult issue, at least initially. Gottlieb and Dean (1981) provided an excellent service in their paper, which presents how thoroughly and candidly they discussed sexual issues between them as co-therapists of a girls' group. I expect that this type of candid discussion in supervision groups about our reaction to children's sexuality would also be invaluable. It is incongruous, no matter how often we see it, to observe sexuality in children. It is also personally upsetting to interact with erotophilic (sexualizing) families for any length of time. After a session with a family of this type, the therapist has to fight off an uncontrollable urge to scrub the walls and chairs of the room with a disinfectant. This reaction certainly goes counter to acceptance, a therapeutic necessity.

Also related to sexuality is the role we choose to take in discussing sexuality with the parental couple or with the child victim. For example, when helping a child disclose abuse experiences, how much is a function of a necessary therapy process, how much is voyeurism, and what might we miss due to our own discomfort with sexuality?

Self-protectively, I grew more remote and less involved with an intensely provocative 9 year old who both irritated me and made me feel uncomfortable because of her sexualized manner. Her inappropriate behavior at school and in her foster home escalated because I, along with her foster parent and teacher, did not know how to deal with her.

In retrospect, I could have done much more, both in the therapy hour and in working with the other adults in her life. However, at this stage in my therapy with these children, I still was not comfortable being direct with her about her sexual behavior, preferring to hide behind a nondirective approach. In addition, I was immediately aware of her foster mother's discomfort with sexuality, whether child or adult, and was not able to talk clearly with her about even monitoring the girl's behavior. After several months of increasing frustration, she was moved to a group home some distance away. Approximately eight years have passed since I last saw her and I occasionally will think about her and wonder how she is doing. She is difficult to "let go" because I feel unresolved about our time together.

In another manner, a child whose normal empathy is impaired due to the abuse and other faulty parent-child interactions is also aversive. I have to struggle with my own anger and feelings of hopelessness as I work with children already prematurely hardened against sensitivity and compassion. It is so easy to see into the future for these children, write them off, and move on to some more hopeful child. Who wants to feel defeated before he even begins? Even when I tell myself, "This child has never had a model for empathy and caring. Feel some sympathy for her plight," something to counter this initial pep talk will happen in therapy, or I will hear about her trying to strangle an infant in the foster home where she lives. This more positive frame of her then becomes very difficult to maintain.

With children like this, you have to make your goals of what constitutes an acceptable outcome more realistic. By being consistently therapeutic and empathic to her, you are providing an alternative set of experiences that she may be more able to receive later on. It is only the rare instance in which you can have the time and resources to do much more than help to make her more receptive for future therapeutic or other healing and corrective relationships.

In addition, by helping to bring about an improvement in her behavior, a family may be able to care for her more empathically and for a longer time. Your therapy success may be measured simply, in that because you helped out at this time in the child's life, she will get shuttled around to fewer foster homes during her time in the system. The benefit is that she may come to see herself and relationships more positively, because she experiences less rejection.

One child came to see me after three failed adoptions. Only 6 years of age, blond, blue-eyed, and of above average intelligence, she was a walking time bomb. She had been massively physically and sexually abused and tortured in her birth home. At least two dead family pets, five instances of sexual abuse of a younger or same-age child (all involv-

ing attempted penetration with an object), countless instances of stealing, and one fire were attributed to this child. In addition, she was the
probable suspect in the deaths of all the fish in a large aquarium at the
last adoptive home. A more thorough evaluation was requested and I
completed that and agreed to see her in therapy.

I tried very hard to like her and to develop a mutual relationship, but
when she was adopted again more than 14 months and 60+ therapy
sessions later, I was still wary when I was with her. For example, just
eight months earlier she had jammed a tack into my back. Yet I was
reasonably sure she no longer was stealing, fire-setting, or killing family
pets. The foster family and I instinctively wanted to be gentle with her,
but we had to substitute that with a mini-police state in her life. And we
felt she was now more ready for adoption than during the three previous
attempts.

Fifth, failure is difficult for any therapist. I have felt more successful
with many of the schizophrenic families I have seen than with many of
the sexually abusive families. Only in my work with anorectic families
have I felt such routine failure, and for different reasons. Our goals
defining what is meant by successful treatment must be constantly revised.

Mrazek (1981) attempted a three-year follow-up of the young girls
she saw in group therapy. The excellent case studies of each child are
worth reading because they illustrate how truly negative the impact of
abuse can be in these children, all of whom were from problematic
families, and several of whom were lost to follow-up because the child
had been moved out-of-state with the original perpetrator.

For example, I feel some success when the mother is giving her son his
Ritalin more regularly and his special education teacher reports that he
is now more manageable in class. We never got to the child's abuse
issues, and she has denied her own abuse, but in one area of parenting
she has been assuming more control for three months. By accepting that
level of change, are you buying into the system, developing burnout, or
being realistic? There is a different answer for each therapist-family
combination. Sometimes success is that family members are more likely
to seek help the next time they need it because they thought you helped
them.

A sixth reason is that no matter how we may struggle with it, we
become agents or extensions of the court and social service systems. It is
a necessary by-product of working in this area. However, this muddies
our relationship with the families and, quite importantly, forces an
adversarial posture more like the legal system than the therapeutic,

compromise-conciliation focus that we are trained should be evident in true therapy.

We also cannot let these families just drift away no matter how obnoxious they may be and despite our subconscious wishes that the family would do just that.

When I have individual adult neurotic patients quietly drift away from therapy, I rarely pursue them, particularly if I feel able to trust that they are leaving knowing that they could return. I cannot just do that in families in which sexual abuse is an issue and the likelihood of revictimization is so high. I need to check in with their caseworker and again arrange another appointment that may not be kept, or if it is, I am now more clearly viewed as the enemy. Or, rather than have the family drift away, we may be the culprit. Think about, for example, how we communicate our disinterest to our child clients, e.g., answering the telephone during the session, cutting the sessions short, playing repetitive board games that do little to develop either the relationship or allow for therapeutic work. We do not do these things with the adult clients we see. But we may communicate our disinterest far too often with children.

Finally, the repeated stress from these cases potentiates our tendency for black-white thinking, and we do find ourselves thinking about who is good and who is bad in these families. I have to continually remind myself not to (a) automatically distrust the perpetrator's therapist and to (b) view neglectful mothers as needy of my intervention, despite their seeming complicity in their child's abuse. It is easy to acquire an adversarial view of the world, almost like policemen who become particularly jaded and cynical over the course of their careers.

An excellent therapist in this area, from Minneapolis-St. Paul, Paul Gerber, once told me that we all run the risk of adopting the world view that there are three camps of people: (a) the enlightened few, who think like us; (b) the poor ignorant, who need to be enlightened; and (c) "them" (the enemy). Once we adopt this stance, we lose objectivity and risk rigidity.

Sometimes the "enemy" is our fellow therapists, who do things a bit differently from the way we do. Do we distrust them because we know we are "right," or because we are not capable of realizing that there may be some other options in this complex treatment field that work with diverse clients? Whatever the reason, it can result in personal and professional isolation and should be guarded against.

I hope that the reader can appreciate that many questions have been raised and will continue to be raised in the last portion of this chapter, but not very many answers are provided. Part of that is due to the fact that each case is individual, requiring individualistic planning. The other factor is the lack of easy answers. Most of the answers arise as a product of lengthy dialogue, with the goal of the child's/family's best interests as primary. Even then, there can be disputes.

ROLES OF THE THERAPIST

We will now discuss the multiple roles of the therapist, and how these can be managed best professionally and personally. I can think of at least five different roles that the therapist can assume with families of sexually abused children.

The first role is obviously that of a therapist, but the question becomes, whose therapist? And if you are the family therapist, should you become the child's therapist and also see the mother individually? What if there are few other therapists in the community and you are one of the few who has any expertise in this area? Is that enough rationale to blend these different roles? Probably it is but are you then prepared to deal with the likelihood of your therapy role being minimized or sabotaged? Krieger et al. (1980) stated that as therapists we "must avoid allying with the child solely as a victim, an alliance which would hinder an understanding of the child's motivation and subsequent guilt." Apparently, simple advocacy is not a broad enough definition of the therapist's role.

The second role that comes to mind is that of investigator or forensic mental health professional. One of the features of incest is blurred boundaries. Therapists naturally get co-opted by their clients. Consequently, a parallel process, which includes blurred boundaries, occurs among therapists who treat sexually abused children. I know I have been guilty of wearing two or more hats: the therapist and the investigator. Which comes first? Which is most important? Should the two of them coexist? Are you doing a disservice to the child when you try to wear both hats? Does this make it likely that your input will be discredited in the courtroom setting where the continued safety of the child is in question? If you do wear both hats, when do you switch? Does this make a difference to the child? Does the child feel betrayed, and does this get transmitted into the therapy?

Some states are taking a more active role in legally separating the functions of investigator and therapist. Whether this is simply legal expedience or is therapeutically defensible is another question. However, it does speak to the potential pitfalls that await the therapist who does not respect the various needs and demands in this area.

Two additional roles, both of them complementary, are consultant and educator. As a consultant, you need to provide input to other people who are in this child's life, particularly teachers, day-care providers, and foster parents. The child's acting-out behavior, particularly sexual and aggressive, is sure to prompt an outcry from other parents and children who are involved in the child's life. As an educator you need to help various people appreciate the frequency of abuse and educate them as to their needed reactions to the child. These include other professionals who will vary widely in their understanding of abuse dynamics and what constitutes appropriate intervention.

Finally, the therapist is also a systems player. It is imperative that you identify who is involved in the system and establish an open relationship with them (Sgroi, 1982a). Are you going to take a perpetrator's therapist's recommendation that his client become involved in your child client's life if you do not know who the therapist is? What if you disagree with the treatment method? It is not good to wait until the last minute to start voicing your objections. Are you aware of other potential abusers in the child's life? A child's persisting problems may be due to continuing abuse.

We also too often fail to appreciate the larger systems that operate in our clients' lives. Economic deprivation is a routine matter in the families I see. In fact, it could be argued that economic assistance would be as helpful as any therapy. Economic deprivation adds to the powerlessness the child and family experience. Ethnic issues are too often ignored, but again children of color feel powerless and stigmatized (two of Finkelhor's traumagenic factors), before first experiencing sexual abuse. These economic and racial factors are further evidence for the observation, made several times in this book, that sexual abuse occurs within a larger abusive context. To ignore these dimensions is to hamper therapy.

STAYING ALIVE

The problem of child sexual abuse is not going to go away; in fact there is evidence that it may be increasing in frequency (Russell, 1984). There will always be families and children in need of our services. Yet, many of the best-trained mental health professionals are not involved in providing services in this area, and treatment is frequently relegated to a continually changing group of novice therapists. By the time they have the experience needed to do as good a job as possible, they move out of the field or into administration or work with a completely different client pool. It is difficult to stay alive in an area in which ideally positive outcomes are so rare and in which you are not being fed by your successes or by the clients you see. Rather, you are feeding them. So what do we do? We can only delay gratification for so long.

The gender of the therapist may be related to the issues that emerge as one attempts to stay vital and therapeutic. Males are socialized to be more directive, make more maturity demands, and desire greater control. When in doubt, or overworked, these characteristics may get emphasized in the therapy and generate considerable frustration. The socialization of the female, on the other hand, emphasizes the development of a nurturing, relational posture that may also not be as good a fit with some children and families as we would like.

As a male therapist, I am also keenly aware of the fact that among sexual abuse therapists, I am in a minority: victimization is naturally seen as a woman's issue. I have been asked, directly and indirectly, about my motivation in seeing children and families, and whether, as a purportedly sensitive therapist, I am not being insensitive in seeing either female or male victims who have been abused by a male. This is a good question and is directly related to the issue of emotional regulation I have discussed in several places. Doesn't a child, abused by a male, subsequently have greater difficulty working with a male therapist?

There are two appropriate replies. The first is that a sensitive, well-trained male therapist will appreciate the potential of being an adverse stimulus to the child. The creation of a working relationship will help the child to relearn trust and view the world more accurately and complexly. The second reply is to remind ourselves that abuse occurs within a context. The child is likely to have as much ambivalence about nonprotective parents, whether male or female, as she has about abusive parents or adults. Both male and female therapists bring baggage; both can provide opportunities to the child.

One answer to staying vital in this type of therapy is to learn to set limits, to cut back on the sheer number of cases you see. Yet I know of many therapists for whom that is not possible. They work in a child-family service of an agency or an HMO, and sexual-abuse referrals predominate. To make matters worse, they may have a maximum of 8 to 12 sessions to rectify the situation. Yet the work is absolutely necessary. This is hardly the arena for ideal therapy, and it is also difficult to create a more balanced caseload. Some combination of clients, so that failures can be balanced with successes, is important. For example, it is difficult for most of us to see more than one or two individuals with a borderline diagnosis at a time. Similarly, despite my enthusiasm for family therapy, I cannot see only families. I need to create a mix of individuals and families, and think over who I am seeing and for how long before I set up new appointments.

Another partial solution may be to recognize what you do best and practice within that area of expertise. For example, a therapist whose personal issues were not as well resolved as they needed to be did not do well with family work, particularly mother-daughter pairs. But she was an excellent group therapist for preadolescent and adolescent victims and found many rewards in her work with them. Sometimes I do more assessments and less therapy, and then I switch, depending on my needs.

Part of the solution is to know yourself as well as you can. This cannot be the arena in which we are working out our own problems. I am not limiting "problems" simply to a previous abuse history. That does not necessarily preclude good therapy, particularly if the person has worked on the victimization in therapy. But other potential blind spots or suspect motives exist.

For example, what are my motivations for seeing children? I can think of both positive and not so positive reasons. It is enlivening to be part of the child's optimism and witness the resilience of childhood. Children can be both spontaneous and blunt. Less positive motivations are my insecurities regarding my abilities—it is easier to be with children than adults. Other personal issues concern power, managing seduction, personal boundaries, and knowing how to take care of ourselves. Each of these can get in the way of good therapy.

Something else that keeps me going in this area is a belief in the resilience of individuals and a deep empathy for individuals who have been depleted. I enjoy seeing them make progress, seemingly against insurmountable odds. I also enjoy watching the coping process in action, as children demonstrate their resilience and growth potential (Masten and O'Connor, 1989).

It is also important to create supportive and collegial relationships. Steward et al. (1986) described a long-term group-therapy program with sexually abused preschoolers that included home visits and other support for the parents. Built into this top-quality service delivery, however, were regular supervision groups. She reported that not only were there no instances of "burnout" in the therapists, but the therapists persisted in their work even after rotational obligations had moved them out of that service. The supervision opportunity seemed to meet many levels of needs, including personal support and intellectual growth. We have to figure out how to do that better for ourselves.

Our therapy with sexually abused children and their families goes counter to their isolation and victimization and introduces the healing power of relationships. Some work settings can be both isolating and victimizing; this simply continues the process that we are struggling against. The degree to which we can create these same supportive relationships with colleagues in our workplace is the degree to which we can continue to do this most essential therapy.

Appendix

CHILD SEXUAL BEHAVIOR INVENTORY, VERSION 1

Please circle the number that tells how often your child has shown the following behaviors *recently or in the last 6 months:*

Never		Less than 1/month	1–3 times/month	At least 1/week
0		1	2	3

1.	0 1 2 3	Dresses like the opposite sex
2.	0 1 2 3	Talks about wanting to be the opposite sex
3.	0 1 2 3	Touches sex (private) parts when in public places
4.	0 1 2 3	Masturbates with hand
5.	0 1 2 3	Scratches anal or crotch area, or both
6.	0 1 2 3	Touches or tries to touch mother's or other women's breasts
7.	0 1 2 3	Masturbates with object
8.	0 1 2 3	Touches other people's sex (private) parts
9.	0 1 2 3	Imitates the act of sexual intercourse
10.	0 1 2 3	Puts mouth on another child's or adult's sex parts
11.	0 1 2 3	Touches sex (private) parts when at home
12.	0 1 2 3	Uses words that describe sex acts
13.	0 1 2 3	Pretends to be the opposite sex when playing
14.	0 1 2 3	Makes sexual sounds (sighing, moaning, heavy breathing, etc.)
15.	0 1 2 3	Asks others to engage in sexual acts with him or her
16.	0 1 2 3	Rubs body against people or furniture
17.	0 1 2 3	Inserts or tries to insert objects in vagina or anus
18.	0 1 2 3	Tries to look at people when they are nude or undressing
19.	0 1 2 3	Imitates sexual behavior with dolls or stuffed animals
20.	0 1 2 3	Shows sex (private) parts to adults

21.	0	1	2	3	Tries to view pictures of nude or partially dressed people (may include catalogs)
22.	0	1	2	3	Talks about sexual acts
23.	0	1	2	3	Kisses adults not in the family
24.	0	1	2	3	Undresses self in front of others
25.	0	1	2	3	Sits with crotch or underwear exposed
26.	0	1	2	3	Kisses other children not in the family
27.	0	1	2	3	Talks in a flirtatious manner
28.	0	1	2	3	Tries to undress other children or adults against their will (opening pants, shirts, etc.)
29.	0	1	2	3	Asks to view nude or sexually explicit TV shows (may include video movies or HBO-type shows)
30.	0	1	2	3	When kissing, tries to put tongue in other person's mouth
31.	0	1	2	3	Hugs adults he or she does not know well
32.	0	1	2	3	Shows sex (private) parts to children
33.	0	1	2	3	If a girl, overly aggressive; if a boy, overly passive
34.	0	1	2	3	Seems very interested in the opposite sex
35.	0	1	2	3	If a boy, plays with girls' toys; if a girl, plays with boys' toys
36.	0	1	2	3	Other sexual behaviors (please describe)

A. _____

B. _____

References

Achenbach, T. M., & Edelbrock, C. (1983). *Manual for the child behavior checklist and revised child behavior profile*. Burlington: University of Vermont Department of Psychiatry.

Adams, P. L. (1982). *A primer of child psychotherapy* (2nd ed.). Boston: Little Brown.

Adams-Tucker, C. (1984). The unmet psychiatric needs of sexually abused youths: Referrals from a child protection agency and clinical evaluations. *Journal of the American Academy of Child Psychiatry, 23*, 659–667.

Alexander, J., & Parsons, B. V. (1982). *Functional family therapy*. Monterey, CA: Brooks/Cole.

Alexander, J. F., Waldron, H. B., Barton, C., & Mas, C. H. (1989). The minimizing of blaming attributions and behaviors in delinquent families. *Journal of Consulting and Clinical Psychology, 57*, 19–24.

Alexander, P. C. (1985). A systems theory conceptualization of incest. *Family Process, 24*, 79–88.

Alexander, P. C., Neimeyer, R. A., Follette, V. M., Moore, M. K., & Harter, S. (1989). A comparison of group treatments of women sexually abused as children. *Journal of Consulting and Clinical Psychology, 57*, 479–483.

American Psychiatric Association. (1987). *Diagnostic and statistical manual of mental disorders* (3rd ed., rev.). Washington, DC: Author.

Anderson, L. M., & Shafer, G. (1979). The character-disordered family: A community treatment model for family sexual abuse. *American Journal of Orthopsychiatry, 49*, 436–445.

Andolfi, M., Angelo, C., Menghi, P., & Nicolò-Corigliano, A. M. (1983). *Behind the family mask: Therapeutic changes in rigid family systems*. New York: Brunner/Mazel.

Arroyo, W., Eth, S., & Pynoos, R. (1984). Sexual assault of a mother by her preadolescent son. *American Journal of Psychiatry, 141*, 1107–1108.

Arthur, B., & Kemme, M. L. (1964). Bereavement in childhood. *Journal of Child Psychology and Psychiatry, 5*, 37–49.

283

Axline, V. M. (1969). *Play therapy*. New York: Ballantine.

Baker, E. L. (1981). An hypnotherapeutic approach to enhance object related-ness in psychotic patients. *International Journal of Clinical and Experimental Hypnosis, 29*, 136–147.

Bandura, A. (1977). *Social learning theory*. Englewood Cliffs, NJ: Prentice-Hall.

Barnard, C. P. (1983). Alcoholism and incest: Improving diagnostic comprehensiveness. *International Journal of Family Therapy, 5*, 136–144.

Barrett, M. J., Sykes, C., & Byrnes, W. (1986). A systemic model for the treatment of intrafamily child sexual abuse. In T. S. Trepper, & M. J. Barrett (Eds.), *Treating incest: A multiple systems perspective* (pp. 67–82). New York: Haworth Press.

Bates, J. E., Skilbeck, W. M., Smith, K. V. R., & Bentler, P. M. (1974). Gender role abnormalities in boys: An analysis of clinical ratings. *Journal of Abnormal Child Psychology, 2*, 1–16.

Baumrind, D. (1982). Are androgynous individuals more effective persons and parents? *Child Development, 53*, 44–75.

Beck, A. T., Rush, A. J., Shaw, B. F., & Emery, G. (1979). *Cognitive therapy of depression*. New York: Guilford Press.

Becker, J. V. (1988). The effects of child sexual abuse on adolescent sexual offenders. In G. E. Wyatt, & G. J. Powell (Eds.), *Lasting effects of child sexual abuse* (pp. 193–207). Beverly Hills: Sage.

Behar, L., & Stringfield, S. (1974). A behavior rating scale for the preschool child. *Developmental Psychology, 10*, 601–610.

Bellak, L. (1975). *The T.A.T., C.A.T., and S.A.T. in clinical use* (3rd ed.). New York: Grune & Stratton.

Bene, E., & Anthony, J. (1976). *Manual for the children's version of the Family Relations Test*. Windsor, England: NFER Publishing Company.

Benedek, E. P. (1989, April). *Definition and description of children who murder*. Paper presented at the Fourth National Symposium on Issues in Child and Adolescent Psychiatry, Minneapolis.

Benward, J., & Densen-Gerber, J. (1975). Incest as a causative factor in antisocial behavior: An exploratory study. *Contemporary Drug Problems, 4*, 323–340.

Berlin, I. N. (1987). Some transference and countertransference issues in the playroom. *Journal of the American Academy of Child and Adolescent Psychiatry, 26*, 101–107.

Berliner, L. (1989). Another option for victims: Civil damage suits. *Journal of Interpersonal Violence, 4*, 107–109.

Berliner, L., & Ernst, E. (1984). Group work with preadolescent sexual assault victims. In I. Stuart, & J. Greer (Eds.), *Victims of sexual aggression: Treatment of children, women, and men* (pp. 105–124). New York: Van Nostrand Reinhold.

Berliner, L., Manaois, O., & Monastersky, C. (1986). *Child sexual behavior disturbance: An assessment and treatment model*. Seattle: Harborview Sexual Assault Center.

Berliner, L., & Wheeler, R. J. (1987). Treating the effects of sexual abuse on children. *Journal of Interpersonal Violence, 2*, 415–434.

Bierman, K. L. (1983). Cognitive development and clinical interviews with children. *Advances in Clinical Child Psychology, 6*, 217–249.

Billings, A. G., & Moos, R. H. (1981). The role of coping responses and social resources in attenuating the stress of life events. *Journal of Behavioral Medicine, 4,* 139–157.

Blick, L. C., & Porter, F. S. (1982). Group therapy with female adolescent incest victims. In S. M. Sgroi (Ed.), *Handbook of clinical intervention in child sexual abuse* (pp. 147–175). Lexington, MA: Lexington Books.

Boat, B. (1987, June). Personal communication.

Boat, B. W., & Everson, M. D. (1986). *Using anatomical dolls: Guidelines for interviewing young children in sexual abuse investigations.* Chapel Hill: University of North Carolina.

Bograd, M. (1986). Holding the line: Confronting the abusive partner. *Family Therapy Networker, 10,* 44–47.

Bolton, F. G., Morris, L. A., & MacEachron, A. E. (1989). *Males at risk: The other side of child sexual abuse.* Newbury Park, CA: Sage.

Boniello, M. J. (1986). The family as "stage" for creating abusive children. *Connections, 1,* 4–5, 20.

Boszormenyi-Nagy, I., & Spark, G. M. (1973). *Invisible loyalties: Reciprocity in intergenerational family therapy.* New York: Harper & Row.

Bourque, L. B., & Back, K. W. (1977). Life graphs and life events. *Journal of Gerontology, 32,* 669–674.

Bowen, M. (1978). *Family therapy in clinical practice.* New York: Jason Aronson.

Bowlby, J. (1969). *Attachment and loss* (Vol. 1). London: Hogarth Press.

Bowlby, J. (1980). *Attachment and loss* (Vol. 3). New York: Basic Books.

Bowman, E. S., Blix, S., & Coons, P. M. (1985). Multiple personality in adolescence: Relationship to incestual experiences. *Journal of the American Academy of Child Psychiatry, 24,* 109–114.

Brady, C. A., & Friedrich, W. N. (1982). Levels of intervention: A model for training in play therapy. *Journal of Clinical Child Psychology, 11,* 39–43.

Briere, J. (1989a, August). *Moderators of long-term symptomatology in women molested as children.* Paper presented at the 97th annual convention of the American Psychological Association, New Orleans.

Briere, J. (1989b). *Therapy for adults molested as children: Beyond survival.* New York: Springer.

Brown, D. P., & Fromm, E. (1986). *Hypnotherapy and hypnoanalysis.* Hillsdale, NJ: Lawrence Erlbaum.

Brown, G. W., & Harris, T. O. (1978). *Social origins of depression: A study of psychiatric disorder in women.* New York: Free Press.

Browne, A., & Finkelhor, D. (1986). Impact of child sexual abuse: A review of the research. *Psychological Bulletin, 99,* 66–77.

Burgess, A. W., Hartman, C. R., & McCormack, A. (1987). Abused to abuser: Antecedents of socially deviant behaviors. *American Journal of Psychiatry, 144,* 1431–1436.

Burgess, A. W., McCausland, M. P., & Wolbert, W. A. (1981). Children's drawings as indicators of sexual trauma. *Perspectives in Psychiatric Care, 14,* 50–58.

Burke, J. D., Jr., Moccia, P., Borus, J. F., & Burns, B. J. (1986). Emotional distress in fifth-grade children ten months after a natural disaster. *Journal of the American Academy of Child Psychiatry, 25,* 536–541.

Caplan, P. J., & Hall-McCorquodale, I. (1985). Mother-blaming in major clinical journals. *American Journal of Orthopsychiatry, 55*, 345–353.

Caruso, K. R. (1987). *Basic manual (version 1): To accompany projective storytelling cards.* Redding: Northwest Psychological Publishers.

Ceci, S. J., Toglis, M. P., & Ross, D. F. (1987). *Children's eyewitness memory.* New York: Springer-Verlag.

Cicchetti, D. (1987). Developmental psychopathology in infancy: Illustration from the study of maltreated youngsters. *Journal of Consulting and Clinical Psychology, 55*, 837–845.

Cicchetti, D., & Rizley, D. (1981). Developmental perspective on the etiology, intergenerational transmission, and sequelae of child maltreatment. *New Directions for Child Development, 11*, 31–55.

Cohen, F. W., & Phelps, R. E. (1985). Incest markers in children's artwork. *The Arts in Psychotherapy, 12*, 265–283.

Cohn, A. H., & Daro, D. (1987). Is treatment too late: What ten years of evaluative research tell us. *Child Abuse and Neglect, 11*, 433–442.

Cole, C. H., & Barney, E. E. (1987). Safeguards and the therapeutic window: A group treatment strategy for adult incest survivors. *American Journal of Orthopsychiatry, 57*, 601–609.

Cole, P. M. (1986). Children's spontaneous control of facial expression. *Child Development, 57*, 1309–1321.

Cole, P. M., Stadler, J. G., & Mahnke, M. L. (1989, August). *Strategies for ending sexual abuse and their relation to adult adjustment.* Paper presented at the 97th annual convention of the American Psychological Association, New Orleans.

Conte, J. R. (1984). Progress in treating the sexual abuse of children. *Social Work, 29*, 258–263.

Conte, J. R. (1986). Sexual abuse and the family: A critical analysis. In T. Trepper, & M. J. Barrett (Eds.), *Treating incest: A multiple systems perspective* (pp. 113–126). New York: Haworth Press.

Conte, J. R. (1989, August). *Treating incest victims and offenders: Applying recent research.* Paper presented at the 97th annual convention of the American Psychological Association, New Orleans.

Conte, J. R., & Schuerman, J. R. (1987). Factors associated with an increased impact of child sexual abuse. *Child Abuse and Neglect, 11*, 201–211.

Conte, J. R., Wolf, S., & Smith, T. (1989). What sexual offenders tell us about prevention strategies. *Child Abuse and Neglect, 13*, 293–301.

Curry, J. F. (1989, August). *Cognitive-interpersonal models of group psychotherapy for children and adolescents.* Paper presented at the 97th annual convention of the American Psychological Association, New Orleans.

Damon, L., Todd, J., & Crespo, A. E. (1989). *Responsibility and self-blame in young sexually abused children.* Manuscript submitted for publication.

Damon, W. (1988). *The moral child: Nurturing children's natural moral growth.* New York: Free Press.

Dell, P. F. (1989). Violence and the systemic view: The problem of power. *Family Process, 28*(1), 1–14.

Derogatis, L. R. (1983). *SCL-90-R: Administration scoring & procedures manual – II for the r(evised) version and other instruments of the psychopathology rating scale series.* Baltimore: Clinical Psychometrics Research.

de Young, M. (1984). Counterphobic behavior in multiply molested children. *Child Welfare, 63,* 333–339.

Dollinger, S. J. (1983). A case report of dissociative neurosis (depersonalization disorder) in an adolescent treated with family therapy and behavior modification. *Journal of Consulting and Clinical Psychology, 51,* 479–484.

Earls, F., Beardslee, W., & Garrison, W. (1987). Correlates and predictors of competence in young children. In E. J. Anthony, & B. J. Cohler (Eds.), *The invulnerable child* (pp. 70–83). New York: Guilford Press.

Egeland, B., Jacobvitz, D., & Sroufe, L. A. (1988). Breaking the cycle of abuse. *Child Development, 59,* 1080–1088.

Egeland, B., & Sroufe, L. A. (1981). Attachment and early maltreatment. *Child Development, 52,* 44–52.

Ehrhardt, A. A., Meyer-Bahlburg, H. F. L., Bell, J. J., Cohen, S. F., Healey, J. M., Stiel, R., Feldman, J. F., Morishima, A., & New, M. I. (1984). Idiopathic precocious puberty in girls: Psychiatric follow-up in adolescence. *Journal of the American Academy of Child Psychiatry, 23,* 23–33.

Einbender, A. J., & Friedrich, W. N. (1984). *Physically abused children's response to the Bene-Anthony Family Relations Test.* Unpublished manuscript, University of Washington.

Einbender, A. J., & Friedrich, W. N. (1989). Psychological functioning and behavior of sexually abused girls. *Journal of Consulting and Clinical Psychology, 57,* 155–157.

Eist, H. I., & Mandel, A. (1968). Family treatment of ongoing incest behavior. *Family Process, 7,* 216–232.

Elkind, D. (Ed.). (1979). *The child and society* (pp. 167–183). New York: Oxford University Press.

Elmer, E. (1977). A follow-up study of traumatized children. *Pediatrics, 59,* 273–279.

Eme, R. F. (1979). Sex differences in childhood psychopathology: A review. *Psychological Bulletin, 86,* 574–595.

Erickson, M. F. (1986, August). *Young sexually abused children: Socio-emotional development and family interaction.* Paper presented at the 94th annual convention of the American Psychological Association, Washington, DC.

Erickson, M. F., & Egeland, B. (1987). A developmental view of the psychological consequences of maltreatment. *School Psychology Review, 16,* 156–168.

Erickson, M. F., Egeland, B., & Pianta, R. (1989). The effects of maltreatment on the development of young children. In D. Cicchetti, & V. Carlson (Eds.), *Child maltreatment: Theory and research on the causes and consequences of child abuse and neglect* (pp. 647–684). New York: Cambridge University Press.

Erikson, E. H. (1963). *Childhood and society* (2nd ed.). New York: W. W. Norton.

Eth, S., & Pynoos, R. S. (1985). Psychiatric interventions with children traumatized by violence. In E. Benedek, & D. Schetky (Eds.), *Emerging issues in child psychiatry and the law* (pp. 285–309). New York: Brunner/Mazel.

Everson, M. D., & Boat, B. W. (1989). False allegations of sexual abuse by children and adolescents. *Journal of the American Academy of Child and Adolescent Psychiatry, 28,* 230–235.

Everson, M. D., Hunter, W. M., Runyon, D. K., Edelsohn, G. A., & Coulter, M. L. (1989). Maternal support following disclosure of incest. *American Journal of Orthopsychiatry, 59*(2), 197–207.

Exner, J. E., Jr. (1974). *The Rorschach: A comprehensive system* (Vol. 1). New York: John Wiley.

Fagan, J., & McMahon, P. P. (1984). Incipient multiple personality in children: Four cases. *Journal of Nervous and Mental Disease, 172,* 26–36.

Faller, K. C. (1987, July). *Women who sexually abuse children: A descriptive study.* Paper presented at the Third National Family Violence Research Conference, Durham, NH.

Faller, K. C. (1988). Decision-making in cases of extrafamilial child sexual abuse. *American Journal of Orthopsychiatry, 58,* 121–128.

Feiring, C. (1983). Behavioral styles in infancy and adulthood: The work of Karen Horney and attachment theorists collaterally considered. *Journal of the American Academy of Child Psychiatry, 22,* 1–7.

Finkelhor, D. (1979). *Sexually victimized children.* New York: Free Press.

Finkelhor, D. (1984). *Child sexual abuse: New theory and research.* New York: Free Press.

Finkelhor, D. (1986). Sexual abuse: Beyond the family system approach. In T. S. Trepper, & M. J. Barrett (Eds.), *Treating incest: A multiple systems perspective* (pp. 53–65). New York: Haworth Press.

Finkelhor, D. (1988). The trauma of child sexual abuse: Two models. In G. E. Wyatt, & G. J. Powell (Eds.), *Lasting effects of child sexual abuse* (pp. 61–82). Beverly Hills: Sage.

Finkelhor, D., & Browne, A. (1985). The traumatic impact of child sexual abuse: A conceptualization. *American Journal of Orthopsychiatry, 55,* 530–541.

Folkman, S., Schaefer, C., & Lazarus, R. (1979). Cognitive processes as mediators of stress and coping. In V. Hamilton, & D. W. Warburton (Eds.), *Human stress and cognition: An informational approach* (pp. 265–297). New York: John Wiley.

Fowler, C., Burns, S. R., & Roehl, J. E. (1983). The role of group therapy in incest counseling. *International Journal of Family Therapy, 5,* 127–135.

Freud, A. (1966). *The ego and the mechanisms of defense* (Vol. 2, rev. ed.). New York: International Universities Press.

Freud, A., & Dann, S. (1951). An experiment in group upbringing. *Psychoanalytic Study of the Child, 6,* 127–168.

Friedlander, S., Weiss, D. S., & Traylor, J. (1986). Assessing the influence of maternal depression on the validity of the Child Behavior Checklist. *Journal of Abnormal Child Psychology, 14,* 123–133.

Friedrich, W. N. (1988a). Behavior problems in sexually abused children: An adaptational perspective. In G. E. Wyatt, & G. J. Powell (Eds.), *Lasting effects of child sexual abuse* (pp. 171–191). Beverly Hills: Sage.

Friedrich, W. N. (1988b). Child abuse and sexual abuse. In R. L. Green (Ed.), *The MMPI: Use with specific populations* (pp. 246–258). Philadelphia: Grune & Stratton.

Friedrich, W. N., Beilke, R. L., & Urquiza, A. J. (1987). Children from sexually abusive families: A behavioral comparison. *Journal of Interpersonal Violence, 2,* 391–402.

Friedrich, W. N., Beilke, R. L., & Urquiza, A. J. (1988a). Behavior problems in young sexually abused boys: A comparison study. *Journal of Interpersonal Violence, 3,* 21–28.

Friedrich, W. N., Berliner, L., Urquiza, A. J., & Beilke, R. L. (1988b). Brief diagnostic group treatment of sexually abused boys. *Journal of Interpersonal Violence, 3,* 331–343.

Friedrich, W. N., & Einbender, A. J. (1983). The abused child: A psychological review. *Journal of Clinical Child Psychology, 12,* 244–256.

Friedrich, W. N., Einbender, A. J., & Luecke, W. J. (1983). Cognitive and behavioral characteristics of physically abused children. *Journal of Consulting and Clinical Psychology, 51,* 313–314.

Friedrich, W. N., Grambsch, P., Koverola, C., Hewitt, S., Damon, L., Lemmond, T., & Broughton, D. (1989). *The Child Sexual Behavior Inventory: Normative and clinical findings.* Unpublished manuscript.

Friedrich, W. N., & Luecke, W. J. (1988). Young school-age sexually aggressive children. *Professional Psychology Research and Practice, 19,* 155–164.

Friedrich, W. N., Luecke, W. J., Beilke, R. L., & Place V. (1990). *Group treatment of sexually abused boys: An agency study.* Manuscript submitted for publication.

Friedrich, W. N., & Lui, B. (1985). *An observational rating scale for sexually abused children.* Unpublished manuscript. University of Washington, Seattle.

Friedrich, W. N., & Reams, R. A. (1987). Course of psychological symptoms in sexually abused young children. *Psychotherapy, 24,* 160–170.

Friedrich, W. N., Urquiza, A. J., & Beilke, R. L. (1986). Behavior problems in sexually abused young children. *Journal of Pediatric Psychology, 11*(1), 47–57.

Friedrich, W. N., & Wheeler, K. K. (1982). The abusing parent revisited: A decade of psychological research. *Journal of Nervous and Mental Disease, 170,* 577–587.

Friedrich, W. N., Wilturner, L. T., & Cohen, D. S. (1985). Coping resources and parenting mentally retarded children. *American Journal of Mental Deficiency, 90,* 130–139.

Gagliano, C. K. (1987). Group treatment for sexually abused girls. *Social Casework, 68*(2), 102–108.

Gale, J., Thompson, R. J., Moran, T., & Sack, W. H. (1988). Sexual abuse in young children: Its clinical presentation and characteristic patterns. *Child Abuse and Neglect, 12,* 163–170.

Gallo, A. M. (1979). Early childhood masturbation: A developmental approach. *Pediatric Nursing, 12,* 47–49.

Garbarino, J. (1982). *Children and families in the social environment.* New York: Aldine.

Garbarino, J., Stott, F. M., & Faculty of the Erikson Institute (1989). *What children can tell us.* San Francisco: Jossey-Bass.

Garber, J. (1984). Classification of childhood psychopathology: A developmental perspective. *Child Development, 55,* 30–48.

Gardner, G. G., & Olness, K. (1981). *Hypnosis and hypnotherapy with children.* Orlando: Grune & Stratton.

Garmezy, N. (1983). Stressors of childhood. In Garmezy, N., & Rutter, M. (Eds.), *Stress, coping, and development in children* (pp. 43–84). New York: McGraw-Hill.

Garmezy, N., Masten, A. S., & Tellegen, A. (1984). The study of stress and competence in children: A building block for developmental psychopathology. *Child Development, 55,* 97–111.

Gelfand, D. M., & Peterson, L. (1985). *Child development and psychopathology.* Beverly Hills: Sage.

Gelinas, D. J. (1983). The persisting negative effects of incest. *Psychiatry, 46,* 312–332.

Gelinas, D. J. (1988). Family therapy: Critical early structuring. In S. M. Sgroi (Ed.), *Vulnerable populations* (Vol. 1) (pp. 51–77). Lexington, MA: Lexington Books.

Gelles, R. J. (1974). *The violent home: A study of physical aggression between husbands and wives.* Beverly Hills: Sage.

George, C., & Main, M. (1979). Social interactions of young abused children: Approach, avoidance, and aggression. *Child Development, 50,* 306–318.

Giaretto, H. (1982). *Integrated treatment of child sexual abuse: A treatment and training manual.* Palo Alto, CA: Science and Behavior Books.

Goldston, D., Turnquist, D. C., & Knutson, J. F. (1989). Presenting problems of sexually abused girls receiving psychiatric services. *Journal of Abnormal Psychology, 98,* 314–317.

Gomes-Schwartz, B., Horowitz, J. M., & Sauzier, M. (1985). Severity of emotional distress among sexually abused preschool, school-age, and adolescent children. *Hospital and Community Psychiatry, 36,* 503–508.

Goodman, G., Aman, C., & Hirschman, J. (1987). Child sexual and physical abuse: Children's testimony. In S. J. Ceci, M. P. Toglia, & D. F. Ross (Eds.), *Children's eyewitness memory.* New York: Springer-Verlag.

Goodman, G., & Reed, R. S. (1986). Age differences in eyewitness testimony. *Law and Human Behavior, 10,* 317–322.

Goodman, G. S. (1984). The child witness: Conclusions and future directions for research and legal practice. *Journal of Social Issues, 40,* 157–175.

Goodwin, J., Simms, M., & Bergman, R. (1979). Hysterical seizures: A sequel to incest. *American Journal of Orthopsychiatry, 49,* 698–703.

Goodyer, I. (1981). Hysterical conversion reactions in childhood. *Journal of Child Psychology and Psychiatry, 22,* 179–188.

Gordon, M. (1989). The family environment of sexual abuse: A comparison of natal and stepfather abuse. *Child Abuse and Neglect, 13,* 121–130.

Gottlieb, B., & Dean, J. (1981). The co-therapy relationship in group treatment of sexually mistreated adolescent girls. In P. B. Mrazek, & C. H. Kempe (Eds.), *Sexually abused children and their families* (pp. 211–218). New York: Pergamon Press.

Goyette, C. H., Conners, C. K., & Ulrich, R. F. (1978). Normative data on revised Conners Parent and Teacher Rating Scales. *Journal of Abnormal Child Psychology, 6,* 221–236.

Graham, P. (1979). Epidemiological studies. In H. C. Quay, & J. S. Werry

(Eds.), *Psychopathological disorders of childhood* (2nd ed.) (pp. 185–209). New York: John Wiley.

Gries, L. T. (1986). The use of multiple goals in the treatment of foster children with emotional disorders. *Professional Psychology Research and Practice, 17*, 381–390.

Gross, M. (1979). Incestuous rape: A cause for hysterical seizures in four adolescent girls. *American Journal of Orthopsychiatry, 49*, 704–708.

Groth, A. N. (1979). *Men who rape: The psychology of the offender.* New York: Plenum Press.

Groth, A. N. (1982). The incest offender. In S. M. Sgroi (Ed.), *Handbook of clinical intervention in child sexual abuse* (pp. 215–239). Lexington, MA: Lexington Books.

Gruber, K. J., & Jones, R. J. (1983). Identifying determinants of risk of sexual victimization of youth: A multivariate approach. *Child Abuse and Neglect, 7*, 17–24.

Guntrip, H. J. S. (1969). *Schizoid phenomena, object-relations and the self.* New York: International Universities Press.

Haan, N. (1977). *Coping and defending: Processes of self-environment organization.* New York: Academic Press.

Haley, J. (1973). *Uncommon therapy.* New York: W. W. Norton.

Harter, S. (1977). A cognitive-developmental approach to children's expression of conflicting feelings and a technique to facilitate such expression in play therapy. *Journal of Consulting and Clinical Psychology, 45*, 417–432.

Harter, S. (1980). Children's understanding of multiple emotions: Cognitive developmental approach. In *Proceedings of the Jean Piaget Society.* Hillsdale, NJ: Lawrence Erlbaum.

Harter, S. (1981). A model of intrinsic mastery motivation in children: Individual differences and developmental changes. In W. A. Collins (Ed.), *Minnesota Symposium on Child Psychology* (Vol. 14). Hillsdale, NJ: Lawrence Erlbaum.

Harter, S. (1982). The perceived competence scale for children. *Child Development, 53*, 87–97.

Harter, S. (1983). Cognitive-developmental considerations in the conduct of play therapy. In C. Schaefer, & K. J. O'Connor (Eds.), *Handbook of play therapy* (pp. 95–127). New York: John Wiley.

Harter, S., Alexander, P. C., & Neimeyer, R. A. (1988). Long-term effects of incestuous child abuse in college women: Social adjustment, social cognition, and family characteristics. *Journal of Consulting and Clinical Psychology, 56*, 5–8.

Hartman, C. R., & Burgess, A. W. (in press). Information processing of trauma: A case application of a model. *Journal of Interpersonal Violence.*

Hazzard, A., King, H. E., & Webb, C. (1986). Group therapy with sexually abused adolescent girls. *American Journal of Psychotherapy, 40*, 213–223.

Herman, J. (1983). Recognition and treatment of incestuous families. *International Journal of Family Therapy, 5*, 81–91.

Herman, J. L. (1981). *Father-daughter incest.* Cambridge, MA: Harvard University Press.

Herrenkohl, E. C., Herrenkohl, R. C., & Toedter, L. J. (1983). Perspectives on the intergenerational transmission of abuse. In D. Finkelhor, R. J. Gelles,

G. T. Hotaling, & M. A. Strauss (Eds.), *The dark side of families: Current family violence research* (pp. 305–316). Beverly Hills: Sage.

Hetherington, E. M. (1984). Stress and coping in children and families. In A. Doyle, D. Gold, & D. S. Moskowitz (Eds.), *Children in families under stress* (pp. 7–33). San Francisco: Jossey-Bass.

Hewitt, S. K. (1988, April). Personal communication.

Hewitt, S. K. (in press). Therapeutic management of preschool cases of alleged but unsubstantiated sexual abuse. *Child Welfare.*

Hewitt, S. K., & McNaught, J. (1987). *The impact of child sexual abuse on learning skills.* Unpublished manuscript, Midwest Children's Resource Center, St. Paul, MN.

Hibbard, R. A., Roghmann, K., & Hoekelman, R. A. (1987). Genitalia in children's drawings: An association with sexual abuse. *Pediatrics, 79,* 129–137.

Higgins, E. T. (1987). Self-discrepancy: A theory relating self and affect. *Psychological Review, 94,* 319–340.

Hodges, K., Kline, J., Stern, L., Cytryn, L., & McKnew, D. (1982). The development of a child assessment interview for research and clinical use. *Journal of Abnormal Child Psychology, 10,* 173–189.

Hodges, V. K. (1988, September). Personal communication.

Hoffman, L. (1981). *Foundations of family therapy: A conceptual framework for systems change.* New York: Basic Books.

Horney, K. (1950). *Neurosis and human growth: The struggle toward self-realization.* New York: W. W. Norton.

Jacobvitz, D., & Sroufe, L. A. (1987). The early caregiver-child relationship and attention-deficit disorder with hyperactivity in kindergarten: A prospective study. *Child Development, 58,* 1496–1504.

Jaffe, P., Wolfe, D., Wilson, S., & Zak, L. (1986). Similarities in behavioral and social maladjustment among child victims and witnesses to family violence. *American Journal of Orthopsychiatry, 56,* 142–146.

Jesse, R. C. (1989). *Children in recovery.* New York: W. W. Norton.

Johnson, T. C. (1988). Child perpetrators—children who molest other children: Preliminary findings. *Child Abuse and Neglect, 12,* 219–229.

Johnston, M. S. (1979). The sexually mistreated child: Diagnostic evaluation. *Child Abuse and Neglect, 3,* 943–951.

Jones, D. P. (1986). Individual psychotherapy for the sexually abused child. *Child Abuse and Neglect, 10,* 377–385.

Jones, D. P. H. (1987). The untreatable family. *Child Abuse and Neglect, 11,* 409–420.

Jones, D. P. H., & McGraw, J. M. (1987). Reliable and fictitious accounts of sexual abuse to children. *Journal of Interpersonal Violence, 2,* 27–45.

Jones, J. G. (1980). The child accident repeater. *Clinical Pediatrics, 19,* 284–288.

Justice, B., & Justice, R. (1979). *The broken taboo: Sex in the family.* New York: Human Sciences Press.

Kazdin, A. E. (1987). Treatment of antisocial behavior in children: Current status and future directions. *Psychological Bulletin, 102,* 187–203.

Kegan, R. (1982). *The evolving self: Problem and process in human development.* Cambridge, MA: Harvard University Press.

Kempe, R. S., & Kempe, C. H. (1978). *Child abuse*. Cambridge, MA: Harvard University Press.

Kendall, P. C., & Braswell, L. (1985). *Cognitive behavioral therapy for impulsive children*. New York: Guilford Press.

Kiser, L. J., Ackerman, B. J., Brown, E., Edwards, N. B., McColgan, E., Pugh, R., & Pruitt, D. B. (1988). Post-traumatic stress disorder in young children: A reaction to purported sexual abuse. *Journal of the American Academy of Child and Adolescent Psychiatry, 27*, 645–649.

Kluft, R. P. (1984). Multiple personality in childhood. *Psychiatric Clinics of North America, 7*(1), 121–134.

Knight, R. A., Carter, D. L., & Prentky, R. A. (1989). A system for the classification of child molesters: Reliability and application. *Journal of Interpersonal Violence, 4*, 3–23.

Kohan, M. J., Pothier, P., & Norbeck, J. S. (1987). Hospitalized children with history of sexual abuse: Incidence and care issues. *American Journal of Orthopsychiatry, 57*, 258–264.

Kopp, S. B. (1977). *Back to one*. Palo Alto, CA: Science and Behavior Books.

Kovacs, M., & Beck, A. T. (1977). An empirical-clinical approach toward a definition of childhood depression. In J. G. Schultebrandt, & A. Raskin (Eds.), *Depression in childhood: Diagnosis, treatment, and conceptual models* (pp. 1–25). New York: Raven Press.

Koverola, A. C. (1989). *Initial impact of child sexual abuse: An empirical investigation*. Unpublished doctoral dissertation. Fuller Graduate School, Pasadena, CA.

Krieger, M. J., Rosenfeld, A. A., Gordon, A., & Bennett, M. (1980). Problems in the psychotherapy of children with histories of incest. *American Journal of Psychotherapy, 34*, 81–88.

Kurdek, L. A. (1981). An integrative perspective on children's divorce adjustment. *American Psychologist, 36*, 856–866.

Lamb, S. (1986). Treating sexually abused children: Issues of blame and responsibility. *American Journal of Orthopsychiatry, 56*, 303–307.

Langevin, R. (1983). *Sexual strands: Understanding and treating sexual anomalies in men*. Hillsdale, NJ: Lawrence Erlbaum.

Langley, J., McGee, R., Silva, P., & Williams, S. (1983). Child behavior and accidents. *Journal of Pediatric Psychology, 8*, 181–189.

Lanning, K. V. (1986). *Child molesters: A behavioral analysis*. Washington, DC: National Center for Missing and Exploited Children.

Larson, N. R., & Maddock, J. W. (1986). Structural and functional variables in incest family systems: Implications for assessment and treatment. In T. S. Trepper, & M. J. Barrett (Eds.), *Treating incest: A multiple systems perspective* (pp. 27–44). New York: Haworth Press.

Lindahl, M. W. (1988). Letters to Tammy: A technique useful in the treatment of a sexually abused child. *Child Abuse and Neglect, 12*, 417–420.

Lustig, N., Dresser, J. W., Spellman, S. W., & Murray, T. B. (1966). Incest: A family group survival pattern. *Archives of General Psychiatry, 14*, 31–40.

Maccoby, E. E. (1983). Social-emotional development and response to stressors. In N. Garmezy, & M. Rutter (Eds.), *Stress, coping, and development in children* (pp. 217–234). New York: McGraw-Hill.

MacFarlane, K. (1986). The clinical interview [Videotape]. New York: Guilford Press.

MacFarlane, K., Waterman, J., Conerly, S., Damon, L., Durfee, M., & Long, S. (1986). *Sexual abuse of young children: Evaluation and treatment*. New York: Guilford Press.

Machotka, P., Pittman, F. S., III, & Flomenhaft, K. (1967). Incest as a family affair. *Family Process, 6*, 98–116.

Machover, K. (1948). *Personality projection in the drawing of the human figure*. Springfield, IL: Charles C Thomas.

Maddock, J. W. (1988). Child reporting and testimony in incest cases: Comments on the construction and reconstruction of reality. *Behavioral Sciences and the Law, 6*, 1–20.

Malenbaum, R., & Russell, A. T. (1987). Multiple personality disorder in an 11-year-old boy and his mother. *Journal of the American Academy of Child and Adolescent Psychiatry, 26*, 436–439.

Malz, W., & Holman, B. (1987). *Incest and sexuality*. Lexington, MA: Lexington Books.

Mandell, J. G., & Damon, L. (1989). *Group treatment for sexually abused children*. New York: Guilford Press.

Mannarino, A. P., & Cohen, J. (1987, July). *Psychological symptoms of sexually abused children*. Paper presented at the Third National Family Violence Research Conference, Durham, NH.

Martinson, F. M. (1976). Eroticism in infancy and childhood. *The Journal of Sex Research, 12*, 251–262.

Masten, A. S., & O'Connor, M. J. (1989). Vulnerability, stress, and resilience in the early development of a high risk child. *Journal of the American Academy of Child and Adolescent Psychiatry, 28*, 274–278.

Matheny, A. P., Jr., & Fisher, J. E. (1984). Behavioral perspectives on children's accidents. In M. Wolraich, & D. K. Routh (Eds.), *Advances in developmental and behavioral pediatrics* (Vol. 5) (pp. 221–264). Greenwich, CT: JAI Press.

Maturana, H., & Varela, F. (1987). *The tree of knowledge: Biological roots of human understanding*. Boston: New Science Library.

McArthur, D. S., & Roberts, B. E. (1982). *Roberts apperception test for children*. Los Angeles: Western Psychological Services.

McCarthy, B. W. (1986). A cognitive-behavioral approach to understanding and treating sexual trauma. *Journal of Sex and Marital Therapy, 12*, 322–329.

McCarthy, I. C., & Byrne, N. O. (1988). Mis-taken love: Conversations on the problem of incest in an Irish context. *Family Process, 27*(2), 181–199.

McLeer, S. V., Deblinger, E., Atkins, M. S., Foa, E. B., & Ralphe, D. L. (1988). Post-traumatic stress disorder in sexually abused children. *Journal of the American Academy of Child and Adolescent Psychiatry, 27*, 650–654.

McNeill, J. W., & Todd, F. J. (1986). The operant treatment of excessive verbal ruminations and negative emotional arousal in a case of child molestation. *Child and Family Behavior Therapy, 8*, 61–69.

Meiselman, K. C. (1978). *Incest*. San Francisco: Jossey-Bass.

Melton, G. B. (1987). On humility: Knowing what we don't know. *Division 37 Newsletter*, 2.

Mian, M., Wehrspann, W., Klajner-Diamond, H., LeBaron, D., & Winder, C. (1986). Review of 125 children 6 years of age and under who were sexually abused. *Child Abuse and Neglect, 10*, 223–229.

Miller, L. C., Hampe, E., Barrett, C. L., & Noble, H. (1977). Children's deviant behavior within the general population. *Journal of Consulting and Clinical Psychology, 37*, 16–22.

Miller, P. H., & Aloise, P. A. (1989). Young children's understanding of the psychological causes of behavior: A review. *Child Development, 60*, 257–285.

Miller, T. W., Veltkamp, L. J., & Janson, D. (1987). Projective measures in the clinical evaluation of sexually abused children. *Child Psychiatry and Human Development, 18*, 47–57.

Minuchin, S. (1974). *Families & family therapy*. Cambridge, MA: Harvard University Press.

Money, J., & Ehrhardt, A. A. (1972). *Man & woman, boy & girl*. Baltimore: Johns Hopkins University Press.

Monte, C. F. (1980). *Beneath the mask* (2nd ed.). New York: Holt, Rinehart and Winston.

Moos, R. H., Cronkite, R. C., Billings, A. G., & Finney, J. W. (1983). *Health and daily living form manual*. Palo Alto, CA: Social Ecology Laboratory.

Mowrer, C. (1986). The family worker and the incestuous family: Integrating levels of understanding. Part 1: Issues and models. *Prevention Report, Winter*, 1–3.

Mowrer, C. (1987). The family worker and the incestuous family: Integrating levels of understanding. Part 2: Implications for risk assessment and treatment. *Prevention Report, Spring*, 1–3.

Mrazek, D. A., & Mrazek, P. B. (1981). Psychosexual development within the family. In P. B. Mrazek, & C. H. Kempe (Eds.), *Sexually abused children and their families* (pp. 17–32). New York: Pergamon Press.

Mrazek, P. B. (1981). Group psychotherapy with sexually abused children. In P. B. Mrazek, & C. H. Kempe (Eds.), *Sexually abused children and their families* (pp. 199–210). New York: Pergamon Press.

Mrazek, P. B., & Bentovim, A. (1981). Incest and the dysfunctional family system. In P. B. Mrazek, & C. H. Kempe (Eds.), *Sexually abused children and their families* (pp. 167–178). New York: Pergamon Press.

Mrazek, P. B., & Kempe, C. H. (Eds.). (1981). *Sexually abused children and their families*. New York: Pergamon Press.

Mrazek, P. B., & Mrazek, D. A. (1987). Resilience in child maltreatment victims: A conceptual exploration. *Child Abuse and Neglect, 11*, 357–366.

Murphy, S. M., Saunders, B. E., & McClure, S. (1986, August). *Victims of incest: An individual and family profile*. Paper presented at the meeting of the American Psychological Association, Washington, DC.

Nader, K., & Pynoos, R. (n.d.). *Parent traumatic events questionnaire*. Unpublished manuscript, UCLA Neuropsychiatric Institute, Los Angeles.

Nash, M., & Baker, E. (1984). Trance encounters: Susceptibility to hypnosis. *Psychology Today, 18*(Feb), 72–73.

Nelki, J. S., & Watters, J. (1989). A group for sexually abused young children: Unravelling the web. *Child Abuse and Neglect*, *13*, 369–377.

O'Brien, M., & Bera, W. (1986). Adolescent sexual offenders: A descriptive typology. *Preventing Sexual Abuse*, *1*, 1–4.

Overholser, J. C., & Beck, S. (1986). Multimethod assessment of rapists, child molesters, and three control groups on behavioral and psychological measures. *Journal of Consulting and Clinical Psychology*, *54*, 682–687.

Parker, H., & Parker, S. (1986). Father-daughter sexual abuse: An emerging perspective. *American Journal of Orthopsychiatry*, *56*, 531–549.

Patterson, G. R. (1986). Performance models for antisocial boys. *American Psychologist*, *41*, 432–444.

Patterson, G. R., DeBaryshe, B. D., & Ramsey, E. (1989). A developmental perspective on antisocial behavior. *American Psychologist*, *44*, 329–335.

Patterson, G. R., Redl, J. B., Jones, R. R., & Conger, R. E. (1975). *A social learning approach to family intervention: Vol. 1: Families with aggressive children*. Eugene, OR: Castalia.

Patterson, J. M., & McCubbin, H. I. (1983). Chronic illness: Family stress and coping. In C. R. Figley, & H. I. McCubbin (Eds.), *Stress and the family: Vol. II: Coping with catastrophe* (pp. 21–36). New York: Brunner/Mazel.

Paveza, G. J. (1987, July). *Risk factors in father-daughter child sexual abuse: Findings from a case-control study*. Paper presented at the Third National Family Violence Research Conference, Durham, NH.

Pelletier, G., & Handy, L. C. (1986). Family dysfunction and the psychological impact of child sexual abuse. *Canadian Journal of Psychiatry*, *31*, 407–412.

Pelton, L. H. (1978). Child abuse and neglect: The myth of classlessness. *American Journal of Orthopsychiatry*, *48*, 608–617.

Pescosolido, F. J., & Petrella, D. M. (1986). The development, process, and evaluation of group psychotherapy with sexually abused preschool girls. *International Journal of Group Psychotherapy*, *36*(3), 447–469.

Peters, J. J. (1976). Children who are victims of sexual assault and the psychology of offenders. *American Journal of Psychotherapy*, *30*, 398–421.

Peters, S. D. (1988). Child sexual abuse and later psychological problems. In G. E. Wyatt, & G. J. Powell (Eds.), *Lasting effects of child sexual abuse* (pp. 101–117). Beverly Hills: Sage.

Plionis, E. M. (1977). Family functioning and childhood accident occurrence. *American Journal of Orthopsychiatry*, *47*, 250–263.

Pomeroy, J. C., Behar, D., & Stewart, M. A. (1981). Abnormal sexual behavior in pre-pubescent children. *British Journal of Psychiatry*, *138*, 119–125.

Porter, F. S., Blick, L. C., & Sgroi, S. M. (1982). Treatment of the sexually abused child. In S. Sgroi (Ed.), *Handbook of clinical intervention in child sexual abuse* (pp. 109–145). Lexington, MA: Lexington Books.

Powell, G. (1987). Personal communication.

Purcell, J., Beilke, R., & Friedrich, W. N. (1986, August). *The child sexual behavior inventory: Preliminary normative data*. Paper presented at the American Psychological Association Annual Convention. Washington, DC.

Putnam, F. (1987). *Child dissociative checklist (version 2.1 – 11/87)*. (Available from Frank W. Putnam, Laboratory of Developmental Psychology, National Institute of Mental Health, 9000 Rockville Pike, Bethesda, MD 20892.)

Pynoos, R. S., Frederick, C., Nader, K., Arroyo, W., Steinberg, S., Eth, S., Nunez, F., & Fairbanks, L. (1987). Life threat and posttraumatic stress in school-age children. *Archives of General Psychiatry, 44,* 1057–1063.

Radke-Yarrow, M., Cummings, E. M., Kuczynski, L., & Chapman, M. (1985). Patterns of attachment in two- and three-year-olds in normal families and families with parental depression. *Child Development, 56,* 884–893.

Rae, W. A. (1977). Childhood conversion reactions: A review of incidence in pediatric settings. *Journal of Clinical Child Psychology, 6,* 69–72.

Rasmussen, N. H. (1989, September). *Social skills training with conduct-disordered and attention-deficit disordered children.* Paper presented at the meeting of the Section of Psychology, Mayo Clinic and Mayo Foundation, Rochester, MN.

Reposa, R. E., & Zuelzer, M. B. (1983). Family therapy with incest. *International Journal of Family Therapy, 5,* 111–126.

Richman, L. C., & Lindgren, S. D. (1981). Verbal mediation deficits: Relation to behavior and achievement in children. *Journal of Abnormal Psychology, 90,* 99–104.

Rieker, P. P., & Carmen, E. (1986). The victim-to-patient process: The disconfirmation and transformation of abuse. *American Journal of Orthopsychiatry, 56,* 360–370.

Ritterman, M. (1983). *Using hypnosis in family therapy.* San Francisco: Jossey-Bass.

Roberts, J. (1984). Antidotes for secrecy: Treating the incestuous family. *Family Therapy Networker, 8*(5), 49–54.

Root, M. P., & Fallon, P. (1988). The incidence of victimization in experiences in a bulimic sample. *Journal of Interpersonal Violence, 3,* 161–173.

Root, M. P. P., Fallon, P., & Friedrich, W. N. (1986). *Bulimia: A systems approach to treatment.* New York: W. W. Norton.

Rosenfeld, A., Bailey, R., Siegel, B., & Bailey, G. (1986). Determining incestuous contact between parent and child: Frequency of children touching parents' genitals in a nonclinical population. *Journal of the American Academy of Child Psychiatry, 25,* 481–484.

Rothbaum, F., & Weisz, J. R. (1989). *Child psychopathology and the quest for control.* Newbury Park, CA: Sage.

Runyan, D. K., Everson, M. D., Edelsohn, G. A., Hunter, W. M., & Coulter, M. L. (1988). Impact of legal intervention on sexually abused children. *Journal of Pediatrics, 113,* 647–653.

Russell, D. E. H. (1984). *Sexual exploitation: Rape, child sexual abuse, and workplace harassment.* Beverly Hills: Sage.

Russell, D. E. H. (1986). *The secret trauma.* New York: Basic Books.

Russell, R. L., & van den Broek, P. (1988). A cognitive-developmental account of storytelling in child psychotherapy. In S. R. Shirk (Ed.), *Cognitive development and child psychotherapy* (pp. 19–52). New York: Plenum Press.

Rutter, M. (1971). Normal psychosexual development. *Journal of Child Psychology and Psychiatry, 11,* 259–283.

Rutter, M. (1980). Protective factors in children's response to stress and disadvantage. In M. Kent, & J. Rolf (Eds.), *Primary prevention of psychopathology. III. Promoting social competence and coping in children* (pp. 49–74). Hanover, NH: University Press of New England.

Rutter, M. (1983). Stress, coping, and development: Some issues and some questions. In N. Garmezy, & M. Rutter (Eds.), *Stress, coping, and development in children* (pp. 1–41). New York: McGraw-Hill.

Rutter, M., & Quinton, D. (1977). Psychiatric disorder: Ecological factors and concepts of causation. In H. McGurk (Ed.), *Ecological factors in human development*. Amsterdam: North-Holland.

Salter, A. C. (1988). *Treating child sex offenders and victims: A practical guide*. Beverly Hills: Sage.

Sameroff, A. J., & Chandler, M. J. (1975). Reproductive risk and the continuum of caretaking casualty. In F. D. Horowitz (Ed.), *Review of child development research* (Vol. 4) (pp. 187–244). Chicago: University of Chicago Press.

Sameroff, A. J., Seifer, F., & Zax, M. (1982). Early development of children at risk for emotional disorder. *Monographs of the Society for Research in Child Development, 47*(1, Serial No. 199).

Sands, S. (1986). The use of hypnosis in establishing a holding environment to facilitate affect tolerance and integration in impulsive patients. *Psychiatry, 49*, 218–230.

Sansonnet-Hayden, H., Haley, G., Marriage, K., & Fine, S. (1987). Sexual abuse and psychopathology in hospitalized adolescents. *Journal of the American Academy of Child and Adolescent Psychiatry, 26*, 753–757.

Saunders, B. E., McClure, S. M., & Murphy, S. M. (1987, July). *Structure, function, and symptoms in father-daughter sexual abuse families: A multilevel-multirespondent empirical assessment*. Paper presented at the Third National Family Violence Research Conference, Durham, NH.

Schafer, R. (1968). *Aspects of internalization*. New York: International Universities Press.

Schiffer, M. (1984). *Children's group therapy: Methods and case histories*. New York: Free Press.

Schoettle, U. C. (1980). Child exploitation: A study of child pornography. *Journal of the American Academy of Child Psychiatry, 19*, 289–299.

Schofield, M. (1965). *The sexual behaviour of young people*. London: Longmans.

Schwartz, S., & Johnson, J. H. (1985). *Psychopathology of childhood: A clinical-experimental approach* (2nd ed.). New York: Pergamon Press.

Sexton, M. C., Hulsey, T. L., Harralson, T. L., & Nash, M. R. (1989, August). *Family functioning in childhood sexual abuse*. Paper presented at the annual convention of the American Psychological Association, New Orleans.

Sgroi, S. M. (Ed.). (1982). *Handbook of clinical intervention in child sexual abuse* (a, pp. 81–108; b, pp. 241–268). Lexington, MA: Lexington Books.

Singer, K. I. (1989). Group work with men who experienced incest in childhood. *American Journal of Orthopsychiatry, 59*, 468–472.

Smets, A. C., & Cebula, C. M. (1987). A group treatment program for adolescent sex offenders: Five steps toward resolution. *Child Abuse and Neglect, 11*, 247–254.

Smith, H., & Israel, E. (1987). Sibling incest: A study of the dynamics of 25 cases. *Child Abuse and Neglect, 11*, 101–108.

Smith, W. R., Monastersky, C., & Deisher, R. M. (1987). MMPI-based personality types among juvenile sexual offenders. *Journal of Clinical Psychology, 43*, 422–430.

Solin, C. A. (1986). Displacement of affect in families following incest disclosure. *American Journal of Orthopsychiatry, 56*, 570–576.

Solyom, A. E., Austad, C. C., Sherick, I., & Bacon, G. E. (1980). Precocious sexual development in girls: The emotional impact on the child and her parents. *Journal of Pediatric Psychology, 5*, 385–393.

Spanos, N. P., Weekes, J. R., Menary, E., & Bertrand, L. D. (1986). Hypnotic interview and age regression procedures in the elicitation of multiple personality symptoms: A simulation study. *Psychiatry, 49*, 298–311.

Spinetta, J. J., & Deasy-Spinetta, P. (1981). *Living with childhood cancer*. St. Louis: C. V. Mosby.

Sroufe, L. A., Jacobvitz, D., Mangelsdorf, S., DeAngelo, E., & Ward, M. J. (1985). Generational boundary dissolution between mothers and their preschool children: A relationship systems approach. *Child Development, 56*, 317–325.

Sroufe, L. A., & Ward, M. J. (1980). Seductive behavior of mothers of toddlers: Occurrence, correlates, and family origins. *Child Development, 51*, 1222–1229.

Stanton, M. D., & Todd, T. C. (1981). Engaging "resistant" families in treatment. *Family Process, 20*, 261–293.

Steele, B. F., & Alexander, H. (1981). Long-term effects of sexual abuse in childhood. In P. B. Mrazek, & C. H. Kempe (Eds.), *Sexually abused children and their families* (pp. 223–234). New York: Pergamon Press.

Steinglass, P. (1987). *The alcoholic family*. New York: Basic Books.

Stern, M. J., & Meyer, L. (1980). Family and couple interaction patterns in cases of father-daughter incest. In *Sexual abuse of children: Selected readings*. Washington, DC: Government Printing Office, Pub. # (OHDS) 78-30161.

Steward, M. S., Farquhar, L. C., Dicharry, D. C., Glick, D. R., & Martin, P. W. (1986). Group therapy: A treatment of choice for young victims of child abuse. *International Journal of Group Psychotherapy, 36*(2), 261–277.

Storms, M. D. (1981). A theory of erotic orientation development. *Psychological Review, 88*, 340–353.

Strassberg, Z., & Dodge, K. A. (1989). Identification of discriminative stimuli for aggressive behavior in children. *Behavior Therapist, 12*, 195–199.

Sullivan, H. S. (1953). *The interpersonal theory of psychiatry*. New York: W. W. Norton.

Summit, R. C. (1983). The child sexual abuse accommodation syndrome. *Child Abuse and Neglect, 7*, 177–193.

Summit, R. C. (1988). Hidden victims, hidden pain: Societal avoidance of child sexual abuse. In G. E. Wyatt, & G. J. Powell (Eds.), *Lasting effects of child sexual abuse* (pp. 39–60). Beverly Hills: Sage.

Swanson, L., & Biaggio, M. K. (1985). Therapeutic perspectives on father-daughter incest. *American Journal of Psychiatry, 142*, 667–674.

Swenson, W. M., & Morse, R. M. (1975). The use of a self-administered alcoholism screening test (SAAST) in a medical center. *Mayo Clinic Proceedings, 50*, 204–208.

Terr, L. (1988). What happens to early memories of trauma? A study of twenty children under age five at the time of documented traumatic events. *Journal of the American Academy of Child and Adolescent Psychiatry, 1*, 96–104.

Terr, L. C. (1981). "Forbidden games": Post-traumatic child's play. *Journal of the American Academy of Child Psychiatry, 20*, 741–760.

Tong, L., Oates, K., & McDowell, M. (1987). Personality development following sexual abuse. *Child Abuse and Neglect, 11*, 371–383.

Trepper, T. S. (1986). The apology session. In T. S. Trepper, & M. J. Barrett (Eds.), *Treating incest: A multiple systems perspective* (pp. 93–101). New York: Haworth Press.

Troy, M., & Sroufe, L. A. (1987). Victimization among preschoolers: Role of attachment relationship history. *Journal of the American Academy of Child and Adolescent Psychiatry, 26*, 166–172.

Tsai, M., Feldman-Summers, S., & Edgar, M. (1979). Childhood molestation: Variables related to differential impacts on psychosexual functioning in adult women. *Journal of Abnormal Psychology, 88*, 407–417.

Tuber, S., & Coates, S. (1989). Indices of psychopathology in the Rorschachs of boys with severe gender identity disorder: A comparison with normal control subjects. *Journal of Personality Assessment, 53*, 100–112.

Tuber, S. B. (1983). Children's Rorschach scores as predictors of later adjustment. *Journal of Consulting and Clinical Psychology, 51*, 379–385.

Tyler, A. H., & Brassard, M. R. (1984). Abuse in the investigation and treatment of intrafamilial child sexual abuse. *Child Abuse and Neglect, 8*, 47–53.

Uherek, A. (1986). *The ritually victimized child: Symptoms and treatment.* Paper presented at the mid-winter meeting of Divisions 29, 42, and 43 of the American Psychological Association, New Orleans.

Veronen, L. J., & Kilpatrick, D. (1986). *The impact of event scale.* Unpublished manuscript, Medical University of South Carolina, Charleston.

Wahler, R. G. (1980). The multiply entrapped parent: Obstacles to change in parent-child problems. In J. P. Vincent (Ed.), *Advances in family intervention, assessment and theory* (Vol. 1) (pp. 29–52). Greenwich, CT: JAI Press.

Wallerstein, J. S., & Kelly, J. B. (1980). *Surviving the breakup: How children and parents cope with divorce.* New York: Basic Books.

Weiss, M., Sutton, P. J., & Utecht, A. J. (1985). Multiple personality in a 10-year-old girl. *Journal of the American Academy of Child Psychiatry, 24*, 495–501.

Weisz, J. R., Weiss, B., Alicke, M. D., & Klotz, M. L. (1987). Effectiveness of psychotherapy with children and adolescents: A meta-analysis for clinicians. *Journal of Consulting and Clinical Psychology, 55*, 542–549.

Werner, E. E., & Smith, R. S. (1982). *Vulnerable but invincible: A longitudinal study of resilient children and youth.* New York: McGraw-Hill.

Werner, H. (1948). *Comparative psychology of mental development.* New York: International Universities Press.

Westfelt, J. A. R. (1982). Environmental factors in childhood accidents. *Acta Paediatria Scandinavica Supplement, 291,* 1–75.

White, S. (1987). *Child sexual abuse assessment: The investigatory interview* [Videotape]. Cleveland: Child Guidance Center.

White, S., Halpin, B. M., Strom, G. A., & Santilli, G. (1988). Behavioral comparisons of young sexually abused, neglected, and nonreferred children. *Journal of Clinical Child Psychology, 17,* 53–61.

Winnicott, D. W. (1975). *Through paediatrics to psycho-analysis.* London: Hogarth Press.

Wolfe, D. A. (1989, October). *Discussion of treatment papers.* Paper presented at the Institute for the Prevention of Child Abuse Research Conference, Toronto.

Wolfe, D. A., & Mosk, M. D. (1983). Behavioral comparisons of children from abusive and distressed families. *Journal of Consulting and Clinical Psychology, 51,* 702–708.

Wolfe, V., Wolfe, D., & LaRose, L. (1986). *The children's impact of traumatic events scale.* Unpublished manuscript, University of Western Ontario.

Wolfe, V. V., Gentile, C., & Wolfe, D. A. (in press). The impact of sexual abuse on children: A PTSD formulation. *Journal of Interpersonal Violence.*

Wolfe, V. V., & Wolfe, D. A. (1988). The sexually abused child. In E. J. Mash, & L. G. Terdal (Eds.), *Behavioral assessment of childhood disorders* (2nd ed.) (pp. 670–714). New York: Guilford Press.

Wolpe, J. (1973). *The practice of behavior therapy* (2nd ed.). Elmsford, NY: Pergamon Press.

Wright, L. (1975). Outcome of a standardized program for treating psychogenic encopresis. *Professional Psychology, 6,* 453–456.

Wurtele, S. K. (1987). School-based sexual abuse prevention programs: A review. *Child Abuse and Neglect, 11,* 483–495.

Wyatt, G., & Mickey, M. R. (1988). The support by parents and others as it mediates the effects of child sexual abuse. In G. E. Wyatt, & G. J. Powell (Eds.), *Lasting effects of child sexual abuse* (pp. 211–226). Beverly Hills: Sage.

Wyatt, G. E., & Newcomb, M. (in press). Women's internal and external mediators of child sexual abuse. *Journal of Consulting and Clinical Psychology.*

Wyatt, G. E., & Powell, G. J. (Eds.). (1988). *Lasting effects of child sexual abuse.* Beverly Hills: Sage.

Wynne, L. C., Ryckoff, I. M., Day, J., & Hirsch, S. I. (1958). Pseudomutuality in the family relations of schizophrenics. *Psychiatry, 21,* 205–220.

Yalom, I. D. (1975). *The theory and practice of group psychotherapy* (2nd ed.). New York: Basic Books.

Yates, A. (1982). Children eroticized by incest. *American Journal of Psychiatry, 139,* 482–485.

Zeitlin, S. (1980). Assessing coping behavior. *American Journal of Orthopsychiatry, 50,* 139–144.

Zimet, S. G., & Farley, G. K. (1986). Four perspectives on the competence and self-esteem of emotionally disturbed children beginning day treatment. *Journal of the American Academy of Child Psychiatry, 25,* 76–83.

Zivney, O. A., Nash, M. R., & Hulsey, T. L. (1988). Sexual abuse in early versus late childhood: Differing patterns of pathology as revealed on the Rorschach. *Psychotherapy, 25,* 99–106.

Name Index

Subject Index